Business-Driven
Digital Transformation

Business-Driven
Digital Transformation

Efficiency, Scaling, and Innovation

Vivek Kale

┃┃BEP

BUSINESS EXPERT PRESS

Leader in applied, concise business books

Business-Driven Digital Transformation:
Efficiency, Scaling, and Innovation

Cover design by Cassandra Kronstedt

Interior design by S4Carlisle Publishing Services, Chennai, India

First published in 2025 by
Business Expert Press, LLC
222 East 46th Street, New York, NY 10017
www.businessexpertpress.com

ISBN-13: 978-1-63742-866-5 (paperback)
ISBN-13: 978-1-63742-867-2 (e-book)

Information Systems Collection

First edition: 2025

10 9 8 7 6 5 4 3 2 1

EU SAFETY REPRESENTATIVE
Mare Nostrum Group B.V.
Mauritskade 21D
1091 GC Amsterdam
The Netherlands
gpsr@mare-nostrum.co.uk

Description

Business-Driven Digital Transformations (BDDTs) are the transformation of business and organizational activities, processes, competencies, and models to fully leverage the changes and opportunities of a mix of digital technologies and their accelerating impact across industries strategically and in a prioritized way, with present and future business and technology shifts in mind. Business-Driven Digital Transformations are not so much about technologies, but they are a way for enterprises to do business differently, to remain competitive, and be disruptive in their market space. BDDT can be of three types: digitization, smartization, and metamorphosis.

BDDT is not so much about technologies as fundamentally about building Built_to_Change organizations. This book devolves this theme into three ambidextrous development goals for digital transformations: implementing Efficient, Scalable, and Innovable digital transformation models or design blueprints. This book provides details of these design blueprints for achieving their respective goals using specific technologies suitable for specific contexts. The three digital transformation models correspond respectively to the vision of "Enterprise as a Machine," i.e., an *automated enterprise*; "Enterprise as an Organism," i.e., a *sentient enterprise*; and, lastly, "Enterprise as a Brain," i.e., a *cognitive enterprise*.

Digital Transformation Model I relates to enterprises adopting the "efficient" transformation models or design blueprints aimed at efficient operations opportunities and maximizing profitability. Digital Transformation Model II relates to enterprises adopting the "scaling" transformation models or design blueprints aimed at volume growth opportunities and maximizing value appropriation through mass customization. Digital Transformation Model III relates to enterprises adopting the "innovable" transformation models or design blueprints aimed at business growth opportunities and market share maximization through mass innovation. Correspondingly, BDDT focuses in Parts I, II, and III of this book respectively on three types of artifacts: business processes, business architectures, and business models.

As part of *digital transformation*, when organizations implement the latest technologies like Artificial Intelligence (AI), Machine Learning (ML), Internet of Things (IoT), Software-Defined Networks (SDN), Web 3.0, 5G/6G communications, edge computing, and metaverse—which are discussed in this book—they are not only responding to market and competition but are also inherently being Built_to_Change! Digital transformation enables organizations to withstand a heavy combined onslaught of dynamic changes in profitability, delivery structures, and competitiveness, till triggered by dramatic unforeseen changes either in the go-to-market conditions or the technology or the market competitiveness itself, it is time for another *iteration of digital transformation*.

Contents

List of Figures and Tables

Figures

Tables

Testimonials

"Vivek Kale has once again created a leading-edge book that successfully addresses one of today's most critical challenges that businesses face. Business-Driven Digital Transformation *provides executives and managers in a wide variety of industries valued insights on enhancing business efficiencies, business scaling, and business model innovation. Rather than focus mainly on the "what," Vivek provides valuable insights into the "why" and the "how," thus enabling leaders to not only provide a rationale and motivation for digital transformation, but also insights into the techniques and approaches to help ensure its success. Clearly, the cost of the book is a tiny price to pay for access to such valuable practical expertise!"*—**Prof. Gregory Dess, University of Texas at Dallas**

"Business-Driven Digital Transformation *has the potential to make a significant impact on the way organizations approach and implement digital transformation. It provides a much-needed holistic view of the process, addressing the challenges and opportunities that come with it. If you must transform your business to thrive in a digital world, start with this book!"*—**Lex Sisney, business scaling coach and author of** *Organizational Physics: The Science of Growing a Business*

"Business-Driven Digital Transformation (BDDT) *written by Vivek Kale is highly insightful not only for practitioners but also for academic researchers. The most distinctive feature, compared to other books on digital transformation, is that it proposes BDDT based on strategy management theories, specifically, activity-based, resource-based, and market-based views. He positions the role of information technology (IT) as the core of business activities and directly incorporates IT into competitive strategy. In addition, he presents a transformation model comprising three phases: enterprise as a machine, enterprise as an organism, and enterprise as a brain. This theory-based model serves as a comprehensive roadmap for companies pursuing digital transformation, targeting not only operational efficiency, but also growth and innovation."*—**Prof. Dr. Mikihisa Nakano, Professor of Business Administration, Kyoto Sangyo University**

Foreword 1

Why Digital Transformation Is About Mindset Transformation

In *Business-Driven Digital Transformation*, Vivek Kale challenges the traditional approach to digital evolution. It's not about upgrading technology or work processes—it's about transforming the mindset and the very DNA of the organization. This is what I have referred to as Stage 5 maturity in digital transformation in my book, *Why Digital Transformations Fail*. Kale adds a layer on top about how to execute this.

Kale introduces three levels of transformation: digitization (streamlining processes), digitalization (architectural evolution), and digital metamorphosis (reinventing business models). The companies that succeed aren't just reacting to disruption—they're built to change. The book explores how organizations can develop Efficient, Scalable, and Innovable transformation models, ensuring not just profitability but long-term market leadership. Kale emphasizes agility over rigidity, distinguishing between planned adaptation and dynamic, real-time responses to change. Leveraging strategic frameworks—such as Michael Porter's strategy principles—he provides actionable insights into resilience, ambidexterity, and digital maturity, essential for navigating volatile, uncertain, and complex environments.

Ultimately, this isn't just a book about digital transformation—it's a guide to rethinking business itself. If leaders embrace a mindset of adaptability and innovation, they won't just survive the digital era—they'll define it.

– Tony Saldanha, is a globally renowned author, adviser, and founder. He ran Procter & Gamble's famed multibillion-dollar GBS and IT operations in every region across the world during a 27-year career. Tony is CEO and co-founder of Inixia, the global standards and certification body for the Shared Services industry. His books, Why Digital Transformations Fail and Revolutionizing Business Operations, are acclaimed bestsellers. Tony advises about 20 of the Fortune 100 organizations on digital strategy at the board or CXO levels. www.transformant.io

Foreword 2

In *Business-Driven Digital Transformation*, Vivek Kale offers an insightful exploration of how enterprises can thrive amidst the digital revolution. This book transcends conventional approaches to digital transformation by focusing on actionable frameworks and strategic insights that enable organizations to leverage digital tools for sustained competitiveness.

It introduces three core transformation models—Efficient, Scalable, and Innovable Design Blueprints—each tailored to address profitability, growth, and innovation. Kale's approach emphasizes building "Built-to-Change" organizations, which adapt seamlessly to evolving market dynamics. With in-depth case studies, including organizations like Amazon and Netflix, the book delves into how leading firms have successfully reimagined their processes, architectures, and business models. From exploring the nuances of digitization to embracing digital metamorphosis, Kale provides practical methodologies grounded in Porter's strategy frameworks.

Packed with key insights on enterprise agility, advanced planning systems (APSs), and cutting-edge technologies like AI and IoT, this book serves as a strategic compass for leaders, managers, and students alike.

Whether you're initiating a digital transformation or refining an ongoing process, *Business-Driven Digital Transformation* equips readers with the tools to navigate the complexities of a digital-first business landscape.

– Prof. Roberto Moro-Visconti, is an academic and consultant who specializes in valuation, corporate finance, and digital transformation. He is a professor of Corporate Finance at the Catholic University of Milan and combines his extensive research with hands-on experience advising companies on strategic finance and digital innovations. morovisconti.com/en

Preface

While wrapping up my last book *Unleashing the Startup Unicorn*, I suddenly had an epiphany on the primary reason why all companies, small-, medium-, and large enterprises, across the world were hit by the tsunami wave of digital transformations—every organization had been compelled to transform progressively, if not immediately, into a *digital company*, that is, both a *digital enterprise* (i.e., as an organization) and *digital business* (i.e., in operations) (Kale 2024). This was fueled primarily by the iconic successes of top successful Silicon Valley startups like Google, Facebook, LinkedIn, and Twitter. They had all been legendary pioneering unicorns of their times and were products of a digital storm that had blown away many traditional, well-entrenched iconic industrial companies.

In the past few years, newly minted firms have grown from startups to international multibillion-dollar companies like Google, Uber, Airbnb, and so on—surpassing even the long-standing iconic blue-chip companies like IBM, GE, and so on—with much of their success credited to their innovative business models and smart use of the accessible surrounding digital ecosystem(s) environment coupled with customer co-created, co-customized and co-innovated digital customer-centric products, compelling services, and enthralling experiences. Customers have begun to expect products, services, and experiences to perform at a level comparable to the front-runners of digitalized companies. Firms increasingly need to maintain, on an ongoing basis, a variety of innovation efforts to operate more efficiently and effectively, as well as to continuously strive to deliver greater and greater value to their customers. *Digital technology changes the very basis of competition across most industries.* Hence, staying competitive leads to an increased focus on keeping the firm's business model current and in line with the leading digitalized or digitally transformed companies. An enterprise's business model reflects the design of the value creation, capture, and value-delivery (and realization) mechanism that a firm deploys; it is about how it organizes itself to create, capture, and profitably deliver value.

How Is the Book Different?

This book enables business and information technology (IT) managers to get a clear understanding of what Business-Driven Digital Transformations (BDDT) means, what it can do for them, and why it is currently relevant. BDDT is not so much about technology as about fundamentally building a Built_to_Change organization, a *digital company* that is both a *digital enterprise* (i.e., as an organization) and a *digital business* (i.e., in operation) at the same time. There are more failed projects in digital transformation than successes (Saldanha 2019; Venkatraman 2017). This is caused because of the following reasons:

1. There is no widely applicable definition of digital transformation.
2. There is a lack of a coherent strategy for achieving the dual objective of *digital enterprise* and *digital business* simultaneously for embarking on digital transformation.
3. There is an absence of an effective digital transformation plan.
4. There is no clear framework for digital transformation implementation that can guide enterprises through different segments or stages of their digital transformation journey.

Several books speak about cloud, AI, and data analytics in silos, but no book provides a harmonized view of what organizations *need* in order to embark on their digital transformation journey and be successful.

> Most of the books on digital transformation do not address the WHY and HOW questions: *why* is digital transformation required at all and *how* to go about executing it? Even the selection of ICT components for consideration in a BDDT project is *ad hoc,* which begs another important question: *why only those select ICT components, why not some others?*

The author never subscribed, even before the advent of the internet, to the stance that IT strategy is merely an enabler of business strategy (also termed as "Business and IT Strategy Alignment")—always believing that IT was an independent value creator in its own right. Indeed, in light of the ascending role of extended reality systems (AR/VR [augmented reality/virtual reality] systems) and cyber-physical systems (CPS) envisaged in the future, it is clear that business strategy will primarily be driven by *IT reality* rather than *business reality per se*, because, in the future, it is only IT that will empower the creation of a *digital company*, i.e., a digital enterprise as well as a digital business, i.e., new business opportunities, and become its growth engine. Hence, the author also fundamentally believes that the IT vision cannot but emerge only from the shifting preferences and priorities of the customers alone—and not from the shifting travails and tribulations of even relevant technology regimes. Consequently, the pathway to and the initiative for digital transformation originates only from customer preferences and choices and the consequent challenges in business rather than from the perceived threat of being left behind in some mythical, hypothetical, or ad hoc race of technology. The author wanted to write a book presenting the vision of cyber-physical, systems-enabled, experience-based learning enterprises—the outcome is the book that you are reading now. Thank you!

This book believes that hereafter only IT-driven business strategy that targets achieving transformation of every organization into a *digital company*, that is, a *digital enterprise* and a *digital business,* will succeed—traditional business-driven business strategy is bound to fail. Consequently, every digital transformation must have the dual objective of simultaneously transforming every organization into a *digital enterprise* and a *digital business simultaneously.* Like any other digital company such as Google, Facebook, LinkedIn, etc., Amazon has always been a *digital business* with retail operations (including a marketplace for selling and procuring, e-commerce, etc.) and also a *digital enterprise* providing broad-based infrastructure-metaphor services like (say) cloud computing services (including Amazon Web Services [AWS]). The IT-driven strategy must target achieving the dual strategy of addressing both the requirements of digital enterprise and digital business—it would not be incorrect to term them software-defined enterprises (SDE) and software-defined businesses (SDB). Using the author's decades of experience in supporting transformation and innovation, this book lays out a path to a progressive iteration of business change and value realization, balancing the perspectives of change-enabling transformations and revolutionary performance optimizations (Kale 2024; Callan 2024; Overby and Audestad 2018, 2021).

Thus, it is singularly important to have the IT strategy emerge from the same process that traditionally gives rise to the business strategy. This book explains how M. Porter's standard approach to strategy management can also be used as the basis for determining the very need for BDDT *strategy* as the eligible types of digital transformation models that would address the twin objectives of achieving both *digital enterprise* (i.e., as an organization) and *digital business* (i.e., in operation). It is important that the BDDT blueprints adopted in this book must emerge not on an ad hoc basis but most naturally from (say) M. Porter's standard approach to strategy management. As shown in this book, undertaking such an exercise results in identifying three main strategies for fundamentally realizing Built_to_Change enterprises:

- Activity-Based View (ABV) (Porter 1985; Sheehan and Foss 2009)
- Resource-Based View (RBV) (Barney 1991, 1997)
- Market-Led or Market-Based View (MBV) (Porter 1980)

Motivation for Writing This Book?

The author's journey in exploring the characteristics of digital transformation started with an earlier published book, *Inverting the Paradox of Excellence* (Kale 2015a). This book states that over time, overemphasis and adherence to the same proven routines that helped an organization succeed can also lead to its decline, resulting from organizational inertia, complacency, and inflexibility. Drawing lessons from one of the best models of success, the evolutionary model, that book explains why organizations must proactively seek out changes or variations continuously to ensure excellence by testing out a continuum of opportunities and advantages at any moment. In other words, to maintain excellence, the company must be in constant flux! This book provided the groundwork for the challenges confronted by enterprises in the VUCA (Volatility Uncertainty Complexity Ambiguity) market environment discussed in Chapter 1. The next book, *Agile Network Businesses: Collaboration, Coordination, and Competitive Advantage* (Kale 2017a), is a book on network and e-business business models. These two titles provided the groundwork and foundation required for Part III of the present book.

The author's next book, *Enterprise Process Management Systems: Engineering Process-Centric Enterprise Systems using BPMN 2.0* (Kale 2018c), addresses aspects related to the digital transformation of processes. The following book *Enterprise Performance Intelligence and Decision Patterns* (Kale 2018a) is relevant for a digital transformation initiative. These two titles provided the groundwork and foundation required for Part I of the present book.

The last book in this group, *Digital Transformation of Enterprise Architecture* (Kale 2019), proposes that to withstand the disruptive digital storms of the future, enterprise architecture (EA) brings about digital transformation, i.e., exponential change (amplification or attenuation), in any performance measure of the constituent attributes of technical architecture (TA). In addition to the conventional attributes of TA, like interoperability, scalability, and availability, this book identifies additional attributes of mobility, ubiquity, security, analyticity, and usability. TA affects the digital transformation of interoperability, scalability, availability, ubiquity, security, analyticity, and usability through service orientation, cloud, big data, context-awareness, Internet of Things (IoT), blockchain, and soft and interactive computing technologies. This title, and the book, *Creating Smart Enterprises: Leveraging Cloud, Big Data, Web, Social Media, Mobile and IoT Technologies* (Kale V. 2018b; 2017b; 2015b) provided the groundwork and foundation required for Part II of the present book.

How Is the Book Organized?

To succinctly cover all aspects of a contemporary digital transformation effort, this book has been organized to reflect the natural grouping of activities that are usually applicable to a typical digital transformation initiative with a dual objective of creating both a *digital enterprise* and a *digital business*. As indicated earlier, digital transformations are strategic initiatives; this book adopts M. Porter's standard approach to strategy management for this initiative. The resulting strategies and corresponding activities have been grouped into three separate parts.

Chapter 1 elaborates on the ascent of the *digital company*, that is, digital enterprises and digital businesses simultaneously. It sets the context for the whole book by introducing the VUCA market environment, characteristics of enterprise agility and resilience, and digital transformation. Built_to_Change organizations mandate agile and resilient enterprises. This chapter also establishes the origin of the theme of the three digital transformation models and design blueprints discussed throughout this book. The chapter explains why the digital transformation imperatives require all organizations to iteratively undertake digital transformations to adapt to ongoing digital disruptions and to effectively compete both as a digital enterprise and digital business (Kale 2024; Sinclair 2021).

Chapter 2 describes details of Built_to_Change strategy management. It presents an overview of M. Porter's approach to strategy management and the resulting Activity-Based View (ABV), Resource-Based View (RBV), and Market-Based View (MBV) strategies that are relevant for a Built_to_Change enterprise. These are devolved further to map respectively onto Efficient, Scalable, and Innovable Design Blueprints. This chapter ensures the selection of the appropriate digital transformation models and design blueprints suitable for the organisational priorities identified in addressing the challenges envisaged in their businesses.

Parts I, II, and III consist of two parallel chapters focusing respectively on the visions of the digital transformation models and the specifics of the corresponding design blueprints. The first set of chapters (Chapters 3, 5, and 7) gives the *big picture* or the *clairvoyant bird's eye view* of the three digital transformation models. The second set of chapters (Chapters 4, 6, and 8) gives the *ruminant giraffe's eye view* of the reframing and corresponding means of digital transformations. There is a certain degree of overlap between the various aspects of the three digital transformation models and design blueprints—after all, the three digital transformation models or design blueprints refer to the different organizational parts or different times of the *same organization.*

Part I presents *Digital Transformation for Efficient Design* that involves automated processes, and tighter intra- and inter-integration and interoperability within the enterprise. It mainly deals with business process transformations related to attaining the next level of enhanced efficiency aspects of the enterprise, i.e., business process reengineering (BPR) and change management issues of the enterprise (Kale 2018c; Saldanha and Passerini 2023; Kale 2018a).

Constrained by the overall objective of keeping the book small, some topics when introduced in chapters of Parts I, II, and III may seem to either overlap with topics in another Part's digital transformation model(s) or design blueprint(s), or may seem disjointed or even incongruent with neighboring subsections. However, the reader should be reassured that the chapters in Parts I, II, and III of the book focus on those aspects and technologies that are predominantly and distinguishingly characteristic of a particular digital transformation model and design blueprint only.

Part II explains the *Digital Transformation for Scalable Design* that deals with attaining the next level of enhanced volume growth effectiveness aspects of the enterprise, i.e., augmentation of resources via enterprise architecture (EA) adaptability and adoptability issues of the enterprise, and partnership networks. The trifurcation of supply chain networks into decision, information, and logistics networks enables each one of them to establish and maintain independent partner networks in their own right (Kale 2017a). This also addresses advances in the areas of availability, scalability, ubiquity, security, analyticity, and so on, of the corresponding systems. Thus, this part mainly deals with technological advances related to scalability, like service-oriented architecture (SOA), big data, cloud, and Internet of Things (IoT) (Kale 2019, 2018c, 2017b, 2015b; West 2017).

Part III delineates the *Digital Transformation for Innovable Design* that deals with business model innovations (BMIs) to target business growth, i.e., comparative blue ocean business opportunities for maximization of total market share. Thus, this part mainly deals with advances related to dimensions of business models in the areas of experiences, customer and employee empowerment, and so on (Mitchell and Coles 2003; Linz et al. 2021; Kale 2017a; Hirooka 2006; Wagner 2014; Kirschner and Gerhart 2005; Pfenning and Pfenning 2012).

A comment on the significance of references in this book. Much of the burden of maintaining the shorter length of this book has been shouldered by pointers to the relevant references. On any placeholder topic within the digital transformation framework, while the requisite *necessary* details have been presented in this book, *sufficient* details are made accessible by pointing to the relevant references for the sake of completeness.

Who Should Read This Book?

All stakeholders of a BDDT project can benefit from reading this book.

All stakeholders who are involved with any aspect of a BDDT project will find this book very useful. They will profit by using this book as a framework to make a more meaningful contribution to the success of their BDDT project without getting intimidated by the complexities involved, getting swamped by the multiplicities of competencies required, or getting mired in cross-dependencies to make prudent decisions. This book delineates, depending on the chosen digital transformation model and design blueprint, which aspects or factors need to be relatively prioritized and which aspects or factors can be relatively ignored.

This book will be useful to the following categories of stakeholders of a BDDT project:

- Business and technology leaders
- Executives, business, operational and technical Managers
- Business, project, and process owners
- Project managers and project leaders
- Technology and software managers
- Business, functional, and technical members of business analysis (BA)/information technology (IT)/information services (IS), networking (NT), and communications (Comm.) teams
- Academicians and research scholars in the areas of economics, management, sciences, computer science and engineering, information technology, and engineering, and so on
- Students of mathematics, data science and statistics, computer sciences, information technology and management, business administration and management courses.

Acknowledgments

I want to thank all those who helped me with their clarifications, criticism, and valuable information while writing this book. I would like to especially thank Dr. Mathias Kirchmer, Dr. Cor Molenaar, Dr. Harald Øverby, Dr. V. Kumar, Dr. Carsten Linz, Dr. Mikihisa Nakano, and Neeraj Athalye.

Tony Saldanha's experience with Procter & Gamble's GBS and IT operations in every region across the world during a 27-year career was a reality check for the digital transformation models and design blueprints proposed in this book. This book posits that "digital" is associated more with intangible, virtual, and extended reality than with technology per se (which underlies the whole of Part III). Dr. Roberto Moro-Visconti has worked extensively in the area of intangible valuations. I thank Tony Saldanha and Roberto Moro-Visconti for their reviews, feedback, suggestions, and especially for writing a foreword to this book.

Thanks to Scott Isenberg for making this book happen and Charlene Kronstedt for guiding it through production to completion.

I thank our beloved daughters, Tanaya and Atmaja, for their understanding and support. And finally, to my wife, Girija, I am grateful, beyond measure, for her continuous loving support and help. This book is dedicated to Miheer and Atmaja at the start of their life together.

Prologue

Organizational resilience is a property that allows an organization to retain its original function, structure, and identity despite changing environments. Resilience relates to those capabilities and capacities built into an organization's design that allow it to survive and thrive, regardless of the adverse external pressures and forces exerted upon it. In the context of elasticity, this implies that resilience is an ability that organizations possess where changes can be absorbed, and, as long as the organization does not reach its elastic limits, it is not required to transform dramatically. When an organization is stretched toward its elastic limits, a process of *elasticity*, i.e., incremental adaptation, comes to the fore (Cantor 2020a; Molotnikov and Molotnikova 2021). As in Darwinian biology, those organizations that survive in changing circumstances go through a slow process of adaptation. This process itself is built on the foundation of resilience and is reflected in an innate capacity to alter function, structure, and identity, and, whether spontaneous or planned, prepares an organization for the world it faces.

However, when the stresses and strains imposed by highly turbulent, dynamic environments push an organization beyond its elastic limits, *plasticity*, i.e., adoption, becomes the only viable option (Cantor 2020b; Molotnikov and Molotnikova 2021). Unlike adaptation, which is about changes of degree, adoption represents a *metamorphosis*—a qualitative change in kind. Unlike adaptation, adoption entails several nonlinear processes that require a creative, as opposed to a designing, mind. Without the precursors of resilience and adaptability being in place, organizations that go for such transformational change are unprepared for this, and the likelihood of this high-risk strategy working successfully is limited. Such a highest-level BDDT is the result of prerequisite lean and agile transformations combined with information, communication, and technology (ICT)-assisted transformation processes that are more akin to the "metamorphosis" of a caterpillar into a butterfly (Ryan 2011).

Hence, to succeed in the age of disruption, companies must change their basic approach. They need to shift their emphasis from perpetuating stability to disrupting themselves. Instead of excelling at doing the same things better, faster, and cheaper, they need to challenge themselves to continually do different things; and to continually do them differently. They need to learn to value learning over success, and to value the ability to change direction over the ability to maintain course. In other words, they need to shift their core competency from *efficiency* to *adaptability* to *adoptability*.

In the past few years, new firms have grown from startups to international multibillion-dollar companies, with much of their success credited to their innovative business models and smart use of the accessible surrounding digital ecosystem(s) environment. Customers have begun to expect products, services, and experiences to perform at a level comparable to the front-runners of digitalized companies. Firms increasingly need to maintain, on an ongoing basis, a variety of innovation efforts to operate more efficiently and effectively, as well as to continuously strive to deliver greater and greater value to their customers. *Digital technology changes the very basis of competition across most industries.* Hence, staying competitive leads to an increased focus on keeping the firm's business model current and in line with the leading or digitalized, or digitally transformed companies. An enterprise's business model reflects the design of value creation, capture, and value-delivery (and realization) mechanism that a firm deploys: it is about how it has organized itself to create, capture, and profitably deliver value.

An organization's behavior reflects its management hypothesis about what customers want, how they want it, and how an enterprise can organize to best meet those needs, get paid for doing so, and make a profit. In other words, business-driven digital transformations (BDDT) entail digital transformations of **processes, architectures, partner networks and business models continually to achieve a digital company i.e. digital enterprise and digital business aspects of an organization simultaneously.**

After reading the book, if the reader concludes that the preceding spectrum of business-driven digital transformation models and design blueprints is the most natural choice for any contemporary digital transformation, then it would have achieved its objective.

CHAPTER 1

Ascent of Digital Organizations

*This chapter sets the context for the book focusing on the rationale for continuous digital transformations. It also establishes the origin of the theme of three digital transformation models or design blueprints discussed throughout this book. Built_to_Change organizations mandate agile and resilient enterprises; but Built_to_Change organization is not a state of being but of becoming—it is a continual process. Agile enterprises can only be achieved through iterative digital transformations to a digital company via **both aspects** of an organization, namely, digital enterprise and digital business, hence, the zeal for iterative digital transformations to perpetuate Built_to_Change organizations.*

Enterprise Agility

Agility is the ability to respond to (and ideally benefit from) unexpected change. We must distinguish between agility and flexibility: flexibility is scheduled or planned adaptation to unforeseen yet expected external circumstances, while agility is unplanned and unscheduled adaptation to unforeseen and unexpected external circumstances. The enterprises that can best respond to the fast and frequently changing markets have better competitive advantages than those that fail to sustain the pace dictated by the process of globalization. This can be realized through enterprises acquiring better control and efficiency in their ability to manage the changes in their business processes, business architectures, and business models.

Enterprises primarily aim progressively for efficiency, flexibility, and innovation, in that order. The Model Builder, Erector Set, and LEGO kits are illustrations of enterprises targeting efficiency, flexibility, and innovation (i.e., agility), respectively.

Ambidextrous Enterprises

The word *ambidextrous* is used to describe people who can use both right and left hands at the same time with equal dexterity or versatility. This is also used as a metaphor to describe versatile organizations that can benefit from their existing competencies as well as search out new opportunities with differing competencies with equal proficiency. Being ambidextrous as an organization means being both-handedly skilled, not unlike being able to handle a recurring activity like everyday business with the left hand, while developing a non-recurring activity like developing a new product (or service or experience) with the right hand. When talking about organizational ambidexterity, the reference is to an organization skilled in managing day-to-day business efficiently, while still being agile enough to react and develop the business of tomorrow (O'Reilly and Tushman 2004b).

The concept of organizational ambidexterity is closely related to the concepts of exploitation and exploration: exploitation aims at making a profit from the results while also improving the productivity and efficiency of the operations, while exploration seeks to search and experiment. Exploitational and explorational activities are mutually contradictory; an organization that is focusing on exploitation tends to focus on stability rather than flexibility, whereas an organization that is focusing on exploration tends to go for flexibility and adaptability more than stability (Hannan and Freeman 1984). Organizational ambidexterity is very hard to pursue as an organization, since it needs a balancing act between being exploitative and explorative at the same time.

There are three solutions for solving the issue of becoming an ambidextrous organization. One solution is structural ambidexterity, which implies the separation of exploitation and exploration within the organization to address paradoxical demands. In this solution, formal and informal integration mechanisms should be used to ensure the flow of knowledge across exploitative and explorative units. The second solution is to be contextually ambidextrous as an organization, or even as the individuals working within it, depending on the current need(s). The last solution is to be an ambidextrous organization through leadership, where the leaders guide the organization through the cycles of exploitation and exploration.

Ambidextrous organizations inherently have two competing objectives within the same organization, and both need to be pursued. This requires a differentiated structuring and management of the activities addressed by each objective. Duncan (1976) suggested the creation of separate units to pursue exploitative or exploratory activities, since each type of activity requires different organizational setups and possibly different cultures. The separate units could be new projects, outsourced functionalities, or even suitable startup acquisitions depending on their feasibility (Cuatrecasas 2019; Frankenberger et al. 2021). Organizations that tend toward the exploitative side should invest in explorative activities and vice versa to maintain a balanced optimum. While exploitation aims for current income that in turn allows it to invest in exploration, exploration creates new opportunities designed to assure the long-term survival of an organization.

Organizational ambidexterity needs to reach a certain balance between efficiency and adaptability so that a company is not taking risks to only innovate without earning money through exploitation, nor being very efficient without assuring future earnings through exploration. The tremendous organizational challenge for organizations that have invested solely in one of those sides is to change their focus later on and attempt to establish competencies on the other side. However, organizational ambidexterity might not always be desirable or needed in the first place, since a focus on either exploitation or exploration might dominate *under certain circumstances*.

The concept of organizational ambidexterity is closely related to the major challenges of the *innovator's dilemma* (Frankenberger et al. 2021; O'Reilly III and Tushman 2021). This interpretation of the *innovator's dilemma* dictates that many of the older business models remain with their originating project(s) or division(s) until the newer digitally transformed business model(s) or design blueprint(s) is tested and proven in the market and has taken a firm foothold in their originating project(s) or division(s). But there are exceptions to this. With the core mainframe products faltering in 1992, the newly appointed CEO of IBM, L. Gerstner, instead of working toward progressively phasing out the mainframes, reversed direction to aim for the consolidation of mainframe hardware, software, systems integration, and services for steadily improving and enhancing the mainframe business!

Strategic agility and organizational resilience capability (and capacity) are complementary capabilities that enable organizations to deal with the turbulent environments in which they operate. Strategic agility, that is, the capacity for moving quickly, flexibly, and decisively, needs to be complemented by organizational resilience, that is, the ability to anticipate, initiate, and take advantage of opportunities while aiming to avoid any negative circumstances of change. Together they enable firms to prepare for changing circumstances, restore their vitality after excruciating setbacks, and become even more effective as a result of the joint effort. Together, they represent an organization's adaptive and adoptive capacity, that is, its *changeability*.

In a context where change is a key aspect of the business environment for the foreseeable future, organizations must become Built_to_Change (Lawler III and Worley 2006). If change is to happen effectively, people at all levels need to:

- embrace change, that is, the willingness to adopt change;
- have a desire or a mindset oriented to manage change;
- have an ability or a way of acting upon change, that is, to adapt to change.

All three aspects can be developed to prepare individuals, groups, and organizations for change, to render organizations more agile, more responsive, and more resilient to change than they might previously have considered possible (Klein 2010).

Construction toys offer a useful metaphor because the enterprise, e-business, or cognitive systems we are concerned with must be configured and reconfigured constantly—precisely the objective of most construction toys. An enterprise system architecture and structure consisting of reusable components reconfigurable in a scalable framework can be an effective base model for creating variable (or Built_to_Change) systems. To achieve this, the nature of the framework appears to be a critical factor. The framework/component concept can be introduced by looking at three types of construction toys and observing how they are used in practice, namely, Model Builder, Erector Set, and LEGO kits (Kale 2019).

The Model Builder's kit has a tight framework: a precise construction sequence, no part interchangeability, and high integration. Erector Set has a loose framework that does not encourage interaction among parts and insufficiently discriminates among compatible parts. In contrast, each component in the LEGO system carries all it needs to interact with other components (the interaction framework rejects most unintended parts), and it can grow without end.

You can build virtually anything over and over again with any of these toys, but fundamental differences in their architecture give each system unique dynamic characteristics. All consist of a basic set of core construction components, and also have an architectural and structural framework that enables connecting the components into an unbounded variety of configurations. Nevertheless, the Model Builder is not as reusable in practice as the Erector Set, and the Erector Set is not as reusable, reconfigurable, or scalable in practice as LEGO, and LEGO is more reusable, reconfigurable, and scalable than either of them. LEGO is the dominant construction toy of choice among preteen builders, who appear to value experimentation and innovation.

> Enterprise (re-)engineering is a holistic and pragmatic approach to building (and changing) an organization to increase its profitability, scalability, and competitiveness in meeting its mission, goals, and objectives. It is concerned with identifying the most appropriate business processes, architectures, and models while establishing the most effective change methods and vice versa (Martin 1995; Verma 2024).

Agile Enterprises

The concept of agility was first used in the "Twenty-First Century Manufacturing Enterprise Strategy Report" published in 1991. This report was prepared with the aim of finding solutions to the problems of the decline and loss of competitiveness in the U.S. manufacturing industry. Roger Nagel, Operations Director of Lehigh University, Iacocca Institute, established the concept of *agile production* as a new production system. The concept of agile production entailed responsiveness, speed, alertness, ability, systematic approach, flexibility, innovation, excellence, social sensitivity, economy, and environmental awareness. Although agility was initially developed regarding production strategies, it has become a concept, a perspective, and a management approach that deals with the entire organization, and coupled with strategic agility and organizational agility, it has become associated with strategic management.

An organization is not only expected to be effective and efficient but should also be able to adapt to the frequent changes in the market environment driven by technology, regulation, and competition—in other words, a *digital company* i.e. it should be agile both in digital enterprise (Rogers 2023) and digital business (Rogers 2016). Enterprise agility has become even more important in these times of globalization, particularly in periods of continuous organizational change that are often caused by an increasing pace of innovation, collaboration with other organizations, new challenges in the market, mergers and acquisitions, societal changes, and/or technology advancements. The organization that can best respond to the fast and frequently changing markets will have better competitive advantages than those that fail to sustain the pace dictated by the process of globalization. This can be realized through organizations acquiring better control and efficiency to manage the changes in their business activities and processes, business architecture, and business models.

Agility has become a pinnacle ability of enterprises. The pace at which customers demand changes, laws and regulations are introduced that affect services and processes, and competitors that can copy services, leads to tremendous pressure—to change to reduce cost, scale up, and adopt. True agility of an organization requires that the workforce, products/services/experiences, business processes, systems, infrastructure, and other elements that make up the enterprise can easily adapt and adopt to changing circumstances (Holbeche 2023; Ozbayrac 2022). The focus on change as the driving factor means that agility is *not a state of being agile but of becoming agile,* since the increased uncertainty and unpredictability in the business environment means that how enterprises respond to their environment itself *needs to be adaptive.*

The three main sources or providers of enterprise agility are (Lank-horst 2012) process, system, and business agility.

1. Process agility entails organizations and processes focused on activities, value delivery, and responsiveness to change. If the current process does not achieve the envisaged goals, they can be changed to achieve the same. Processes have an iterative, incremental way of working, involving all relevant stakeholders.
2. System agility entails systems (both technical and organizational) that are easy to change, like scale. This reduces the effort in system changes and facilitates offline simulation and testing to forecast the effects of changes.
3. Business agility entails using change as an essential part of the business strategy. True enterprise agility starts at the top of the organization. Management is focused on rapid recognition of changes in the environment, speed in responding, and value delivery. It recognizes the value of agility and strategically uses shorter time to market, smarter partnering strategies, lower development costs, and higher customer satisfaction to stay ahead of the competition.

There is a strong connection between the IT competencies of an enterprise, the options this creates, the type of agilities resulting from these options, and the competitive actions the enterprise can take. The three sources of enterprise agility described above are the basis for the three digital transformation models or design blueprints proposed in Chapter 2.

When the environment is changing slowly or predictably, traditional models are adequate. However, as the rate of change increases with increasing globalization, technological breakthroughs, associative alliances, and regulatory changes, enterprises have to look for greater agility, flexibility, and innovation from their companies. Instead of pursuing strategies, structures, and cultures that are designed to create long-term competitive advantages, companies must seek a string of temporary competitive advantages through an approach to organization design that assumes change is normal. With the advent of the Internet and the accompanying extended *virtual* market spaces, enterprises are now competing based on intangible assets such as identity, intellectual property, the ability to attract and stick to customers, and their ability to organize, reorganize frequently, or organize differently in different areas depending on the need. Thus, the need for changes in strategy and organization is much more frequent, and excellence is much more a function of possessing the ability to change. Enterprises need to be built around practices that encourage change, not thwart it. Instead of having to create change efforts, disrupt the status quo, or adapt to change, enterprises need to be Built_to_Change.

Strategic Agility

Strategic agility is defined as an organization's ability to forecast and detect changes in its operating environment through the opportunities and threats it faces, and proactively take action by recombining the resources, processes, and strategies to regain the competitive advantage in the market. The strategic agility of organizations is characterized by:

1. competencies in organization, human resources, technology resources, planning, etc. (ability to meet goals and intentions)
2. flexibility (ability to be adaptable to changing market and environmental conditions with its resources)
3. responsiveness (ability to be sensitive to recognize changes, perceiving opportunities and threats, being able to meet changing customer demands)
4. quickness (ability to use these abilities promptly, that is, as quickly as possible).

Operationalizing Agility

Considering that organizations are open systems in constant interaction with their environment, an agile organization needs to have some organizational characteristics to respond quickly to changing internal and external environmental conditions. Organizations are not only in a dynamic environment consisting of many systems, larger or smaller than themselves, but also a whole consisting of many subsystems that interact dynamically with each other. Organizational agility is typified by three metaphors:

1. The *machine metaphor* represents organizations as rational instruments designed to achieve the purposes of their owners or controllers. Machine organizations are structures where clearly defined hierarchy gains importance, expert roles are distributed within this hierarchical order, and orders and instructions flow from top to bottom. Job descriptions are clear, rules are strict, and everyone is expected to follow procedures and protocols.

2. The *organism metaphor* looks at organizations as wholes made up of interrelated parts. These parts function in such a way as to ensure the survival of the organization as an organismOrganic organizations have a minimum level of hierarchy and flexible structures. They perform the coordination not with hierarchical commands, but at the lateral level through consulting. The ideas of employees are taken into account; this in turn, paves the way for teamwork and strengthens existing teams. There are no rigid job descriptions; instead, there is a strong central communication network. There is a shared set of values and goals rather than managed behavior, instructions, and rules. Downward communication from senior executives has the characteristics of advisory input rather than instruction.

3. The *brain metaphor*, deriving directly from cybernetics, emphasizes active learning rather than the rather passive adaptability that characterizes the organismic view.
   This involves the ability to incorporate and enable human-computer integrated systems. Cognitive organizations have vital elements of knowledge, learning, and core competence.
   - Explicit knowledge learning is the ability to obtain knowledge from external sources, but accessing knowledge in this way is not an institutional core competence. However, if knowledge is captured, imbibed, internalized, and used in the organization's practice in its area of expertise, it can be a core capability of the business to a certain extent and represent a potential core competence.

- Tacit knowledge learning refers to the knowledge in the minds, that is, non-coded, non-formal knowledge, and can be shared experientially and transferred by mutual learning. This form of learning can provide connectivity to core competence and expand the scope of the core competencies. To become explicit knowledge, tacit knowledge should be put on the record. However, this requires the sharing of information in a reliable environment and the integration of information.
- Work learning, also referred to as process learning, is "learning by doing." During the process of carrying out a job, all kinds of transactions and activities performed allow one to gain experience and information. This is of great importance for an organization as it broadens the scope of knowledge and core competence.
- R&D (research and development) learning can be considered as the most important form of learning, because it is not possible for innovation to develop without R&D, and at the same time, innovation is the basis and source of sustainable advantage.

Resilient Enterprises

Organizational resilience is the capacity to deploy different forms of strategic agility when confronted with the unexpected and to respond effectively to changing conditions. It involves taking prompt, creative, situation-specific, robust, and transformative actions to minimize the impact of powerful events that are not avoided or avoidable and that have the potential to jeopardize the organization's long-term survival.

In a future defined by volatility, unpredictability, complexity, ambiguity, nonlinearity, emergence, multiple stakeholders, and rapid change, organizations need resilience to respond to severely disruptive change. Darwin's principle of *survival of the fittest* for the life sciences applies to the ever-changing business world that is subjected to unexpected variations as well; only systems that can successfully reorganize these factors and beat these challenges will survive.

Charles Darwin made an important point in The Origin of Species in early 1859: "It is neither the strongest of a species that survives, nor the most intelligent. Rather, it is those who can best adapt to change." Digital Darwinism always sets in when *technologies and society change faster than the ability of companies to adapt to these changes.*

Forecasts regarding the longevity of S&P-500 companies assume that the average period that a company belongs to this group will continue to shorten over the next decade. Based on the Innosight study, the average length of belonging to the group of S&P-500 companies or *retention period* has decreased significantly (Scott et al. 2018):

- In 1965, the *retention period* was 32 years.
- By 2016, the *retention period* had decreased to 24 years.
- By 2030, the *retention period* will shrink to only 14 years.

Conventional VUCA organizational risks are as follows:

a. *Volatility*: It is a term that indicates extreme and rapid fluctuations in a business environment. The pace, the volume, and the magnitude of change define the degree of turbulence it creates in the business or industrial environments. Examples are price volatility that can cause supply chain risk, or lack of availability of the commodity in contrast to its demand flow that can cause price risks, etc.

b. *Uncertainty*: The lack of knowledge about situations causes uncertainty in any field which results in an unpredictable future and affects the long-term growth of that organization. Examples are never-ending customer needs and changes in customer tastes and preferences; technological changes; introduction of new trade policies and multiple barriers to trade; launching of new products as a substitute for currently used products in the market, etc.

c. *Complexity*: With rapid industrialization, complexity arises due to the interconnected parts, networks, and procedures within the organization; the external business environment might even be unidentifiable and contradict each other, leading to complexity in decision making. The more interrelatedness in an organization, the more difficult it is to understand the cause of the problem and the statement of risks. An example is a successful consumer goods company that contains different brands, products, an efficient network of global distribution, etc., that may lead to complexity in understanding the cause of future risks.

d. *Ambiguity*: If the problem statement lacks clarity, confidence in probability assessments, and the diversity of potential results in which the outcome cannot be clearly described, then it is termed as ambiguity in the business environment. Examples are when a new product plan or technology is introduced in the market, then the diversity in customers' expectations and behaviors may cause ambiguity in decision-making for an organization.

Unlike stable environments, where things are linear and expected, in a nonlinear world, it is hard to ascertain the cause and effect, the output is not proportional to the change in the input, and it is, therefore, hard to plan or manage the unexpected. The environment is complex because of the multiplicity of stakeholders involved, the number of interactions, and the sheer number of linkages and dependencies. It is not clear who all the stakeholders are, and the primary stakeholders (i.e., customers) are indecisive—they do not know what they want. Scope, requirements, solutions, and stakeholders are emergent and unpredictable from the bottom up; consequently, it is hard to plan top-down in a continually shifting landscape.

Rapid Response

Resilient organizations are able to address impactful events that affect their business because they anticipate and are alert to both internal and environmental changes—opportunities as well as challenges—and effectively respond to those changes using available resources in a timely, flexible, affordable, and relevant manner.

Restoration

An organization demonstrates resiliency when it experiences a severe, life-threatening setback but can reinvent itself around its core values. At the organizational level, this is about the robustness of systems, which is the capacity for resisting, absorbing, and responding, even reinventing if required, in response to fast and/or disruptive change that cannot be avoided. Different levels of resilience may result in different organizational outcomes. While modest levels of resilience should enable a firm to recover from disruptions and resume normal operations, high levels of resilience may place an organization ahead of its competition since it has learned to adopt to environmental disruptions and can create new options and capabilities while undergoing a robust transformation in the face of adverse events and circumstances.

> Central to an organization's resilience capacity is its relationship with its workforce, and how the workforce feels "engaged" or not with the organization and its fortunes. While people are often stated as being a company's greatest asset, few businesses have a clear model of leadership that improves engagement, removes barriers to innovation, and uncovers hidden strengths in people and the organization (Lardi 2023).

Anti-Fragility

Naseem Taleb introduced the concept of anti-fragility to analyze and explain why it is not enough for large natural or man-made systems to be robust enough to handle predictable events with large impacts. In an unpredictable world, systems must be able to handle randomness, volatility, and unforeseen large-impact events. Learning from incidents is needed to prevent systems from developing fragilities over time (Taleb 2012).

The research literature has long categorized complex adaptive systems as fragile or robust to incidents with a particular type of impact. Fragile systems are vulnerable to the impact of these incidents, while robust systems withstand or absorb them. Unlike robust systems, anti-fragile systems learn from such incidents how to function in-creasingly well in a changing environment (Miles 2016). Anti-fragile systems need incidents to remain well-adapted to their environments. Without the ability to learn from incidents, anti-fragile systems be-come fragile over time as the systems themselves and their environ-ments change. The human immune system, with its ability to adapt and self-repair, is a prime example of a system that is anti-fragile to many types of impact.

Building the Agile Enterprise Through Digital Transformations

Sustaining an agile enterprise is not a matter of searching for the strat-egy but continuously strategizing, not a matter of specifying an orga-nization design but committing to a process of organizing, and not generating value but continuously improving the efficiency and effec-tiveness of the value generation process. It is a search for a series of temporary configurations that create short-term advantages. In turbu-lent environments, enterprises that string together a series of temporary but adequate competitive advantages will outperform enterprises that stick with one advantage for an extended period. The key issue for the Built_to_Change enterprise is orchestration, or coordinating the mul-tiple changing subsystems to produce high levels of current enterprise performance.

Being agile means being proficient at change. Agility allows an en-terprise to do anything it wants to do whenever it wants to—or has to—do it. This can be achieved through *digital transformation*. Thus, an agile enterprise can employ business process reengineering (BPR) as a core competency and can hasten its conversion to lean production when greater efficiencies are useful; it can deploy greater resources and render up-scaling or out-scaling competency when greater performance is essen-tial, and it can continue to succeed when constant innovation becomes the dominant competitive strategy. Agility can be wielded overtly as a business strategy as well as covertly as a sustainable-existence competency through *digital transformation*.

Digital Maturity Model (DMM)

There is a strong link between transitions from digital transformation maturity to digital maturity. A company's readiness for technological transformation is determined by an assessment of the level of compliance with fundamental processes and their management methods of using the accumulated information. Determining the level of maturity of the management system, one can characterize the stage of the company's readiness for digital transformation, identify the company's potential for development, and choose the direction of modernization and growth (Carrijo et al. 2023).

The *Digital Maturity Model (DMM)* is:

- Level 1—Computerization: Systems have been introduced to enable process automation by any IT system. Entering data into the system is carried out manually. Basic infrastructure and technologies do not give correct business functionality by themselves, but are necessary for the introduction of advanced technologies, e.g., enterprise systems like SAP ECC 6.x.
- Level 2—Connectivity: Systems have been introduced to enable operational data of the processes to enter the system automatically, without human intervention. Adjacent systems and technologies have been integrated. The control action is carried out remotely, e.g., e-business systems like mySAP.com.
- Level 3—Transparency: Systems have been introduced to enable key process indicators (KPIs) visualization and tracking in real time. Predictive systems have been introduced to predict the future state, e.g., SAP Analytics.
- Level 4—Adaptability: Systems have been introduced that have a corrective effect on infrastructure and technologies either independently or within a corporate system to maximize efficiency, e.g., SAP HANA.
- Level 5—Adoptability: Systems have been introduced that have correct native functionality either independently or within a corporate system to maximize effectiveness, e.g., SAP Leonardo with SAP S/4HANA.

> Stata argued that the bottleneck of many U.S. companies was man-
> agement innovation, rather than technological innovation (Stata
> 1989). Management innovation is a particular prerequisite of inno-
> vation strategy, and facilitates the efficient use of process innovations
> and technical products, thus improving organizational performance
> through productivity, lead times, quality, and flexibility (Lin 2018).

A company that works effectively and efficiently achieves a stable state in the global market and has a high index of readiness for digital transformation. The management of such companies can: identify weaknesses that need improvements and innovations through IT technologies, organize monitoring of changes in the environment, increase satisfaction of the needs and expectations of stakeholders, and improve structural goals.

Digital Transformation

To achieve the highest level of digital maturity, the approach is the improvement and implementation of business models and IT technologies in enterprises, which takes as a basis a detailed analysis of business and processes down to operational activities. New modern technologies are taken as the basis for optimization. Thus, the output is a detailed program for the digital transformation of the main business models, architecture, and processes to improve the effectiveness and efficiency of the enterprise (Hess 2022).

Fortunately, there is a wonderful metaphor that can be used to understand digital transformation based on how nature expresses the highest degree of drastic and dramatic change through the process of *metamorphosis*. The grasshopper, exemplifying partial metamorphosis, grows progressively bigger through several stages, looking like a version of the adult at every stage. This is an excellent metaphor for applying new technology to optimize existing ways to get bigger, faster, and more efficient. There is significant value for organizations in optimization through automation, analytics, predictive modeling, machine learning (ML), and smart decision-making. Yet a poor or outdated process, which is well optimized, is still a poor or outdated process, necessitating sometimes the need to go beyond (Perkin and Abraham 2021; Evans 2017).

The caterpillar, exemplifying complete metamorphosis, undergoes a comprehensive change in anatomical and physiological form as it progresses through a series of life stages to emerge as a butterfly. This is an excellent metaphor for true transformation—reinventing and redesigning business processes, structures and architectures, business models, and mindsets because new technology creates new possibilities. Yet this process of transformation from a *caterpillar to a butterfly* brings with it some critical challenges, including navigating the "messy middle" stage of transformation, which is likely to be characterized by higher levels of uncertainty and complexity, and necessitating the need to unlearn some behaviors to become a different but functioning whole again (Pismen 2020).

Defining Digital Transformation

Digital transformation can be defined as follows (modified from the version in Solis et al. 2014):

Digital transformation is the realignment of processes (ways of working and cultures, and enterprise systems); technologies (infrastructure and application systems, and e-business systems); and business models (value proposition and revenue models, and cognitive systems) to more effectively engage digital customers at every touch point in the customer experience life cycle.

Digital transformation utilizes digital technologies to fundamentally change business operations, scaling, and value delivery (along with concomitant customer experiences). It's about integrating digital technology into all areas of a business, leading to significant improvements in efficiency, scaling, and value innovation. Digital transformation reshapes how organizations streamline processes, engage with their exponentially multiplying customers, and compete in the digital age.

Digital transformations can be of three types, namely, digitization, digitalization, or smartization, and digital metamorphosis. *Digitization* refers to the process of converting or switching from analog to digital format. It would be a misconception to think that the digitization phase has already been completed and done with; with the advent of metaverse (including augmented reality [AR] and virtual reality [VR]; see Chapter 8, Section "Metaverse"), it is easy to envisage charting of newer areas of digitization like computer vision, visualization, visual recognition and so on, in the future. *Digitalization or smartization* refers to the waves of changes that empower society through the increased utilization of digital technology. Finally, introducing a new term, *digital metamorphosis* refers to the adaptations and adoptions that firms make to thrive in an increasingly digital world.

Smartization incorporates the characteristics and effects of digitization, and, in turn, digital metamorphosis incorporates the characteristics and effects of concerned smartization(s) and digitization(s). In the contemporary enterprise context, *digitization* majorly focuses on business processes, *smartization* majorly focuses on business architecture, and *metamorphosis* majorly focuses on business models. Accordingly, digital metamorphosis recursively, cumulatively, and comprehensively incorporates the characteristics, technologies, and effects of preceding constituent smartization(s) and digitization(s). Thus, in this book, digital transformations refer to three types of digital transformations, namely, digitizations, smartizations, and metamorphosis. Correspondingly, business-driven digital transformations (BDDT) focus on three types of artifacts, namely, business processes, business architectures, and business models, respectively.

Parts I, II, and III focus respectively on Efficient, Scalable, and Innovable Digital Transformation Models or Design Blueprints for achieving the respective goals of efficiency (profitability), scaling (volume growth), and innovation (business growth, i.e., maneuvering to comparatively blue ocean business opportunities), leveraging relevant technologies that are suitable in specific contexts. They correspond respectively to the comparatively/relatively enhanced focus on:

- Part I   Digitization, profit maximization, and mass production
- Part II   Digitalization or smartization, value appropriation maximization, and mass customization
- Part III   Digital metamorphosis of business models, market share maximization, and mass innovation

Historically, digital transformations have spanned decades, moving from efficiency/profitability-driven business/enterprise processes in the 1990s to scalability/availability-driven business/enterprise architectures in the 2010s, onto customer-centric customized/innovated business/enterprise models in the 2030s. Not discounting elements of processes, architectures, and business models in *each* of these three parts, these approximately correspond to Part I, Part II, and Part III of this book.

The author would hasten to add that it would be wrong to think that an *efficient* digital transformation model or design blueprint (i.e., Part I) is *old or old-fashioned* or *non-modern*. It is just that some parts of all businesses, now and in the future, will continue to be *defined and managed by business processes to enhance efficiency*. An efficient digital transformation model or design blueprint will entail even the latest technologies like Cyber-Physical Systems (CPS). It should be highlighted that in the second track of chapters (Chapters 4, 6, and 8), the technologies specified in the "Means of Digital Transformation" subsection are only the characteristic minimum required to become placeholders in a particular digital transformation model or design blueprint. Nothing stops the organization from upgrading the technologies in specific categories beyond what has been indicated. For example, in Chapter 3, it has been indicated that double-entry accounting (DEA) should be adequate to deliver the envisaged level of governance. However, nothing prevents the organization from leapfrogging to implement triple-entry accounting (TEA) to deliver enhanced auditable governance via blockchain technology. Similarly, in Chapter 4, Section "Means of Digital Transformation for Efficiency," it has been indicated that an upgrade to SAP ECC 6.x and SAP NetWeaver should be adequate to deliver the envisaged level of features and functionality. However, nothing stops or bars the organization from upgrading even further to SAP S/4HANA and SAP HANA—if the focus of the transformation is *enhancing business efficiency*, it will continue to be "Efficiency Design Blueprint" regardless of what higher technologies are being deployed per se. An organization can also have all three models prevalent simultaneously albeit in different projects or business divisions. Moreover, now and in the future, the *innovator's dilemma* may dictate continuance with any of these models, in their originating project(s) or division(s), till such time that the digitally transformed model(s) or design blueprint(s) is tested and proven in the market and taken a firm foothold in their originating project(s) or division(s).

Here are the characteristic features of this approach:

1. It identifies three parts of effort for any *business-driven digital transformation (BDDT)*: Business Efficiency, Business Scaling, and Business Model Innovation (BMI). It highlights that the consequent three digital transformation models or design blueprints involve three different artifacts, viz., business processes, business architectures, and business models.

2. It addresses the WHY & HOW questions of *digital transformations* for achieving the *digital company*, i.e., the dual objective of *digital enterprise* and *digital business* that traditionally remain unaddressed in such exercises. This book uniquely explains how M. Porter's standard approach to strategy management reveals the primary objectives for any BDDT effort: Efficient, Scalable, and Innovable digital transformation models or design blueprints.

3. It is presented in two parallel tracks of chapters in Parts I, II, and III, focusing respectively on the part's overarching strategic vision, and corresponding reframing efforts and applicable transformative actions. Again, in each of these parts, M. Porter's approach to strategy management is used to map the vision and objectives obtained from the first track of chapters *directly onto the respective IT strategies* in the second track of chapters.

4. It demonstrates how BDDT design blueprints seamlessly incorporate not only past transformation efforts like change management and business process reengineering (BPR) but also the envisioned latest e-business and innovative technological strategies.

5. It combines the best of concepts and theories of business management with the latest concepts and frameworks of IT without getting entrapped in the traditional duality or dichotomy between

business and IT. The envisaged role of cyber-physical systems (CPS) and extended reality systems (AR/VR systems) in future enterprises belie maintaining any such duality or dichotomy between business and IT. This also paves the way for a new, more holistic view of organizational strategy, of not business aligned with IT, but business and IT working to drive change synergistically.

6. It incorporates the latest themes of customer centricity (mass innovation), customer experiences (emotion & attention), and multiple business (value) models that are critical for BDDT. Thus, it adds *experiences* within the spectrum of enterprise offerings on par with traditional offerings like products and services. Products can be customized limitlessly with services; similarly, experiences can be innovated limitlessly with services. Correspondingly, services can be productized, and experiences can be servicized for better administration and management.

This chapter presents a *unified approach* encompassing all such digital transformations by combining them through a business-driven strategy management approach. It explains *why* and *how* the digital transformation imperative compels all organizations to iteratively undertake digital transformation to adapt to ongoing digital disruption and compete effectively as a *digital company*, i.e. a combination of *digital enterprise* and *digital business*. Not discounting elements of processes, digital enterprise, and digital business in each of the three parts, broadly, Part I corresponds to top-down strategy making, Part II corresponds to bottom-up strategy making, and Part III corresponds to horizontal or lateral strategy making. Similarly, not discounting elements of processes, digital enterprise, and digital business in each of the three parts, broadly, Part I corresponds to the digitization of data and business processes (Saldanha and Passerini 2023; Schank 2023; Hess 2022); Part II corresponds to digitalization, i.e., smartization of a *digital enterprise* (architecture and infrastructure) and a *digital business* (E-business & E-commerce systems) (Rogers 2023; Wang 2024; Shivakumar 2024; Hoe 2023), and, finally, Part III corresponds to a *digital company* i.e. a digital metamorphosis of a *digital enterprise* (software-defined networks (SDN) and edge computing) and a *digital business* (business model with customer-, partner-, and employee specificity) (Rogers 2016; Evans 2017; Tardieu et al. 2020; Linz et al. 2021, 2017; Mitchell and Coles 2003; Lardi 2023).

1. Business-Driven Digital Transformation (BDDT) is not a state of *being* but of *becoming*—it is a continual process.
2. The BDDT framework suggested in this book enables addressing *multiple and heterogeneous* granularity/levels of business efficiencies, business scaling, and business models innovation within the same enterprise—it is too involved an issue to be described here and is beyond the scope of this book.
3. There is a certain degree of historicity to the sequence of BDDT. However, initiatives in the three identified design blueprints do not have to be run sequentially per se, and can be initiated within any part, any time, and at any level of the organization to run concurrently, provided they are all collated and eventually aligned sequentially within the overall elapsed time frames indicated above.
4. The attendant issues of leadership, change management, people management, talent management, etc., and changes in their nature *even during the extended durations of the enterprise-wide BDDT initiative itself*, are important and significant (Lardi 2023); but for the benefit of limiting the size of the book, these are again considered beyond the scope of this book, which is focused primarily on proposing a fundamental framework for the digital transformation models or design blueprints of BDDT.
5. Within a digital transformation, there is a certain degree of historicity to the sequence of technologies, techniques, and tools. For instance, the framework incorporates a hint of the historical evolution of digital enterprises and digital businesses. A chapter in Parts I, II, and III presumes inclusion (and availability) of all preceding technologies, i.e., technologies explained in chapters before the chapter concerned.

Digital Transformation Iterations

In the past few decades, there has been a misconception regarding the mystery of *missing productivity* despite immense investments in IT, software, and services, leading to what has been termed as the "productivity paradox" (Bessen 2022). The enigma gets resolved only when it is realized that a major portion of IT productivity is *transmuted* into the organization's ability (i.e., flexibility, reconfigurability, adaptability, and adoptability) to respond to the market changes without majorly disrupting the normal business operations. This is effectively *technical credits,* opposite to the concept of *technical debts* (Lawless et al. 2021).

This chapter demonstrates that digital transformation towards a digital company, involving both components of digital enterprise and digital business, also engineers its enterprise agility (i.e., flexibility, adaptations, and adoptions) to address and respond effectively to market changes and challenges in the organization's profitability, delivery structures, and competitiveness.

Digital transformation enables organizations to withstand a heavy combined onslaught of dynamic changes in profitability, delivery structures, and competitiveness, till triggered by unforeseen dramatic changes either in the go-to-market conditions or the technology or the market competitiveness itself, it is time for another *iteration* of *digital transformation.*

Across a few iterations of digital transformation, an organization strives to rapidly become a *digital company* where the distinctions become blurred and *digital business* is indistinguishable from the *digital enterprise.* For instance, retail banking branches were digitally transformed by ATMs (Automated Teller Machines), which in turn were digitally transformed by fully 'metamorphesized' electronic payment systems. Organizations strive to rapidly become a fully *digital companies* because, otherwise, their operations may be rapidly decimated just like retail banking branches or ATMs. Kodak did not comprehend the converging power of *digital camera* vis-a-vis their mainstay category of *photo films* till it was too late to take impactful corrective action. Similarly, Nokia did not comprehend the converging power of *smart phones* vis-a-vis their mainstay category of feature phones till it was too late to take impactful corrective action. Smart phones that were effectively a *digitally transformed* general-purpose PC with internet access in one's hand, were combined with mobile communication, authenticated identity, time watch, teleconference node, email, video communication, camera, payment node, locational device, healthcare device, and so on. This converged device decimated many disparate services and companies that were earlier independently viable businesses on their own like Sony Walkman, Blackberry, Skype, and so on.

Conclusion

This chapter sets the context for the whole book, focusing on the rationale for continuous digital transformations. It also established the origin of the theme of three transformation models or design blueprints discussed throughout this book. Built_to_Change organizations mandate agile and resilient enterprises, but a Built_to_Change organization is not a state of *being* but of *becoming*—it is a continuous process.

This chapter substantiates why agile enterprises can only be achieved through iterative digital transformation to a digital company via both aspects of an organization, namely, digital enterprise and digital business. This chapter presents a unified approach encompassing all such digital transformations by combining them through a business-driven strategy management approach, hence the zeal for iterative digital transformations to perpetuate Built_to_Change organizations.

CHAPTER 2

Enterprise Strategy Management

This chapter presents the three options of a business-driven digital transformation strategy based on the traditional M. Porter's approach to enterprise strategy. It explains the triad of activity-based, resource-based, and market-based views of digital transformation strategy and what each entails. This background ensures the selection of the appropriate digital transformation models or design blueprints suitable for the priorities identified in addressing the challenges envisaged by organizations in their businesses. It presents a framework to understand the underlying seven dimensions of any digital transformation effort, namely, the type of strategy operations, network business model, architecture, connecting mechanism, communications, social networks, and analytics. These seven dimensions are employed across all chapters in Parts I, II, and III to enable a comparative perspective across the three digital transformation models or design blueprints. This chapter ensures a uniform evaluation criterion across the three digital transformation models or design blueprints.

Built_to_Change Strategy Management

Strategy management is the management of an organization's long-term purpose. A distinction is often made between strategic management and operations. Strategic management is also about managing an organization, including the extent to which operations serve the strategic needs of the organization's strategy. Organizations need to have a common purpose. Purpose is the primary and basic reason for an organization's existence. Purpose is the basic reason for an organization's long-term existence, and it is the starting point for understanding an organization in its entirety. Purpose is articulated at the top level, and it is communicated from there through purpose statements of vision, mission, and values. This is important if everybody in an organization is to work effectively together. Senior managers spend considerable time clarifying and making the purpose meaningful. This is done not only to inspire the organization but also to help employees in an organization develop their priorities and roles, and to understand the priorities and roles of others they work with.

A situation analysis evaluates an organization's current external and internal situations; these are used to develop strategic objectives. The strategy used to achieve strategic objectives is conditioned by the scale and nature of an organization's activities, whether single-business, multi-business, or global in orientation. Implementation of strategy includes organizing for managing strategic control and change, including feedback and learning through strategic performance management. In the end, the effectiveness of an organization's strategic management depends on the strategic leadership, including the nature and commitment of the top management.

Five Forces Analysis

The strength of these forces and the way they influence each other determine an industry's profitability and shape its structure. The central force is the intensity of the rivalry between existing competitors; this is influenced by four other forces: the threat of new business, the bargaining power of customers, the bargaining power of suppliers, and the threat of substitute products and services. If they are weak, above-average returns are possible. If the competitive forces are intense, an organization is unlikely to earn attractive returns on its investment. It is important to realize that the five competitive forces are factors that apply in the long term.

   a. Force 1—Risk of Entry from Potential Competitors: The challenge for new entrants is to find ways to overcome the entry barriers without the heavy costs of investment that cancel out the profitability of operating in the industry. If entry barriers are low and industry profitability is high, new businesses can enter the industry and drive down prices and raise costs for the existing competitors. New competition from outside brings additional capacity pressures on existing market shares that influence prices, costs, and investment in an industry.

b. Force 2—Threat of Substitute Products: The threat of substitutes influences an industry's profitability because it may enable an industry's customers to go elsewhere. The threat of substitutes is high if it is apparent that alternatives offer an attractive price-performance trade-off to the industry's offer.

c. Force 3—Bargaining Power of Suppliers: The strength of suppliers will influence the profitability of customer organizations; if this is strong, suppliers can negotiate higher prices to their advantage.

d. Force 4—Bargaining Power of Buyers: Powerful customers or groups of customers can force suppliers in the industry to lower prices, demand more customized features, and force up service and quality levels. This activity drives down an organization's profitability and shifts the balance of power and value in favor of buyers.

e. Force 5—Rivalry among Established Companies: Rivalry is strong when competitors are roughly of equal power and size, and are numerous. In this case, it is difficult for any organization to win customers without taking them from rivals. Unless the industry has a leader which sets the competitive conditions for the industry, competition is likely to be unstable and costly for the industry as a whole.

> In view of the increasing and decisive role of regulatory bodies, there is a need to add another force:
>
> Force 6—Regulators: Regulators strongly influence not only the offerings, sales, pricing, and so on, but also the competitive conditions for the benefit of end customers.

Generic Strategies

Strategic management aims to provide a strong, long-term competitive position that, over time, will benefit an organization's stakeholders more lastingly than short-term profitability. The external environment will likely be subject to sudden shocks as well as continuous change, so it is necessary to ensure that strategic priorities are constant and consistent so that the organization as a whole is clear about its purpose and can adjust to change accordingly. Michael Porter (1980) refers to these as generic strategies; when an organization targets a whole industry, a strategy is either a cost-leadership generic strategy or an industry-wide differentiation generic strategy. When an organization targets a part of an industry, such as a market segment, a generic strategy is focused on either cost or differentiation.

a. Cost-Leadership Generic Strategy: Low-cost leaders often sell a standard or no-frills product and/or service. They place considerable emphasis on taking advantage of scale but are also likely to take advantage of any other opportunities to lower costs. A low-cost leader does not necessarily have to lower its prices below those of its rivals. It may do this to win more customers and to reap more economies of scale, but if its costs are lower than the industry's average, all it has to do to earn above-average returns is to command prices at or near the industry average.

   Walmart and Southwest Airlines have earned strong market positions because of the low-cost advantages they have achieved over their rivals. Low-cost provider strategies can produce a durable competitive edge when rivals find it hard to match the low-cost leader's approach to driving costs out of the business. If an organization has a larger share of its industry's markets than its rivals, it can achieve relatively greater economies of scale and scope. Economies of scale are obtained through cost savings that occur when higher volumes allow unit costs to be reduced. Economies of scope involve cost savings that are available as a result of separate products sharing the same facilities.

b. Differentiation Industry-Wide Generic Strategy: A differentiation industry-wide generic strategy offers unique value for an industry's customers in a way that more than offsets the costs of differentiation, which enables an organization to earn above-average profits for the industry. Unlike cost leadership, there can be more than one successful industry-wide differentiation competitive position in an industry. This happens when there are significantly different and distinctive customer groups that value product and service attributes in contrasting ways. The organization concerned will seek to reduce its costs but only in a way that does not affect the sources of differentiation and the value it creates.

Successful adopters of broad differentiation strategies include Johnson & Johnson in baby products (product reliability) and Apple (innovative products). Differentiation strategies can be powerful so long as a company is sufficiently innovative to thwart rivals' attempts to copy or closely imitate its product offering. The development of an industry's markets over time tends to favor differentiation, especially if the industry is associated with consumers with preferences that change frequently and who are affluent. In general, as consumers become more affluent, lower prices may be considered secondary to quality and branding.

c. Cost-Focused Strategy: This involves concentrating on a narrow buyer segment (or market niche) and outcompeting rivals by having lower costs than rivals and thus being able to serve niche members at a lower price. Private-label manufacturers of food, health, beauty products, and nutritional supplements use their low-cost advantage to offer supermarket buyers lower prices than those demanded by producers of branded products.

d. Differentiation-Focused Strategy: This involves concentrating on a narrow buyer segment (or market niche) and outcompeting rivals by offering niche members customized attributes that meet their tastes and requirements better than rivals' products. Louis Vuitton and Rolex have sustained their advantage in the luxury goods industry through a focus on affluent consumers demanding luxury and prestige.

The prefix 'Built_to_Change' in the Section heading has been used to highlight the changed context while discussing Porter's conventional approach to strategy management and strategy. The significance of this context would become apparent at the time of implementing these strategies (see Epilogue **'Implementing a Transformation Model'**). Digital transformation implements the chosen strategies only via digital technologies. It is the digital technologies employed and deployed for implementing the designated strategies *that are inherently Built_to_Change because of their inherent modularity, portability, multi-layered architecture, service-oriented architecture, and extensive interoperability*

> *enabled by Application Programming Interfaces (APIs), etc. (Kale 2018c, 2019, 2017a, 2020).* To give an analogy, this goes much beyond the capabilities of LEGO kits because LEGO does not enable player-defined changes or creation of *new LEGO bricks (see p.5). LEGO would be on par with the concept of digital transformation if it routinely incorporated a 3D printer (with allied systems and materials) that would make possible changes or the creation of new LEGO bricks.*

Activity-Based View of Strategy

According to Porter's activity-based view (ABV) of strategy, creating unique and valuable market positions can be achieved in three ways:

a. Access-based positioning: to serve the broader needs of many customers in a narrow market
b. Variety-based positioning: to serve a few needs of many customers
c. Needs-based positioning: to serve the broader needs of a few customers

In Porter's view, strategy rests on the unique activities performed by a firm. A firm's uniqueness is based on its ability to create a unique and valuable position involving a different set of activities; a successful strategy pinpoints a different set of activities to deliver a unique mix of value. The individual activities a firm performs do not necessarily generate a unique mix of customer value; rather, it is how the activities are performed and combined that explains a firm's superior performance. Indeed, how well all the activities of a firm complement each other is more important than how well a company performs in "core competencies, critical resources, and key success factors." Southwest Airlines can offer a unique mix of value to passengers (low price, fun, convenience, quick aircraft turnaround at airports) primarily because of the activities it performs (operating on a point-to-point basis, no worker unions, a culture that stimulates employees to help each other, offering no meals or seat assignments).

A strategic position requires trade-offs. A firm should not and will not succeed if it tries to take more than one position. For example, an airline can either provide full-scale service or scaled-down service, but it cannot do both at the same time. The reason for trade-offs is primarily due to a firm's activities. It is difficult for a firm to configure itself to be flexible enough to support more than one market position. For example, an airline cannot and will not succeed if it tries to position itself as a low-cost carrier while operating as a full-service carrier. The problem stems from limits on internal control and coordination, and a high risk of confusion in delivering more than one type of service to customers.

Resource-Based View of Strategy

Inside-out perspectives center on an organization's internal environment and the resource-based view (RBV) of strategy. Strategic resources are those organizational attributes that combine to give a unique competitive advantage; they are typically core competencies that, over time, require dynamic capabilities to manage them. The aim is to manage an internal fit of strategic resources to create and sustain a unique competitive difference. According to the RBV, firm-specific resources matter most to the competitive difference.

Core competencies are the organization-specific competencies people have that are shared and used in common in ways that give the organization its competitive advantage. Core competencies produce a different way of working and a competitive difference that rivals cannot emulate. An organization's core competencies are characterized as bundles or patterns of skills, knowledge, and supporting resources that give the organization its signature pattern of competencies that are characteristic of its uniqueness.

The VRIO approach, developed by Barney (Barney 2002), serves the identification of core competencies, which can be understood as the highest possible manifestation of competitive advantage. The term "VRIO" stands for the initials of the following four key questions, which are used for the identification of core competencies:

i. The value question: Do the respective resources and abilities of a company permit an adequate reaction to opportunities and threats from the company environment? Answering yes to this question means that the respective resources and abilities are valuable for the company.

ii. The rarity question: Are only a few (or no) competitors in possession of the respective resources or abilities? If yes, these are classified as rare.

iii. The imitability question: Is it impossible, or hardly possible (i.e., only at a high cost) for competitors to imitate the resources and abilities of a company?

iv. The organization question: Is a company organized in such a way that its valuable, rare, and inimitable (or hardly imitable) resources and abilities can be optimally exploited? If this question can be answered with yes, the highest possible manifestation of a competitive advantage for the respective resource or ability—and therefore a core competency—has been achieved.

Table 2.1 demonstrates the logic of the VRIO approach as a whole (Barney 2002). If a resource or ability is not valuable, questions about rarity, imitability, and optimal usage by the company are irrelevant—there exists a competitive disadvantage. If a resource or ability is valuable, but not rare, a competitive parity is given. If a resource or ability is rare but easy to imitate, then there is only a temporary competitive advantage. A sustained competitive advantage exists if the question of whether the respective resource or ability is optimally exploited is the only one to be answered with no. If this question can also be answered in the affirmative, a core competency exists, based on the logic of the VRIO scheme.

Table 2.1 The VRIO scheme

Value?	Rare?	Difficult to Imitate?	Exploited by Organization	Competitive Implications
No	–	–	–	Competitive disadvantage
Yes	No	–	–	Competitive parity
Yes	Yes	No	–	Temporary competitive advantage
Yes	Yes	Yes	No	Sustained competitive advantage
Yes	Yes	Yes	Yes	Core competency

Dynamic capabilities are an organization's ability to renew and recreate its strategic capabilities (including core competencies) to meet the needs of a changing environment. Toyota Production System is an example of dynamic capability. All automakers now have lean production systems similar to that of Toyota, which may suggest that it is no longer a uniquely distinctive capability and cannot be a strategic resource in that sense. However, dynamic capabilities are often similar across different organizations, and the real competitive differences are in the details of their application—factors such as timing, cost, and learning effects—which can produce remarkable differences in performance. Lean activities, including total quality management (TQM), business excellence, benchmarking, and organizational learning, are closely integrated, complementary activities that together add value that exceeds the sum of their parts. An organization's dynamic capability, if it involves a complex integration of these methodologies, is likely to produce markedly superior performance.

Best-cost Differentiation Generic Strategy

Best-cost differentiation generic strategy fits well into the RBV of strategy. The RBV has been contrasted to Porter's ideas about generic strategy. While it aims to minimize its costs through economies of scale, lean production and just-in-time management facilitate a demand-pull rather than a supply-push approach for creating value. Senior executives use top-down strategic priorities that encourage bottom-up operational strategies that are designed to achieve both productivity improvements and continuous improvement in customer value.

The value chain concept can be extended beyond the boundaries of an organization to include strategy-related activities in distribution and the supply chain. The idea is that suppliers should manage their activities in ways that are consistent with the business strategy of their customers. This can be envisaged as a series of linked value chains across relevant distributors and suppliers. Synergies are sought between an industrial customer's core competencies and those of upstream suppliers and between its downstream distributors and customers.

Market-Based View of Strategy

The outside-in perspective is referred to as the market-based view (MBV) of strategy. The most influential work on competitive strategy comes from Michael Porter of the Harvard Business School. His thinking belongs to a well-established industrial organization tradition dating back to the 1960s; this places importance on the external environment as a determining influence for a successful strategy. The aim is to achieve and sustain a strong competitive position within an organization's industry. It starts with an analysis of an industry to determine its attractiveness and the choice of a competitive strategy to take advantage of the opportunities. Strategy-related activities are coordinated and optimized through a value chain.

The strategic management process from the outside in starts with monitoring and review of the background trends to identify and assess opportunities and threats. External conditions are constantly changing, and organizations need to monitor and review strategy continuously to be able to exploit advantageous opportunities and effectively manage any emerging threats. The most comprehensive and most used approach for grouping and reviewing macro-environmental trends in strategic management is PESTEL, which is an acronym for Political, Economic, Social, Technological, Environment, and Legal factors. Coupled and integrated changes over time in any of these areas are liable to lead to the transformation of industries. While PESTEL analysis is primarily about monitoring and reviewing longer-term trends, there are also single events that cannot easily be foreseen. These are structural breaks that subvert trends and change existing behavioral patterns. Like the COVID virus epidemic, some are so potentially catastrophic that a societal and perhaps a global response is required. These will necessitate organizations in general to rethink their purpose and overall strategy.

The industry life cycle likens an industry's life to that of a living organism: markets expand over time, eventually maturing and declining. The life cycle has an introduction, growth, maturity, and decline stages as shown in Figure 2.1.

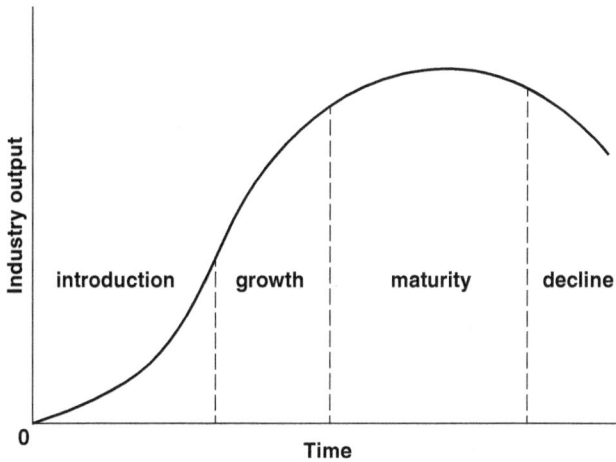

Figure 2.1 Industry life cycle stages

Digital Transformation Strategies

As explained in the Preface, it is singularly important to have the IT strategy emerge from the same process that traditionally gave rise to the business strategy. It is important that the BDDT blueprints adopted in this book must emerge not on an ad hoc basis but most naturally from (say) M. Porter's standard approach to strategy management. Undertaking such an exercise results in identifying three main strategies for fundamentally realizing Built_to_Change enterprises:

  i. Activity-Based View (ABV) (Porter 1985; Sheehan and Foss 2009)
 ii. Resource-Based View (RBV) (Barney 1991, 1997)
iii. Market-Led or Market-Based View (MBV) (Porter 1980)

There are various aspects to each of these views of digital transformation strategies; in the interest of the theme of this book, we focus only on those aspects of these views that majorly contribute to the goal of Built_to_Change organizations—both digital enterprise and digital business. For the digital economy, the aspects that are critical in each of these views are, respectively, reengineering for efficiency, rapid resource augmentation on demand for scaling, and business model innovation (BMI) for survival in the VUCA market environment. The three design blueprints corresponding to these three views are: Design to Efficiency, Design to Scale, and Design to Innovate. i.e., Efficient Design, Scalable Design, and Innovable Design Blueprints, respectively. Thus, the theme of Built_to_Change organizations is devolved into three ambidextrous development goals for the BDDT: realizing efficient design, scalable design, and innovable design blueprints.

There are no good or bad design blueprints or transformation models—an enterprise will hone down to the design blueprint or digital transformation model depending solely upon its priorities in addressing the challenges envisaged in their businesses. This book envisages three types of digital transformation models and design blueprints:

i. Digital Transformation Model I relates to enterprises that would adopt the "efficient" design blueprints or digital transformation models aimed at efficient operations opportunities and maximizing profitability through mass production, i.e., optimizing costs with high quality via (say) lean six sigma business processes management (BPM) (Kale 2018c, 2018a). When the environment changes slowly or predictably, the BPM-focused transformation models are adequate.

ii. Digital Transformation Model II relates to enterprises that would adopt the "scaling" design blueprints or digital transformation models aimed at volume growth opportunities and maximizing value appropriation through mass customization, i.e., explosive user base and stupendous volume growth via enterprise architecture management (EAM) (Kale 2018b, 2019, 2017b). When the operations are envisaged to scale exponentially, only the EAM-focused models are adequate.

iii. Digital Transformation Model III relates to enterprises that would adopt the "innovable" design blueprints or digital transformation models aimed at business growth opportunities, market share maximization through mass innovation, i.e., maneuvering to comparatively blue ocean opportunities via business model innovations (BMI) (Kale 2015a 2017a; Hirooka 2006). When the offerings are envisaged to innovate perennially, only the BMI-focused models are adequate.

The three digital transformation models correspond to the vision of "Enterprise as a Machine," i.e., an automated enterprise; "Enterprise as an Organism," i.e., a sentient enterprise; and lastly, "Enterprise as a Brain," i.e., a cognitive enterprise. The first category of enterprises focuses on maintaining energy flow; the second category of enterprises focuses on maintaining resource flow; and the third category of enterprises focuses on maintaining consistent turbulence-less thought flow.

To dispel any bias regarding the importance of these transformation models or design blueprints, it should be highlighted that their relevance for any BDDT project depends only on the business challenges envisaged as dictated by the targeted customers. For instance, even within an established company within an established sector like the automobile industry, the first model will be more relevant for business divisions targeting individually-owned car customers, the second model will be more relevant for business divisions targeting rental car service and car aggregator service-availing customers, and, finally, the third model will be relevant for business divisions targeting premium brand and luxury brand-owning car customers. The most important artifacts for each of these three digital transformation models (or design blueprints) are business processes, business architectures, and business models, respectively.

The greatest benefit of charting a path from M. Porter's approach to strategy management to IT strategy directly, rather than via business strategy followed by a business and IT alignment (BITA) strategy, is that it makes constellations of concepts and insights garnered from 1980 onward across almost five decades of massive efforts in the fields of business management, operations, and administration accessible and, after appropriate translation, available for deployment and application directly in IT. More significantly, considering the limitless potential of IT strategy (rather than traditional business strategy) for creating gargantuan business opportunities via novel digitalization, digitalization or smartization, and digital metamorphosis strategies, in turn, this also paves the way for IT to become the primary driver of strategy management through iterative business-driven digital transformations in the future (see Preface, Section "Motivation for Writing This Book?").

In a small way, this is not unlike trying to bridge the proverbial gap between the "two cultures" (Science and Arts) that was spoken of in the middle of the twentieth century (Snow 1959). Anyone who is skeptical or in denial of such aspects or issues can refer to the rationale for lately prevalent practices like DevOps for development and operations services (Erder et al. 2021), DevSecOps for development, security, and operations services (Mack 2024), Chaos Engineering for system/software resilience (Rosenthal 2020), and so on. Similarly, at the other end, the perpetual drive toward nature-inspired solutions is also a part of the same trend (Mead 2018; Sisney 2012). This book goes further to assert that the "two cultures" syndrome, that is the widening gap between business and IT, is primarily responsible for a majority of the failed digital transformation projects, and reducing this gap is singularly responsible for the successful ones. In this book, aspects related to the real gap between business and IT have been addressed via Porter's strategy management process and the BDDT framework, and aspects related to the semantic gap between business and IT need to be addressed via leadership (Gobillot 2007) and critical success people factors for BDDT (Kane et al. 2019).

1. This is an appropriate place to request readers' indulgence to enable the author to use terms like "Innovable Design" even though it is either a completely non-existent word or not completely permissible grammatically, or pushes the envelope on the same.

   Innovative design indicates a *state of being*. Something called innovative is usually regarding whatever has come earlier till now—but it may not remain innovative for long. In contrast, innovable design indicates a *state of becoming*—always in the process of becoming innovative, always in the process of continual novelty/renewal. Thus, innovable design indicates an innate capability to get/be innovated again and again. For instance, in design/architecture/software disciplines, innovable design corresponds to evolving while having "open" models, architecture, interfaces, materials, modes, etc., that enable continual re-definition, re-purposing, and reconfiguration.

   In the absence of an appropriate word, the author preferred to coin a new word *innovable*, which means exactly what is defined here and is unlikely to convey any other meanings or connotations at variance with this intended meaning, depending on the perspective of the reader or context in which it is used.

Other words like *smartization, serviceized, serverless,* etc. also fall in the same category.

2. The rationale for the three BDDT blueprints proposed in this chapter is affirmed by the fact that they *naturally incorporate the transformation initiatives of the past,* like business process reengineering (BPR), enterprise architecture management (EAM), and customer-centric customer relationship management (CRM), respectively.

The path from M. Porter's approach to strategy management—from business objectives to IT strategy directly (bypassing the business strategy altogether)—is also followed within each of the three digital transformation models or design blueprints. In Parts I, II, and III, the first track of chapters (i.e., Chapters 3, 5, and 7) focuses on the primary visions for the three digital transformation models: *efficient, scalable,* and *innovable.* Using the identified business vision and objectives for the three models, the second track of chapters (i.e., Chapters 4, 6, and 8) directly maps them to the corresponding IT strategies for these three digital transformation models.

Even business operations strategy can also be envisaged as per the triad of activity-led, resource-led, and market-led views of Built_to_Change strategy (Van Mieghem and Allon 2015).

Business Value Model

The business value model mechanism implements and executes the firm's value strategy, where the value strategy determines where and how the firm competes to achieve a desirable strategic position. The business value model implementation requires the firm to determine which customer segments and customer needs the firm will serve, how the firm will acquire and retain customers, how the firm will create and deliver the customer value, which revenue models and drivers the firm will employ, and what cost structure and drivers will support the value activities. The business value model mechanism acquires and retains customers, creates and delivers customer value, enhances the customer's willingness to pay, optimizes the firm's value activities and cost structure, and thus enables the firm to create, extract, and capture the value created (Kersten 2018). Thus, the value business model mechanism constitutes the firm's value creation and capturing drivers. The value creation is driven by the firm's value opportunities, core resources, and value activities. The value capturing is enhanced by the firm's signaling activities and revenue drivers. The revenue drivers enhance the customer's willingness to pay. The cost drivers must be optimized to achieve the business value model efficiency—the cost drivers lower the activity costs.

Figure 2.2 describes the business value model (Chu 2017).

The customer value design is central to the business value model mechanism. The customer value design constitutes the choice of customer segments the firm will serve, the customer needs they will fulfill, the product or service features the firm may offer, the price point the customer will

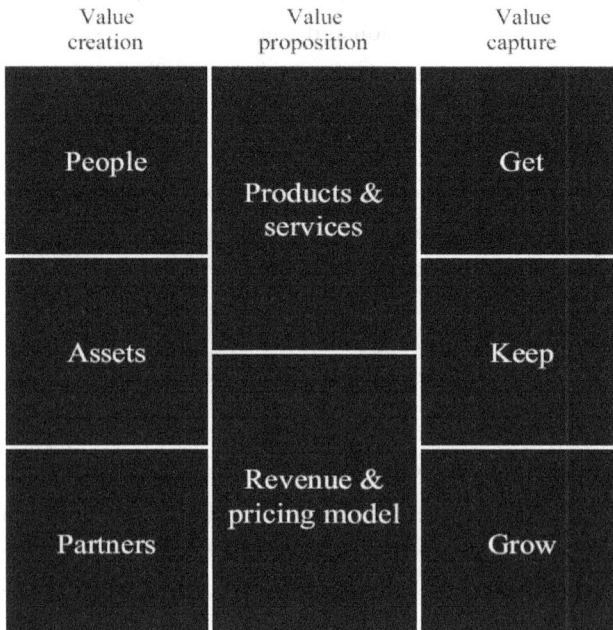

Value creation	Value proposition	Value capture
People	Products & services	Get
Assets		Keep
Partners	Revenue & pricing model	Grow

Figure 2.2 Business value model

be more likely to pay, and the firm's marginal cost to serve a customer. The greater the customer value added and the more of the customer value captured by the firm relative to the competitors, the greater the firm's business model advantage. The business value model mechanism drives the firm's value-creating activities and enables the revenue models and signaling activities to capture the value created. Value activities are the firm's activities that enhance customer value. The customer value is created when the customer cost is lowered or the customer performance is raised, or both. The greater the customer value added by the firm, the greater the customer's willingness to pay for the firm's product, service, or experience. The customer value drivers are at the heart of the firm's business value model design.

The business value model may use several revenue models targeting different customer groups and channels. Each revenue model may contain several revenue streams, and each revenue stream may use more than one price point for product configurations. The revenue model design must be consistent with the customer value design, and the revenue model and its drivers are designed to enhance the customer's willingness to pay. For instance, with the freemium revenue model, the firm provides certain product features at no cost or low cost, and other product features at a premium price. Similarly, in the razorblade model, a product is available at low cost to the customer, but the accessories for the product are offered at a premium price.

The business value model efficiency is enhanced by optimizing the value activities and activity drivers. The business value model sustainability is enhanced when customer and supplier lock-in, business value model novelty and specificity, and business value model tacitness, complexity, and activity complementariness are high. Customer lock-in and supplier lock-in are high when the customer and supplier switching costs are high. Business value model novelty and specificity are achieved when the firm's value activities can be configured in innovative ways to create and deliver customer value. Furthermore, the revenue models and revenue drivers can be configured in innovative ways to extract the customer value created.

The firm's competitive advantage lies in the value creation and capture mechanism powered by superior entrepreneurial advantage for the executives. A firm may have a superior strategy, strategic resources, or superior value opportunities relative to its competitors. Still, without a superior business value model implementation and adequate advantages or incentives for the management, the firm is unlikely to achieve a competitive advantage.

Value Creation Models

Business models may also be classified into a few generic classes based on the embedded value creation model, closely related to the concept of value chain. Value creation models stand for the mechanisms through which the organization and its offerings provide the customer with added value (Table 2.2).

a. Value chain: A typical example of a value chain is a traditional business such as manufacturing, where materials, components, and intermediaries are processed into standard products according to predetermined specifications. The competitive advantage of this value creation model is mostly based on operational excellence.

Table 2.2 Value creation models

Attribute	Value Creation Models		
	Value Chain	Value Shop	Value Network
Deliverable	• Product	• Solution	• Connectivity
Method of production	• Standard products and processes	• Tailor-made products and processes	• Building and maintaining infrastructure
Success factors	• Operational excellence • Volumes	• Problem-solving skills • Effectiveness	• Large network and subscriber base
Marketing challenge	• Selling the problem to the customer to which the product provides a solution	• Justification of high unit costs	• New services: bringing of customers (while offering limited customer value) • Established services: differentiation from competitors
Trade-offs	• Between product differentiation and cost	• Between knowledge depth and breadth	• Between service scope and richness

b. Value shop: A typical example of a value shop is focusing on solving the customer's problem by harnessing the available competencies and resources to the problem-solving process. The competitive advantage of this creation model is not physical or monetary, but typically human, organizational, or relational in nature.

c. Value network: A typical example of a value network are banks, credit institutions, and telecom operators—the more subscribers a telecom operator has, the better the value for the individual subscriber. The more subscribers the operator has, the more incentives there are to expand the network for better coverage, reliability, and, of course, marketability. The competitive advantage of this creation model encompasses a wide range of resources, ranging from physical or monetary, as well as human, organizational, or relational.

Value-Capturing Revenue Models

The revenue model defines the mechanisms through which the offering is expected to capture or monetize value for the company. Revenue models can be divided into two classes:

a. Offering revenue models: This is mostly applied in the direct sales of products, services, or experiences. The customer receives full ownership of the product and may use or resell the product as he or she wishes (e.g., a car). Alternatively, instead of buying the product, the customer may pay only for the actual use of the product or service concerned (e.g., getting his or her car repaired) or for the right to use it (e.g., renting a car for a fixed fee for a fixed period).

Performance-based revenue models call for a customer-centered operating mode, in which the customer is perceived as a partner whose operations and success are also the main concern of the service or experience provider. The idea is to charge the customer based on measured product performance, like:

○ availability (e.g., the fee is inversely proportional to the downtime of a production system)

- ○ production (e.g., the fee is proportional to the amount of commodities produced)
- ○ savings (e.g., the fee is related to verifiable cost savings)
- ○ revenue (e.g., the fee is a certain percentage of the revenue generated through the sales of commodities)
- ○ profit (e.g., the fee is related to the operating income of the customer company)

  It should be highlighted that many actual revenue models are based on different combinations of the simplified archetypes described above.

b. Loss-leader models: This is mostly applied in the areas of software, media, and telecommunications. The loss-leader model itself is not particularly new, as commercial TV stations in the U.S. have operated within this model since the late 1940s. Promotion stands for the sales of advertising space and time for other companies or individuals. The interesting feature of commercial promotion is the fact that the "core" product, e.g., a TV talk show, is not directed at the actual or paying customer (the advertiser who pays for the service provider). The "core" product can be interpreted as an instrument for establishing a connection between the advertiser and the audience (Figure 2.3).

This is the dominant revenue model in Internet-based services today. The customer is essentially offered a package of two or more related

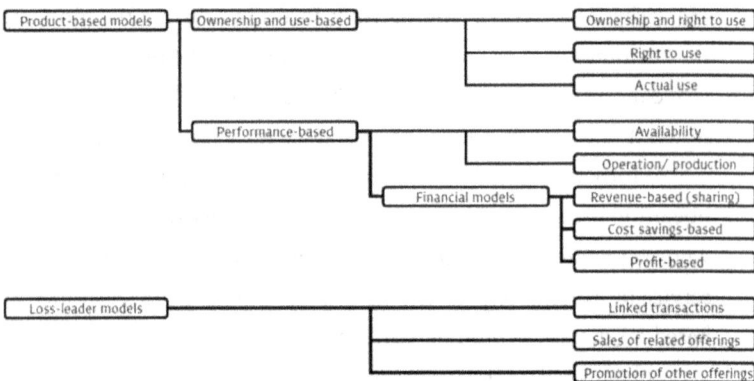

Figure 2.3 Value-capturing revenue models

offerings, of which one (e.g., the Adobe Reader) is provided free of charge, if and only if the customer agrees to purchase the other linked offerings (e.g., Adobe Acrobat Standard, including an editor for creating PDF documents). The idea is that the core product is provided for free to expand the user base and create genuine demand for related chargeable offerings. Similarly, in telecom service provision, one offering is provided free of charge (a mobile phone), if and only if the customer also agrees to purchase the other linked offerings (e.g., a mobile subscription for a fixed term of a minimum of 2 years).

Generic Pricing Models

Pricing is a complex process influenced by a number of factors, but it is based on discernible basic principles.

a. Cost-based pricing: The asking price of the offering is a function of its (estimated) production costs and the targeted profit margin.

b. Market-based pricing: The prices of corresponding offerings in the market, should they exist, constitute the starting point for the exercise. The asking price is then adjusted either downward or upward from the market level, depending on the chosen strategy and business model. For example, a cost-leadership strategy would imply providing the same or an even better offering than what the competitors provide, but at a reduced price. On the other hand, if high quality is seen as the primary source of competitive advantage, the asking price may well exceed the dominant market price.

c. Value-based pricing: The asking price is set between the customer value of the offering and its production costs in such a way that both the customer and the service provider can benefit from the deal. Since it is often challenging to measure, quantify, and justify customer value, value-based pricing schemes mostly apply to tailor-made offerings that cannot be (easily) contrasted with, or are sufficiently different from, other existing offerings.

d. Brand-based pricing: The asking price of a branded offering is defined as the sum of the average market price of corresponding non-branded offerings and the product's brand value. Since brand value is not verifiable, there is no "objective" way of setting the asking price of a branded offering.

Framework for Comparing the Three Design Blueprints

Comparison of the three design blueprints proposed in this book is based on the following dimensions (Slack and Lewis 2017; Van Mieghem and Allon 2015):

a. Type of Strategy Operations
b. Network Business Model
c. Architecture
d. Connecting Mechanism
e. Communications
f. Network Systems
g. Analytics

Conclusion

This chapter presents the three options for a business-driven digital transformation strategy based on the traditional M. Porter's approach to enterprise strategy. It explains the triad of activity-based, resource-based, and market-based views of digital transformation strategy and what each of them entails. This background ensures the selection of the appropriate digital transformation models or design blueprints suitable for the priorities identified in addressing the challenges envisaged by organizations in their businesses.

This chapter explains the triad of Activity-Based View (ABV), Resource-Based View (RBV), and Market-Based View (MBV) of digital transformation strategy and what each entails. The seven-dimensional framework envisaged here is employed across the second track of chapters in Parts I, II, and III (Chapters 4, 6, and 8) for a comparative perspective across the three digital transformation models or design blueprints.

PART I

Efficient Digital Transformation Model and Design Blueprint

CHAPTER 3

Efficient Digital Transformation Model

This chapter provides an overview of salient aspects of the efficiency transformation model and design blueprint. The vision of an automated enterprise highlights aspects like "Enterprise as a Machine," efficiency via Lean, and digitization. Enterprise management highlights enterprise process-oriented business models, mass production, and lean system performance. Distinctive artifacts for this digital transformation model include pattern thinking "out of the box," products, and business processes.

Vision of Automated Enterprise

"Enterprise as a Machine"

The machine view dominated management theory during the first half of the twentieth century and has been remarkably difficult to shift from managers' minds. It represents organizations as rational instruments designed to achieve the purposes of their owners or controllers. The task to be achieved is broken down into parts, and rules are established that govern the behavior of these parts. A hierarchy of authority exercises coordination and control. Efficiency in achieving the predetermined purposes is the most highly valued attribute of the *organization as a machine* (Morgan 1986, 1997). This metaphor is seen as neglecting the individuals who make up the organization and as producing organizational designs that are too rigid in turbulent environments.

Efficiency via Lean

Flow efficiency focuses on the flow unit that flows through the organization for value-receiving inputs regarding the amount of time it takes from identifying a direct or indirect need to satisfying that need (Protzman et al. 2019; Modig and Ahalstrom 2013). A flow unit can be an experience, material, information, or people.

Resource efficiency, i.e., efficient use of resources, has long been the most common way of looking at efficiency. From an economic perspective, because of opportunity cost, it makes sense to strive for the most efficient possible use of resources. Resource efficiency focuses on the value-adding resources, such as staff, sites, equipment, tools, and information systems, that an organization utilizes for a specific period to produce a product, deliver a service, or enact an experience.

Processes

Flow efficiency is created through processes that are a collection of value-receiving activities, with reference to the flow unit, that together create the path for and fulfill the need of a flow unit. A flow unit's throughput time is simply the time it takes for the flow unit to move through the whole process from start to finish. Flow efficiency is the summation of the value-receiving share of and removal of non-value-adding activities, and the optimal share of value-adding resource activities with reference to the throughput time.

   a. *Little's Law:* Throughput time = flow units in process × cycle time
      where:
         Flow units in process are all the flow units within the chosen system boundaries.
         Cycle time is the average time between two flow units completing the process and refers to the pace at which flow units move through the process.
   b. *Constraint Law:* There are stages in the process, in the form of subprocesses or individual activities, that constrain the flow. The law of bottlenecks states that throughput time in a process is primarily affected by the stage of the process that has the longest cycle time.
   c. *Variations Law:* Variations arise from resource utilization (usage ability, malfunctioning, etc.), differing requirements of the flow unit (differing direct or indirect needs), and factors external to the process (like flow unit arrival time at the process).

Throughput time in a process increases in the following ways:

   i. Little's law states that throughput time increases when there is an increase in the number of flow units in process and when the cycle time increases.

  ii. The law of bottlenecks states that throughput time increases when there are bottlenecks in the process.

 iii. The law variations state that throughput time increases as variation in the process increases and the process gets closer to 100 percent utilization.

Process Laws and Flow Efficiency

If throughput time increases, the general rule is that flow efficiency will decrease. This rule applies especially if the increase in throughput time is not met by a corresponding increase in value-adding time.

The following activities improve flow efficiency:

- reducing the total number of flow units in the process by eliminating the causes for the waiting lines;
- working faster, which reduces cycle time;
- adding more resources, which increases capacity and reduces cycle time;
- eliminating, reducing, and managing the different forms of variation in the process.

Efficiency Paradox

The efficiency paradox is explained by superfluous work. By over-focusing on resource efficiency, process laws guarantee that flow efficiency will suffer. If flow efficiency suffers, then several secondary needs will be generated. Activities to meet these secondary needs may seem like value-adding activities, but they would not be necessary if the primary need were already fulfilled. The paradox is that we believe we are utilizing our resources efficiently, but we are being inefficient since much of that utilization comes from superfluous work and non-value-adding activities.

At the core of resolving the paradox is a focus on flow efficiency. By focusing on flow efficiency, an organization can eliminate many of the secondary needs that arise as a consequence of low flow efficiency. More specifically, any decision that decreases throughput time, the amount of flow units in process, and/or the amount of restarts will eliminate superfluous work.

> The vision of *enterprise efficiency* is implemented through enterprise systems, that is, enterprise application programs and enterprise database tables (Scheer 2000, 1998; Davis and Brabänder 2007). Since either of these is present on the enterprise servers, there is no sequence of subprocesses or workflow of programs or postings on the database tables.

Digitization

Digitization refers to the process of converting or switching from analog to digital format (Gong et al. 2024; Carpo 2013). This implies the digitization of not only data but also business processes. The customary enablement of business processes via the enterprise systems (via EPC [event process chain] diagraming in SAP) is a prime illustration of such an approach.

Automation

Automation is the technology by which a procedure or process is accomplished without human assistance. There are mechanical and computational aspects of automation and digitization of systems is often required for automated computation to be made possible (Tella et al. 2024). The human element links mechanization and automation through physical labor as well as cognitive skills and intelligence. In general, repetitive or rule-based tasks can be done by machines, while tasks that require intelligence or higher-level thinking have been done by humans.

Automation maturity ranges from manual operations to connected work systems:

1. Manual operations—Processes are managed on paper or on individual spreadsheets that are difficult to track or trace. Limited (or no) records may be kept.

2. Digitization—Some document repositories, data repositories, or software packages are available to support electronic data entry, retrieval, and possibly visualization.
3. Horizontal integration—Some systems are connected and can be used to exchange information across functional areas of the organization (e.g., sales, marketing, production).
4. Vertical integration—Information and material flows connect the sensor level, control level, production level, and/or enterprise level.
5. Connected work systems—Decisions, information, and materials flow across functional areas and between levels of the automation hierarchy, making it possible for the organization to anticipate, adjust, and adapt to changing circumstances and requirements.

Automation should be considered for:

- Reducing the risk of labor shortages
- Detecting errors faster and more accurately
- Reducing outages and improving time-to-recovery
- Reducing costs by shifting expensive labor to less expensive maintenance
- Increasing flexibility and enhancing the ability to add new products quickly
- Improving product quality and reducing variation in production
- Improving labor productivity and throughput while reducing lead time
- Improving safety by giving more hazardous tasks to robots and nonhumans
- Improving complex tasks that are otherwise slow, labor-intensive, or error-prone
- Accomplishing processes that cannot be done manually

Cyber-Physical Systems (CPS)

CPS can be considered as the development of automation processes at all stages of the life cycle of the enterprise through the introduction of digital technologies (Radziwill 2020; Kudriavtceva 2020). A CPS is a complex distributed system controlled or monitored by computer-based algorithms and tightly integrated with the Internet and its users; CPS has a network structure. Due to several factors, such as a large number of elements and connections between them, the need for real-time processing of large amounts of data, and the environmental influence, it becomes necessary to address the problem of the communication network for such complex distributed systems characterized by uncertainty (not common for uniform networks). A CPS is characterized by tight integration between physical and computational processes within it. Examples of CPS include a smart grid, autonomous automobile systems, automated industrial control systems (Industry 4.0), process control systems, robotics systems, and automatic pilot avionics (Figure 3.1).

The backbone of CPS is physical objects that can communicate with people, machines, or data stores over networks. According to the National Institute of Standards and Technology (NIST, n.d.), CPS are "co-engineered interacting networks of physical and computational components." CPS has a cyber (connected) part and a physical (tangible) part, and disrupts the traditional automation hierarchy in industrial systems by increasing connections between each of the layers (Figure 3.2).

A CPS model can be presented as an aggregation of the CPS's algorithms and structure represented as graphs with the same vertex set (Alekseev 2020). Let the structure graph be defined as the physical graph, as it represents the conditional physical infrastructure allowing for the

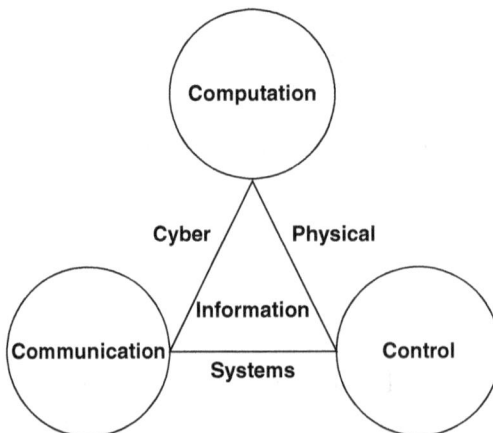

Figure 3.1 Cyber-Physical System (CPS)

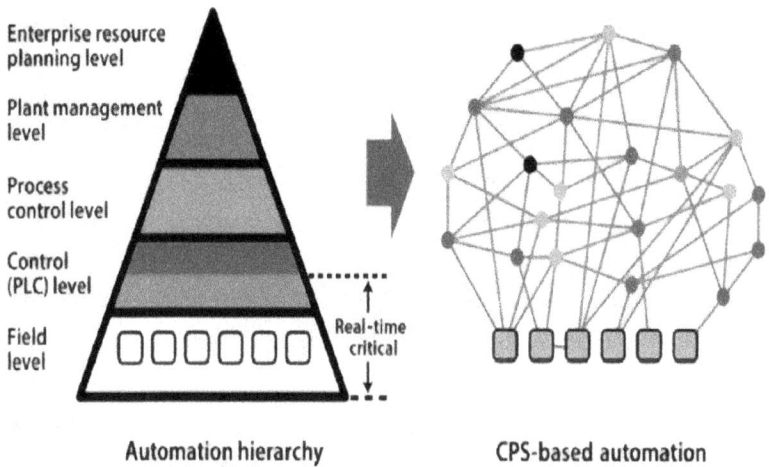

Automation hierarchy   **CPS-based automation**

Figure 3.2 Changed production architectures from hierarchical to networked CPS

information flows. The algorithm graph should then be defined as the logical graph since it represents the structure of the connections between the system's elements, namely their mutual requirements for the information flow. The edges of the graph connect the elements of the system, which pass a flow with specific characteristics from one to the other. Such pairs of elements are called source-sink pairs.

The information flows between a source-sink pair of the logical graph can only go through the channels of the physical infrastructure of the network, i.e., the edges of the physical graph. The kind of network described above is called a multicommodity network because flows of different source-sink pairs are not interchangeable, as every information flow is aimed at a specific addressee and cannot be substituted with any other flow. Information flows between the nodes of the logical graph correspond to different types of products, which go along the edges of the physical graph without interacting.

Learning Organization via Business Intelligence (BI) + Symbolic AI

Learning organizations create, acquire, and transfer knowledge, and modify their behavior to reflect new knowledge and insights (Argote 2013). All organizations are Learning Organizations (LO) to some degree, though not all organizations are equally effective LOs (Banasiewicz 2021). The only real and sustainable competitive advantage organizations have is the rate at which the organizations can learn faster than the competition via its employees empowered with software learning systems.

Narrow AI category follows a rule-based, symbolic understanding of AI (Royce 2025). In this view, AI is expressed in words, numbers, and other symbols that an intelligent entity can understand and manipulate. Despite significant initial promise, its performance has not been able to break through the constraining barriers to match or even surpass human intelligence. Narrow AI (also known as weak AI) is a system that can automate tasks that are typically performed by humans, but do so in a specific narrow knowledge domain. The task could be descriptive, predictive, or prescriptive, and the performance of the machine can be equal to or better than that of the human in those narrow areas (Priyadarshini et al. 2023; Kaliraj and Devi 2022). But even in these narrow areas of validity, the issue is that the system is brittle needing to be updated regularly to be in sync with the updated changes and circumstances.

An expert system is computer software created to solve complicated issues and offer decision-making capabilities similar to those of a human expert. This is accomplished by using both facts and heuristics, and the system retrieves information from its knowledge base per user queries, utilizing reasoning and inference procedures. A conventional problem-solving system has both data structures and programs encoded, whereas an expert system just has data structures hard-coded and does not have any problem-specific information encoded in the program. It emulates human expert decision making through expert knowledge expressed mostly with if-then rules and decision making enabled by reasoning. The majority of expert systems include a user interface and an inference engine. These systems are created for a specific industry, like medicine, mining, and so on. Each expert system shares the feature that, after being fully constructed, it will be evaluated and tested using the same real-world problem-solving scenario. However, not all expert systems contain learning components that allow them to adjust to new circumstances or satisfy new demands.

Governance: Double-Entry Accounting

Double-entry accounting (DEA) is a system so named because every entry to an account (debit) requires a corresponding and opposite entry to a different account (credit) (Kale 2024; Smallwood 2020). If the accounting entries are recorded without error, the aggregate balance of all accounts having debit balances will equal the aggregate balance of all accounts having credit balances. Accounting entries in debit and credit-related accounts typically include the same date and identifying code in both accounts so that in case of error, each debit and credit can be traced back to a journal and transaction source document, thus preserving an audit trail. The accounting entries are recorded in the Books of Accounts. Notwithstanding which accounts and how many are impacted by a given transaction, the fundamental accounting equation of assets equals liabilities plus capital will always hold.

Enterprise Management

In the early 1990s, all software crises underwent a dramatic change with the arrival of Enterprise Resources Planning (ERP) systems. ERPs changed the basic developmental model of implementing computerized systems within enterprises to that of implementing off-the-shelf ready-made packages that covered every aspect of the function and operations of an enterprise. It provided an integrated set of functional modules corresponding to all major functions within the enterprise. It engendered the concept of implementing all these modules as an integrated whole rather than in a piecemeal fashion (Kale 2016). For the first time in the history of IT, ERPs indicated the recognition of the fact that the business processes of an enterprise were much more fundamental than time-invariant data characterizing various aspects of the enterprise (Giachetti 2010; Kale 2016). And, most importantly, the implementation of an ERP within an enterprise was no longer a problem of technology; it was a business problem. ERPs elevated information systems (IS) from a mere enabler of the business strategy of an organization to a significant part of the business strategy itself.

The distinguishing characteristics of ERP are as follows:

1. ERP transforms an enterprise into an information-driven enterprise.
2. ERP fundamentally perceives an enterprise as a global enterprise.
3. ERP reflects and mimics the integrated nature of an enterprise.
4. ERP fundamentally models a process-oriented enterprise.
5. ERP enables real-time enterprise.
6. ERP elevates IT strategy as a part of the business strategy.
7. ERP represents a major advance on earlier manufacturing performance improvement approaches.
8. ERP represents the new departmental store model of implementing computerized systems.
9. ERP is a mass user-oriented application environment.

Mass Production

Each industry revolution was associated with a characteristic exponential phenomenon that powered growth during that period. Even the auto industry had shown similar cost declines during its initial period. At the turn of the twentieth century, cars were luxury items, which typically sold for U.S. $20,000. Henry Ford revolutionized the auto industry with the invention of the assembly line. Ford's efforts resulted in a steady reduction in costs, quickly bringing the cost of manufacturing a car to under U.S. $ 1,000. But even Ford's ability to reduce costs had bottomed out by 1918.

At the beginning of the twentieth century, rapid advances in agricultural techniques, instead of slowing economic growth, buoyed it as they freed up human resources to work on other things, which in turn made possible the industrial age in the latter part of the century. Mechanized transportation allowed centralized manufacturing, so factories could achieve greater economies of scale. This, combined with the mechanization of the factory, greatly enabled improved productivity, thus resulting in greater non-inflationary growth levels. As industry grew to be a larger part of the economy, it pushed economic growth up to an average of about 3 percent, instead of slowing it down to the 1 percent annual economic growth of agricultural economies. Since the latter half of the 1990s, the United States has been able to achieve regular non-inflationary growth of 4 to 5 percent because of productivity gains made possible by the IT industry.

Growth Strategy: Profit Maximization

Growth is defined as an increase in sales, profits, number of employees, market share, penetration into new markets, etc. Here, it should be noted that there is a difference between the words "growth" and "expansion," which are very often used interchangeably in daily conversations. Growth is the first significant increase in sales, profits, and/or number of employees after starting the business; expansion represents a more controlled increase in market share and company size after the growth stage.

The growth of a business can be seen from several perspectives:

1. Strategic growth has to do with the changes that the company makes during its interaction with the environment as a whole. This is related to the way the company develops its ability to exploit opportunities in the market and the ways of using assets to create a sustainable competitive advantage.
2. Financial growth has to do with business growth as a commercial entity and includes the increase in sales, costs, and investments to achieve sales and profits. Financial growth also includes the increase in the value of the company's assets as an important measure of its success.
3. Structural growth is related to the company's changes with regard to the organization of the internal system, in particular, managerial roles and responsibilities, reporting relationships, communication links, and resource control systems.
4. Organizational growth has to do with changes in processes, culture, and attitudes of the company. In particular, attention is given to changes which are related to the entrepreneur's role and style of

leadership as the company "moves" from being a small to a large company.

Management actions that enable accelerated growth are:

- increasing human resources
- increasing production capabilities
- increasing raw material sources
- adding distribution channels
- accessing additional private capital financing
- going public.

Income Statement

The income statement (also called profit and loss statement, the statement of operations, or statement of earnings) shows an organization's income, less its expenses, over some time—it can be anything from a year to a fraction of a year. Profit or net income generated shows how well a company is using the funds it has borrowed and expended. Entrepreneurs, investors, and lenders (both current and potential) use the income statement to track revenues and expenses. It means they can monitor the performance of an organization over a period. It also implies that investors can compare the company's performance across time frames or with other businesses.

The firm's profit (or loss) figure is given by

$$\text{Revenue} - \text{Expenses} = \text{Profit}$$

where:

Revenue is an increase in economic benefits during the accounting period covered in the income statement. This could be in the form of inflows, enhancement of assets, or even decreases of liabilities that result in increases in equity.

Expenses are the opposite, that is, decreases in economic benefits during the accounting period. These might be outflows, depletions of assets, or incurrences of liabilities that result in decreases in equity.

The two main methods of keeping track of a business's income and expenses are as follows:

i. Accrual method is used for regulatory reporting, like filing and tax reporting. This method records revenue when it is earned (for example, when work is done or a product is sold), and expenses when they are incurred (e.g., when an order is actually placed).
ii. Cash method records income at the time the company actually receives the cash. Similarly, this method records expenses at the time the cash is spent.

The primary income statement components are:

a. Revenue: Revenue (or sales or turnover) is inflow of assets, or reduction in liabilities, that comes about because of products and services provided to customers during the year. The customer either pays cash, or promises to pay in the future.
b. Cost of goods sold (or cost of sales) are outflow of assets, or the incurrence of liabilities, that comes about because of delivering or producing goods, provisioning of services, or carrying out business activities. The cost of goods sold is recorded as an expense on the income statement at the time when sales revenue is recorded for the sales of goods. For instance, the main component of a retailer's cost of goods sold is purchases, which are held as inventory awaiting sale at a later period.
c. Selling, general, and administrative expenses (SG&A) are operating expenses that are not directly linked to the company's products or services but come from managing the business or performing general and administrative activities. SG&A expenses include executives' and officers' salaries, legal expenses, payments to utilities (generally known as overheads), insurance, depreciation of office buildings and equipment, stationery, and so on.
d. R&D expenses are operating expenses that are linked directly to future revenues and profitability.
e. Depreciation expenses are operating expenses for purchases of tangible assets recorded on the balance sheet as fixed assets—they are

valued not at the current cost but at the historical cost. During the useful economic life of an asset, the value recorded in the balance sheet gradually reduces to the residual value; this value reduction is termed "depreciation."

In the balance sheet, for any fixed asset, the net book value is the difference between the original value (what we paid for our machine) and accumulated depreciation (the amount of wear so far), which is deducted from the cost of fixed assets.

There are two main methods of depreciation:

i. Straight-line depreciation is where the pattern of the benefits from the fixed asset is viewed as constant over time.
ii. Reducing balance depreciation is where the pattern of the benefits from the fixed asset is viewed as reducing over time.

Shareholders deduce from the income statement how their investment is performing in terms of the earnings per share, which is defined as:

$$\text{Earnings per share} = \frac{(\text{Net income} - \text{Preferred stock dividends})}{\text{Common stock shares outstanding}}$$

Performance: Lean System

Lean System is based on the Toyota Production System, which Toyota has been perfecting for more than five decades. The Toyota Production System (TPS) was inspired by the Ford production system. In 1950, when Toyota Motor Company was in trouble, Eiji Toyoda went to Detroit to learn from the legendary Ford Motor Company how to improve his family's business. He spent 3 months in Detroit, studying Ford's manufacturing techniques in detail and looking for ways to transport them to Toyota. He concluded that while Henry Ford's concept of mass production was probably right for 1913, it was not responsive to the demands of the 1950s. The result was the design of a fundamentally different system, the TPS, which enabled the Japanese automobile industry to overtake Detroit.

Toyota is now recognized as a benchmark of superior performance among the world's best-run, most successful manufacturing companies.

The central organizing concept of Toyota can be described as multiproduct flow. The major difference with Ford, and it is a major one, is that Toyota was not constrained to one product. Toyota applied the principle of flow to a range of products: different models go down the same line without preventing the goals of minimal throughput time and low inventory targets. Toyota still achieved an inventory turn (ratio of sales divided by WIP) approaching 300 (compared to Ford's inventory turns of about 200 and GM's inventory turns of about 8). Toyota took Ford's challenge of synchronization two steps beyond Ford—the first step was to introduce multiproduct flow, and the second was the equalization of the cycle times for every part.

Lean applies a unique process mapping approach called value stream mapping (Gilliam and Taylor-Jones 2005). The current-state value stream map documents material and information flow. Value stream mapping always starts with the customer and includes both material and information flow. In addition, key information is gathered about each value stream operation. The second step is the creation of a future-state value stream map, which is done by assuming that lean practices have been applied to the value stream. Projects are identified based on the changes needed to transform current-state processes into future-state processes. Lean tools are then applied to the improvement projects. When projects are completed, the process is repeated to create a new set of projects. This iterative process continues forever in the pursuit of perfection.

Lean identifies five key concepts:

i. Value is defined by the customer.
ii. Value stream is the information and material flow from suppliers to customers.
iii. Flow is the synchronized, continuous movement of material through the value stream.
iv. Pull is a product usage signal from the customer to other participants in the supply chain.
v. Perfection is the never-ending pursuit of zero waste.

The Lean System is predicated on four clear values and seven principles, and has as its goal eliminating waste and increasing customer value forever by optimizing people, materials, space, and equipment resources. It specifies seven forms of waste to be eliminated:

1. Overproduction—making more than is needed
2. Transport—excessive movement of materials
3. Motion—inefficient movement of people
4. Waiting—underutilization of people
5. Inventory—material lying around unused
6. Overprocessing—manufacturing to a higher quality standard than expected by the customer
7. Defect correction—time spent fixing defects, including the part that gets thrown away, and the time it takes to make the product correctly

Lean is a holistic supply chain operational system best practice with embedded continuous improvement capability linked to customer value. The repetitive cycle of "standardize, level load, stabilize, and create flow" ensures continuous regeneration of improvement opportunities as perfection is pursued. Problem-solving in Lean combines prescriptive standard practices and scientific problem-solving; when none of the existing Lean prescriptive solutions are directly applicable, this allows for the development of new solutions. Lean engages the entire enterprise in the improvement effort, centering around the shop floor operators so that continuous improvement is part of everyone's job. Finally, Lean imparts a continuous improvement system and culture with a common language, tools, goals, and objectives.

Distinctive Artifacts

Pattern Thinking "Out of the Box"

When experts work on a particular problem, it is not common for them to tackle it by inventing a new solution that is completely distinct from existing ones. They adopt pattern thinking wherein they often recall a similar problem they have already solved and reuse the essence of its solution, that is, a pattern to solve the new problem. A pattern describes a particular recurring design problem that arises in specific design contexts, and presents a well-proven generic scheme for its solution; the solution scheme is specified by describing its constituent components, their responsibilities and relationships, and how they collaborate (Bushmann et al. 1996). These problem-solution pairs tend to fall into families of similar problems and solutions, with each family exhibiting a pattern in both the problems and the solutions.

Usually, a good pattern description also includes guidelines for its implementation, that is, a method for creating the solution to a specific problem. Such methods complement general but problem-independent analysis and design methods. Patterns can be realized with almost any programming paradigm and in almost any programming language. Although the context is really of the processes, pattern thinking can also be illustrated by considering the Model-View-Controller (MVC) pattern when developing software with a human-computer interface. Considering that user interfaces are prone to change requests, the challenge can be addressed by apportioning the interactive application into three areas (Figure 3.3):

i. Model component encapsulates core data and functionality. The model is independent of specific output representations or input behavior.

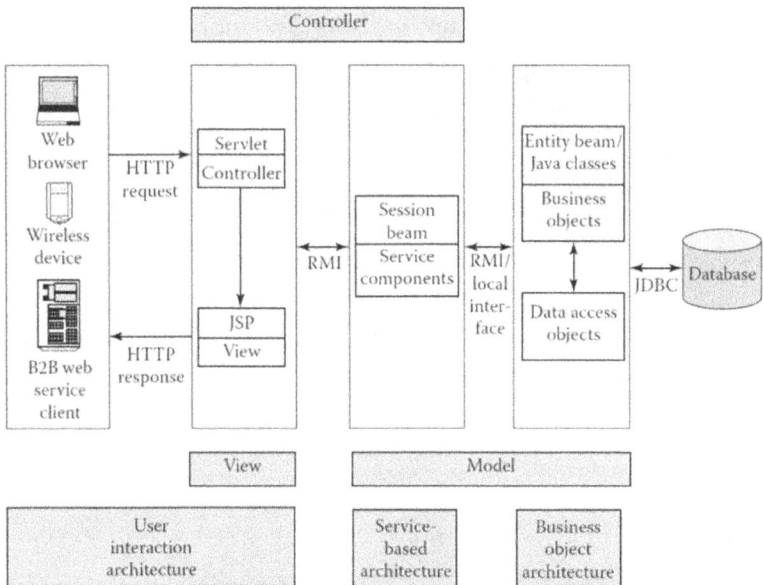

Figure 3.3 MVC and enterprise application architecture

ii. View component displays information to the user. A view obtains the data it displays from the model. There can be multiple views of the model.

iii. Controller component receives input, usually as events that denote mouse movement, activation of mouse buttons, or keyboard input. Events are translated to service requests, which are sent either to the model or to the view. The user interacts with the system only via controllers.

A pattern addresses a recurring design problem that arises in (say) specific design situations, and presents a solution to it (Gamma et al. 1994). The problem is in supporting variability in user interfaces. This problem can be solved by a strict separation of responsibilities—the core functionality of the application is separated from its user interface.

Patterns identify and specify abstractions that are above the level of single classes and instances, or of components. A pattern describes several components, classes, or objects, and details their responsibilities and relationships, as well as their cooperation. All components work together to solve the problem that the pattern addresses, and usually more effectively than a single component. Thus, the MVC pattern describes a triad of three cooperating components, and each MVC triad also cooperates with other MVC triads of the system.

> Pattern thinking describes the overarching vision while designing, architecting, or coding a software system. This helps in implementing this vision while extending and modifying such a system. For example, if a system is known to be structured according to the MVC pattern, it would be evident how to extend the system with a new function—keep core functionality separate from user input and information display.

Products

Products are the traditional carriers of value propositions and value per se (Kale 2024; Cantamessa and Montagna 2023).

Product Attributes

The presence of particular attributes in the product design can not only increase operational efficiency but also contribute directly to customer satisfaction.

The characteristics of successful products are as follows:

a. Functionality: A product with good functionality works to satisfy customers' needs.
b. Validity: The validity attribute of a product deals with generating higher values to customers than the cost (and time) spent by them to acquire the product.
c. Manufacturability: Manufacturability is the degree of ease in making products during the production process. The manufacturability attribute focuses on the efficiency of making the product.
d. Reliability: The quality of the product often relates to how desirable the product is to the final customer. Reliability is an aggregate of multiple related attributes like availability, usability, functionality, flexibility, efficiency, security, compatibility, manufacturability, maintainability, and portability.
e. Serviceability: The serviceability attribute focuses on the ease of performing maintenance or repairs on the product during its effective lifespan.
f. Recyclability: The recyclability attribute considers how the products can be recycled back through the reverse logistics supply chain.

Product Design Approaches

Enterprises can be physically efficient or market-responsive. When customer demand is stable and products are commodities or functional goods with low margins, enterprises need to lower operational costs and maximize their resource utilization. In contrast, when customer demand is unpredictable and subject to sudden changes, the challenge is in the ability to accelerate or decelerate product development and production depending on whether the market is favorable or unfavorable toward new products. Operationally efficient enterprises can employ quality function deployment (QFD) and design for manufacturability (DFM) methods to maximize product performance at minimum cost. In contrast, market-responsive enterprises can utilize concurrent engineering (CE) and design for sustainability (DFS) to reduce the time to market and increase responsiveness to market demand for greener products. The following section details some of these product design methods and explains how each method can support the varying needs of the enterprises.

> A popular term becoming more widely used is the *triple bottom line*. This is a concept that encourages businesses to aim for profitability, positive social involvement, and improved environmental operation as an integrated approach to their business strategies.

> The *digitization* trend is toward an increasingly higher percentage of *digital* products and provisioning through Product as a Software (PaaS)!

Business Processes

It must be highlighted that the business processes referred to here are not the type implemented using business process management (BPM) and workflow applications (Figure 3.3). They are the type implemented through enterprise systems, that is, enterprise applications and enterprise databases (Scheer 2000, 1998; Davis and Brabänder 2007; Brown 2023; Schank 2023; Laguna and Marklund 2025; Escalona et al. 2014). For instance, enterprise modeling for SAP is based on EPC (event process chain) diagrammatic methodology.

The efficiencies gained on account of effectively using such *digitized business processes* are because of:

i. processing through integrated computer application programs, and
ii. digitized data being stored in centrally managed and accessible enterprise databases.

Thus, business processes are effectively a sequence of integrated application programs. The master data required for verification or validation, or transaction data required for updations or reporting, are all available from the centralized enterprise databases.

Enterprise Process-oriented Business Model

The functional business model illustrates the concept of silos of information, which limit the exchange of information between the lower operating levels. Instead, the exchange of information between operating groups is handled by top management, who might not know the functional area (see Figure 3.4A). In the quickly changing markets of the 1990s, the functional model led to top-heavy and overstaffed enterprises incapable of reacting quickly to change. This led to viewing a business as a set of cross-functional processes, as illustrated in Figure 3.4B. In the enterprise process-oriented business model, the flow of information and management activity is horizontal across functions, in

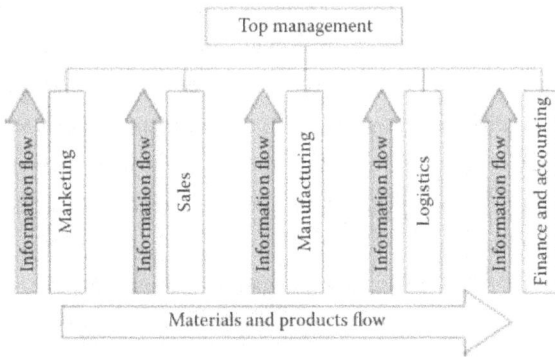

A.

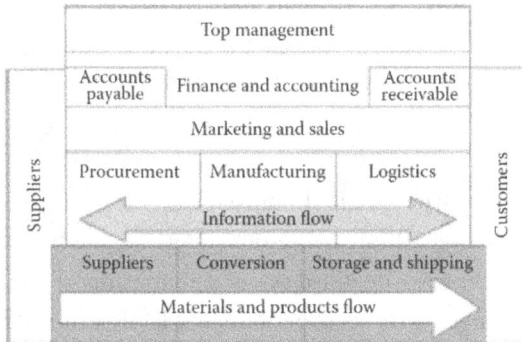

B.

Figure 3.4 Information and material flows. A. Functional business model. B. Business process model

line with the flow of materials and products (Sandkuhl et al. 2014). This horizontal flow promotes flexibility and rapid decision making, and enables managers to see the importance of managing business processes. Now, information flows between the operating levels without top management's involvement. Improvement and enhancements to business processes can lead to a marked improvement in efficiency (Sulis and Taveter 2022; Srinivasan 2017).

Case Study: Digital Transformation at Xerox

Xerox has always developed innovative solutions to improve how people work. The company calls it business engineering. Xerox has around 140,000 employees, as well as offices in more than 180 countries. The portfolio incorporates business services like document management and workplace optimization, as well as office equipment like printers, copiers, multifunction printers and supplies, and production equipment like digital presses, production printers and copiers, wide-format printers, and workflow software.

At the end of the 1980s, Xerox began to thoroughly investigate its internal processes, particularly in terms of their effectiveness and efficiency in customer satisfaction. Xerox realigned its thinking to recognize the importance of business processes and the deficiencies of its segmented, functionally disjointed way of doing business. The company thus became a pioneer of business process management (BPM) techniques, with significant improvement in financial results and its customer satisfaction ratings (Hussey 1998).

1. Phase 1 Immediate Quality Improvement: The company assessed its results in over 200 areas of product, service, and business performance that were identified as key determinants of customer satisfaction. Targets were set at performance levels achieved by world leaders regardless of the industry, and in achieving these benchmark targets, *Team Xerox* also achieved the company's Phase 1 goal of immediate quality improvement.

2. Phase 2 Reengineering Business Processes: Where managers had defined work in terms of processes, they were not only more likely to undertake successful improvement initiatives, but these were much more likely to be cross-functional. Based on these observations, Phase 2 was planned with a particular focus on process improvement, emphasizing cross-functional processes as an area of particular opportunity. Taking a cross-functional view of ways of doing business in support of satisfying customer requirements could lead to breakthrough levels of performance improvement. It was recognized that this approach could yield a quantum of simultaneous improvement in quality, customer satisfaction, and business results.

One example of this process-focused approach was seen in Xerox's supply chain integration efforts. Prominent among these was the process by which Xerox managed its trading assets and ensured that customers' orders were fulfilled in a way that always met the requirements, without the company incurring competitive disadvantage in terms of logistics cost or inventory-carrying cost. Three business processes received priority attention, namely, customer engagement, product design and engineering (soon renamed as time to market), and inventory management and logistics.

Through an important acquisition in 2010, the company has the capability to generate business process outsourcing (BPO) services (Linz et al. 2017). The provision of services has been very successful and caused significant improvements in business, competitiveness, and growth. The company has grown from its origins of delivering on-site, small-scale contracts to being a professional shared service organization delivering substantial outsourcing contracts to its customers, underpinned by its technology.

Xerox's transformation to a service-driven company would be very instructive, but we discussed Xerox's transformation exercise at the end of the 1980s to emphasize the continuity with the *digital transformations* undertaken even during the 1980s, though the term has come into vogue only during recent times.

Conclusion

This chapter provided an overview of the salient aspects of the efficiency transformation model and design blueprint. The vision of an automated enterprise highlights aspects like "Enterprise as a Machine," efficiency via Lean, and digitization. Enterprise management highlights enterprise process-oriented business models, mass production, and lean system performance. Distinctive artifacts for this digital transformation model include pattern thinking "Out of the Box," products, and business processes.

This chapter focuses on characteristics of the enterprise efficiency transformation model or design blueprint, namely, the vision of "Enterprise as a Machine," efficiency via Lean, digitization, products, and business processes.

CHAPTER 4

Efficient Design Blueprint

This chapter discusses digital transformation for an efficient design blueprint in two parts. The first part, on reframing for efficiency, reviews the typical reference state at the commencement of the reframing for efficiency effort. This is in terms of activity-led enterprise operations, network business model (advanced planning systems), enterprise architecture (n-tier architecture), a connecting mechanism (integration brokers), communications (2G mobile communications), network systems (Web 1.0), and analytics (descriptive process analytics). The second part, on means for the digital transformation of efficiency, reviews typical technologies like activity-based view (ABV) of enterprise operations, supply chain network and management, middleware architecture, LAN and WAN networks, 2.5G mobile communications, World Wide Web (WWW), and process analytics management.

Reframing for Efficiency

Activity-led Enterprise Operations

Business operations envisaged as per an activity-led view of operations strategy (Van Mieghem and Allon 2015) have the following aspects:

i. Organization Design
ii. Customer Relationship
iii. Employee Participation
iv. Business Model

All legacy systems like SAP R/3 provide this level of functionality and services through functions like Implementation Guide (IMG), Basis, ABAP for customization, and modules like FI-CO, CRM, HRM, PP, PM, and so on.

Network Business Model: Advanced Planning Systems (APS)

Strategic Network Design covers all four long-term planning sections, especially the tasks of plant location and the design of the physical distribution structure. The design of the supply chain and the elementary material flows between suppliers and customers are determined.

Demand Planning: Further tasks of strategic sales planning (e.g., long-term demand estimates) and mid-term sales planning are usually supported by a module for Demand Planning.

i. Demand Fulfillment & ATP: Most APS providers offer demand fulfillment and ATP (Available To Promise) components that comprise the short-term sales planning. Master planning coordinates procurement, production, and distribution on the mid-term planning level. The tasks distribution, capacity, and mid-term personnel planning are often considered simultaneously. Furthermore, master production scheduling is supported.

ii. Purchasing and Material Requirements Planning: An advanced purchase planning system for materials and components, with respect to alternative suppliers, quantity discounts, and lower (mid-term supply contracts) or upper (material constraints) bounds on supply quantities, is not supported by ERP systems. However, the planning tasks, BOM explosion, and ordering of materials are often left to the ERP systems.

iii. Production Planning and Scheduling: If there are two separate software modules for production planning and scheduling, the first one is responsible for lot-sizing whereas the second one is used for machine scheduling and shop floor control.

iv. Transport Planning and Distribution Planning: Transport planning is covered by a corresponding software module. Sometimes, an additional distribution planning module deals with material flows in a more detailed manner than that can usually be done by master planning.

Figure 4.1 shows the Advanced Planning System (APS) and Execution System. APS covers the long-, mid-, and short-planning aspects, while the execution systems cover the immediate or real time like material

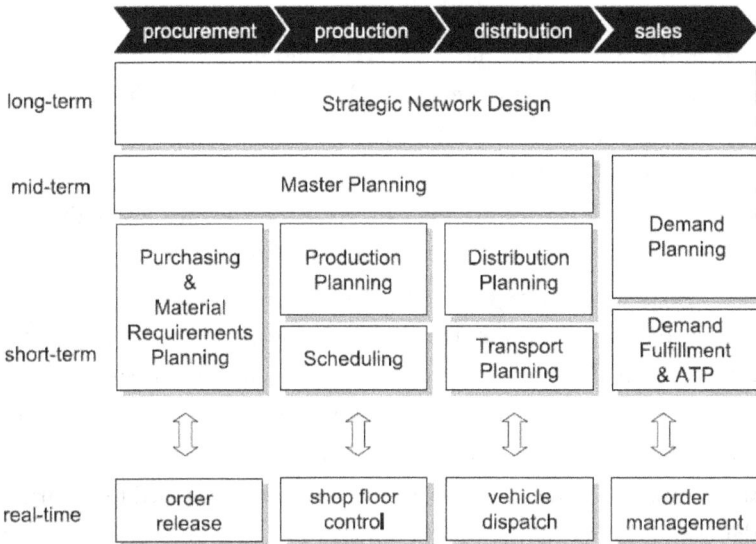

Figure 4.1 Advanced Planning System (APS) and execution system

handling, order transmission to suppliers, shop floor control, transportation execution (including tracking and tracing), and online response to customer requests.

Enterprise Architecture: N-Tier Architecture

The power of the n-tier architecture derives from the fact that instead of treating components as integral parts of applications, components are treated as stand-alone entities, which provide services for applications. Applications exist only as a cooperating constellation of components, and each component in turn can simultaneously be part of many different applications (Myerson 2005). In the 1980s, the prior monolithic architecture began to be replaced by the client/server architecture, which split applications into two pieces in an attempt to leverage new inexpensive desktop machines. Distributing the processing loads across many inexpensive clients allowed client/server applications to scale more linearly than single-host/single-process applications could, and the use of off-the-shelf software like relational database management systems (RDBMS) greatly reduced application development time.

While the client could handle the user interface and data display tasks of the application, and the server could handle all the data management tasks, there was no clear solution for storing the logic corresponding to the business processes being automated. Consequently, the business logic tended to split between the client and the server; typically, the rules for displaying data became embedded inside the user interface, and the rules for integrating several different data sources became stored procedures inside the database. Whereas this division of logic made it difficult to reuse the user interface code with a different data source, it also made it equally difficult to use the logic stored in the database with a different front-end user interface (like ATM and mobile) without being required to redevelop the logic implemented in the earlier interface. Thus, a customer service system developed for a particular client system (like a 3270 terminal, a PC, or a workstation) would have great difficulty in providing telephony and Internet interfaces with the same business functionality.

The client/server architecture failed to recognize the importance of managing the business rules applicable to an enterprise, independent of both the user interface and the storage and management of enterprise data. The three-tiered application architecture of the 1990s resolved this problem by apportioning the application into three distinct layers:

1. Data management: This stores and manages data independent of how they are processed and displayed by the other layers.
2. Business logic: This implements the business logic to process data independent of how they are stored or displayed by the other two layers.
3. Presentation: This formats and displays the data independent of the way they are interpreted/processed, and stored by the other two layers.

With the advent of the Internet in the past few years, the three tiers were split even further to accommodate the heterogeneity in terms of the user interfaces, processing systems, or databases existing in various parts of an enterprise.

The n-tier architecture has many advantages over the more traditional client/server architecture:

- Agile software: The n-tier architecture is useful in creating more flexible and easily modifiable software. By treating software components as stand-alone data providers, middleware service providers, business service providers, and service consumers, the n-tier architecture creates a software infrastructure of reusable parts.
- Maintainable software: The n-tier architecture is useful in creating more maintainable and easily upgradable software. Because software components are stand-alone, reusable parts of business logic, they are used from the same place without the need for multiplication or replication and are therefore easier to change and upgrade, rendering the application as a whole more easily maintainable.
- Reliable software: The n-tier architecture is useful in creating more testable, more easily debuggable, and thus more reliable software. Flexible and maintainable software does not automatically imply reliable software, but because software components are stand-alone packets of business logic, bugs can be localized more easily and their functionality can be calibrated more accurately, rendering the application as a whole more reliable.
- Reduced complexity: The n-tier architecture is useful in creating more streamlined, simplified, and standardized software because the software component paradigm eliminates the need for custom interconnections between disparate constituents of a composite application (which includes existing and legacy systems) that increase in complexity rapidly with the increase in the number of disparate constituents. For instance, for a composite application consisting of n applications and m data sources, the problem of corresponding $n \times m$ interconnections is barely manageable even for small values of n and m. However, in the n-tier architecture, this problem is resolved to a great extent by interfacing all components to (say) a single standardized data bus—this reduces the problem of $m \times n$ interconnections to that of only $n + m$ interconnections! All components can connect via connections to this

singular data bus without the need for multiple customized
single-purpose interconnections between each pair of components.

- Simplified systems management: The n-tier architecture is
  useful in reducing the effort of systems management, especially that of the software, on client machines, particularly
  for large enterprises that may have tens of thousands of client
  machines or even for enterprises that have multilocation and
  decentralized IT/IS operations. For instance, for conventional
  client/server systems, the plan for deploying a new version of
  any application would immediately run into the difficulty of
  choosing between:

  a. changing the entire installed base of clients in a single massive
     effort during which the normal operations come to a complete
     standstill;

  b. undergoing a long and expensive but more regulated phase-in
     of the new software, during which IT/IS would be required
     to support multiple and mutually incompatible versions of
     the server and client codes, and above all, the new application
     would be available to only a part of the target user base.

While n-tier architectures deliver all the advantages associated with
distributed systems, they also have a downside. N-tier systems are work-
able only because of a network-based data bus for communications
between the several tiers. Such a communications layer will have the following adverse effects:

- It will add to the latency of the system and degrade overall
  performance.
- Libraries of software components (and classes) required for interfacing with the data bus will typically increase the size of the
  application.

However, the system architects usually take these problems into account at the time of planning and designing the overall enterprise infrastructure and architecture. And if these problems become noticeable

(because of a dramatic increase in business and transaction volumes) or foreseeable (because of envisaged M&A [mergers and acquisitions] activities, divestures, etc.), the enterprise architecture (EA) is revisited in its entirety.

Connecting Mechanism: Integration Brokers

The interfacing approach of point-to-point interfaces between two applications would be prohibitively expensive for Enterprise Applications Integration (EAI), which may involve tens and hundreds of such interfaces (Kale 2015b). EAIs also adopt the alternate approach of instituting an *information broker* whereby all systems communicate with the information broker by uploading data into the same, while simultaneously translating them into a single format and protocols native to this central broker. Because information is routed through the information broker, rather than going directly among different systems, this simplifies the problem considerably, and it becomes easy to connect disparate systems via their respective adapters for this broker that uses the singular format and protocol of this central broker. Any future systems have to devise only one adapter to integrate with the central broker to start communicating transparently with all other systems.

The exchange of data between the various systems interconnected by EAI is governed by the business rules determined by the user, and the message broker routes the messages according to these rules. However, the data in the messages are translated en route into whatever format is required by the concerned application.

Communications: 2G Mobile Communication

The second generation (2G) of wireless and mobile phone technology gave users the capability to send and receive data in a digital format. Digital technology offers many benefits over analog by offering better service to customers (a service operator can fit more information in a transmission), much-improved clarity of sound (during voice conversations), higher security, and access to future-generation features (Jiang and Han 2024).

However, it led to the creation of three mutually incompatible networks:

i. CDMA: Code Division Multiple Access (CDMA) is a military technology first used during World War II by the English allies to foil German attempts at jamming transmissions. Because Qualcomm Inc. created communications chips for CDMA technology, it was privy to classified information and became the first to patent and commercialize it. CDMA is a digital cellular technology that uses spread-spectrum techniques. CDMA does not assign a specific frequency to each user; instead, every channel uses the full available spectrum. Individual conversations are encoded with a pseudorandom digital sequence. The architecture of CDMA is such that multiple conversations are transpiring at the same time, sharing the same frequency as other CDMA conversations. The CDMA systems decipher each of the conversations so that each listener understands whom he or she is listening to.

Advantages of CDMA over analog systems include:

- Enhanced privacy through the spreading of voice signals
- Improved coverage characteristics, allowing for fewer cell sites
- Increased talk time for portables
- Improved call quality, with better and more consistent sound as compared to AMPS systems
- Capacity gains of 8 to 10 times that of AMPS analog systems
- Simplified system planning through the use of the same frequency in every sector of every cell

ii. TDMA: Time Division Multiple Access (TDMA) was released in 1984. It uses the frequency bands available to the wireless network and divides them into time slots, with each phone user having access to a time slot at regular intervals. TDMA exists in North America at both the 800 MHz and 1900 MHz bands. Major U.S. carriers using TDMA are AT&T Wireless Services, BellSouth, and Southwestern Bell. The TDMA architecture works in a "time slot" format. In other words, one person speaks, and another is listening. For another person to speak, a time slot (channel) must open up. Only one subscriber is assigned a channel at a time, and no other subscriber can access that same channel until the call is ended. Consequently, the total requirement for the number of channels is very high.

Advantages of TDMA include:

- TDMA is the most cost-effective technology for upgrading a current analog system to digital.
- TDMA is the only technology that offers an efficient utilization of hierarchical cell structures (HCSs), offering picocells, micro-cells, and macrocells. HCSs allow coverage for the system to be tailored to support specific traffic and service needs. By using this approach, system capacities of more than 40 times AMPS can be achieved in a cost-efficient way.
- Because of its inherent compatibility with analog systems, TDMA allows service compatibility with dual-mode handsets.
- Unlike spread-spectrum techniques like CDMA, which can suffer from interference among the users, all of whom are on the same frequency band and transmitting at the same time, TDMA's technology, which separates users in time, ensures that they will not experience interference from other simultaneous transmissions.
- TDMA provides the user with extended battery life and talk time because the mobile is only transmitting a portion of the time (from 1/3 to 1/10) during conversations.
- TDMA installations offer substantial savings in base-station equipment, space, and maintenance, an important factor as cell sizes grow ever smaller.

iii. GSM: Global System for Mobile Communications (GSM) is based on an improved version of TDMA technology. In 1982, the Conference of European Posts and Telecommunications (CEPT) began the process of creating a digital cellular standard that would allow users to roam from country to country in Europe. By 1987, the GSM standard was created based on a hybrid of FDMA (ana-log) and TDMA (digital) technologies. GSM engineers decided to use wider 200 kHz channels instead of the 30 kHz channels that TDMA used, and instead of having only three slots like TDMA, GSM channels had eight slots. This allowed for fast bit rates and more natural-sounding voice-compression algorithms. GSM is currently the only one of the three technologies that provides data services such as e-mail, fax, Internet browsing, and intranet/LAN wireless access, and it is also the only service that permits users to place a call from either North America or Europe. The GSM standard was accepted in the United States in 1995. GSM-1900 cellular systems have been operating in the U.S. since 1996, with the first network being in the Washington, D.C. area. Major carriers of GSM 1900 include Pacific Bell, BellSouth, Sprint Spectrum, and so on.

Analog networks still exist today because digital networks like CDMA, TDMA, and GSM cannot readily communicate and interchange information directly with each other. For interchangeable communication, 2G networks have to fall back on 1G analog communication.

Network Systems: Web 1.0

The earliest stage of the web is called the "read-only web." During this period, those desiring to find and purchase products or services switched from offline to online. However, visitors could not interact with the content creation process. Web pages were static and mainly stayed the same. Manufacturers and service providers began posting online catalogs to advertise their products or services. The immediate goal of websites was to publish information for everyone at any moment and to establish an online presence (Avsar 2023).

Most websites are just a collection of static web pages. The Shallow Web, also known as the Static Web, is primarily a collection of static HTML web pages providing information about products or services offered. After a while, the web became dynamic, delivering web pages created on the fly. The ability to create web pages from the content stored on databases enabled web developers to provide customized information to visitors. These sites are known as the Deep Web. Though a visitor to such websites gets information attuned to his or her requirements, these sites provide primarily one-way interaction and limited user interactivity. The users have no role in content generation and no means to access content without visiting the sites concerned. The Shallow Web sites and Deep Web sites, which have no or minimal user interaction, are now generally termed Web 1.0 (Kale 2018b; Sunyaev 2024).

Analytics: Descriptive Analytics

Descriptive analytics is a kind of analytics that delivers the "what happened?" information regarding an organization's processes. It works on past data to identify the changes that have happened in the business. It explains the use of a variety of historical data that helps businesses draw comparisons. If economic metrics are to be considered, then most usually stated monetary metrics occur to be the product of descriptive analytics, like year-over-year change in prices, month-over-month sales progress, the number of consumers, or each subscriber's total income. All these are measures that let businesses know what has happened in a business in a fixed period. It analyzes the raw data to make meaningful conclusions that are valuable for various stakeholders like investors, managers, customers, staff, etc. It utilizes a wide range of data to get a clear idea of what has occurred and how it varies with others. With the help of this wide range of old data, it helps to acquire a comprehensive review of the line of action and efficiency that can be based on business strategy (Zwingmann 2022; Schniederjans et al. 2014).

Aggregation and mining the data are important steps used in descriptive analytics. Data aggregation is done first to gather and sort the data so that the analyst can manage the datasets efficiently. Later, data mining is used to extract meaningful data. It identifies and understands the patterns that have been discovered by applying some intelligent methods. It becomes essential to represent the data visually after transforming, sorting, and analyzing it.

Descriptive analytics can be employed to better understand the customers' behavior by segmenting the customers into dissimilar audiences and then tailoring the marketing strategies. Some other examples of how descriptive analytics can be used include summarizing past events, such as sales and operations data or marketing campaigns. Another example says that if the total number of metal parts manufactured in each month, income on each group of products, and monthly profits are analyzed, then it would help manufacturers to respond to a sequence of "what happened" queries, helping them focus on product classes.

Means of Digital Transformation for Efficiency

Activity-Based View (ABV) of Enterprise Operations

Digital transformation would involve upgrading to the latest functionality, modules, and systems like SAP ECC 6.x and SAP NetWeaver or SAP HANA and S/4HANA (since support for SAP ECC will be discontinued after 2025).

Advanced applications would include:

- Customization and Integration
- Business Process Reengineering (BPR) (Susanto et al. 2019; Srinivasan 2011)
- Robotic Process Automation (RPA) (Tella et al. 2024; Taulli 2020; Fantina et al. 2022; Karwal 2020)

Networks Business Model: Supply Chain Networks and Management

The term *supply chain* came into vogue when many firms realized the benefits of collaboration and relationships between supplier groups and entities within and beyond their operations. The supply chain represents the flow of raw materials provided by suppliers and processed into finished products or services, and consists of activities in different departments like procurement, production, inventory, transportation, warehousing, and sales to create end-products from input materials (Table 4.1).

The management of networks of suppliers is a tactic for organizations to optimize their overall performance; it leads to win–win situations for suppliers and companies. Customers have more choices to satisfy their demands by using different sources from multiple rivals,—nationally and internationally. Although it is possible to acquire lower prices on materials in purchasing, the inefficiencies in production can cause higher

Table 4.1 Evolution of SCM

Evolution stage	Time period	Philosophy	Key driver	Key performance metric
I	Early 1980s	Product driven	Quality	• Inventory turns • Production cost
II	Late 1980s	Volume driven	Cost	• Throughput • Production capacity
III	Early 1990s	Market driven	Product availability	• Market share • Order fill rate
IV	Late 1990s	Customer driven	Lead time	• Customer satisfaction • Value addition • Response time
V	Early twenty-first century	Knowledge driven	Information	• Real-time communication • Business intelligence

costs for the business. It is important to manipulate distribution channel networks and inventory volumes to get maximum customer accessibility with minimum costs.

Supply Chain Management (SCM) coordinates and manages a complex network of processes in the supply chain involved in supplying products or services to end-users in the most efficient and cost-effective ways. SCM is an integration of activities like planning, arranging, and controlling the flow of decisions, information, and materials from suppliers, and transforming them into end-products for customers. SCM focuses on maximizing economies of scale by using particular practices to meet stakeholders' expectations. The implementation of effective SCM reinforces competitive advantages for companies in their industries.

The benefits of SCM are:

i. Better control: When the whole process of business is defined, the organization can readily detect the location of materials and products flowing in the supply chain. The delivery time, number of offers, and purchasing conditions can be controlled quickly and easily.

ii. Fewer delays in processes: Managing the supply chain effectively boosts tight cooperation and transparent communication between organizations, suppliers, and entities that mitigate delays in delivery and production.

iii. Increase in efficiency and competitiveness: When the company integrates SCM systems, it will be able to adjust to changing customers' demands and to fluctuating economies.

iv. More profitability: With increasing reduction in waste, the inventory systems will be adjusted to customers' demand which leads to a reduction of operating costs.

Enterprise Architecture: Middleware Architecture

Middleware is a system service software that executes between the operating system layer and the application layer, and provides services. It connects two or more applications, thus providing connectivity and interoperability to the applications. Middleware is mainly used to denote products that provide the glue between applications, which is distinct from simple data import and export functions that might be built into the applications themselves. Middleware introduces an abstraction layer in the system architecture and thus reduces the complexity considerably. On the other hand, such middleware product introduces a certain communication overhead into the system, which can influence performance, scalability, throughput, and other efficiency factors (Etzkorn 2017; Myerson 2005).

> This is important to consider when designing the integration architecture, particularly if the systems are mission-critical and are used by a large number of concurrent "clients."

Essentially, middleware is a distributed software layer, or platform, that lives above the operating system and abstracts over the complexity and heterogeneity of the underlying distributed environment with its multitude of network technologies, machine architectures, operating systems, and programming languages. The middleware abstraction comprises two layers. The bottom layer is concerned with the characteristics of protocols for communicating between processes in a distributed system and how the data objects, for example, a customer order, and data structures used in application programs can be translated into a suitable form for sending messages over a communications network, taking into account that different computers may rely on heterogeneous representations for simple data items. The layer above is concerned with interprocess communication mechanisms, while the layer above is concerned with message-based and non-message-based forms of middleware:

- Message-based forms of middleware provide asynchronous messaging and event notification mechanisms to exchange messages or react to events over electronic networks.
- Non-message-based forms of middleware provide synchronous communication mechanisms designed to support client-server communication.

Middleware uses two basic modes of message communication:

1. Synchronous or time-dependent: The defining characteristic of a synchronous form of execution is that message communication is synchronized between two communicating application systems, which must both be up and running, and that execution flow at the client's side is interrupted to execute the call. Both sending and receiving applications must be ready to communicate with each other at all times. A sending application initiates a request (sends a message) to a receiving application. The sending application then blocks its processing until it receives a response from the receiving application. The receiving application continues its processing after it receives the response.

2. Asynchronous or time-independent: With asynchronous communication, an application sends (requestor or sender) a request to another while it continues its processing activities. The sending application does not have to wait for the receiving application to be complete and for its reply to come back. Instead, it can continue processing other requests. Unlike the synchronous mode, both application systems (sender and receiver) do not have to be active at the same time for processing to occur.

The basic messaging processes inherently utilize asynchronous communication. There are several benefits to asynchronous messaging:

1. Asynchronous messaging clients can proceed with application processing independently of other applications. Loose coupling of senders and receivers optimizes system processing by not having to block sending client processing while waiting for the receiving client to complete the request.

2. Asynchronous messaging allows batch and parallel processing of messages. The sending client can send as many messages to receiving clients without having to wait for the receiving clients to process previously sent messages. On the receiving end, different receiving clients can process the messages at their speed and time.

3. There is less demand on the communication network because the messaging clients do not have to be connected to the MOM while messages are processed. Connections are active only to put messages to the MOM and get messages from the MOM.

4. The network does not have to be available at all times because of the timing independence of client processing. Messages can wait in the queue of the receiving client if the network is not available. MOM implements asynchronous message queues at its core. It can concurrently service many sending and receiving applications.

Despite the performance drawbacks, synchronous messaging has several benefits over asynchronous messaging. The tightly coupled nature of synchronous messaging means the sending client can better handle application errors in the receiving client. If an error occurs in the receiving client, the sending client can try to compensate for the error. This is especially important when the sending client requests a transaction to be performed on the receiving client. The better error-handling ability of synchronous messaging means it is easier for programmers to develop synchronous messaging solutions. Since both the sending and receiving clients are online and connected, it is easier for programmers to debug errors that might occur during the development stage. Since most developers are also more familiar with programming using synchronous processing, this also facilitates the development of synchronous messaging solutions over asynchronous messaging solutions.

When speaking of middleware products, we encompass a large variety of technologies. For a detailed discussion on the above technologies, refer to the companion volume "Guide to Cloud Computing for Business and Technology Managers" (Kale 2015b).

Connecting Mechanism: LAN, MAN, and WAN Network

Modern networks exist at drastically varying sizes, and it is useful to categorize them into three main classes according to their scale. The three most commonly used terms to describe the scope or scale of a particular network are: the local area network (LAN), metropolitan area network (MAN), and wide area network (WAN), in order of their increasing geographical size. In many cases, there is a hierarchical relationship between these three grades of the network scale. One LAN may be combined with many others in a metropolitan area and can be interconnected to form a MAN; one or more MANs across multiple metropolitan areas may be interconnected to form a WAN (Marcham 2021).

On the other hand, networks at any of these three scales could be created as single networks. This choice is driven by a combination of business and technical factors, depending on the individual parties and technologies involved in a specific area, and is not prescribed by the terms themselves.

The diagram shows multiple LANs within a city, a single MAN covering all of that city, and a WAN that is connecting the two cities despite them being 100 miles apart. A city may have hundreds or thousands of LANs, and there may be multiple MANs and also multiple WANs in that area or between areas, but this example serves to show the difference in scale between typical networks in each of these categories and how one may appear to nest within another from above. There is also not necessarily no direct hierarchical relationship between these network categories at all. For example, depending on the network topology in a particular area, a LAN may just connect directly to a WAN. In another, it may need to connect to a MAN, which itself connects to a WAN. The specifics in this regard are location and implementation choices made by those network operators.

The purposes of each of these types of networks are different from one another as well as a different physical scale. A LAN is typically used to connect endpoints within a single building or campus together or to other network resources, whereas a MAN is often used to connect multiple LANs across an area such as a city. A WAN, then, is typically used to connect one network or endpoint to a network resource that is a significant distance away, hence its "wide area" naming.

Communications: 2.5G Mobile Communications

2.5 Generation networks require a complete overhaul of the wireless network, and the expense to complete the implementation is very high (Jiang and Han 2024). The 2.5G is more of an intermediate solution to third-generation networks. 2.5G networks provide additional functions like:

- Speed of data access
- Identification of the location of the wireless device
- Ability to access customized information based on location
- Ability to store information such as addresses and credit card numbers within personal profiles
- Ability to facilitate mobile online shopping
- Full mobility on the Internet
- Ability to provide business users with access to intranets

2.5G networks are of three types:

i. GPRS: General Packet Radio Services (GPRS) enables true "always-on" capability in the wireless network. Similar to dialing a modem for service to an Internet service provider, in today's cell network, a phone call must be initiated to connect to a network.

Similarly, "always-on" can be compared with broadband-wired connections such as DSL (Digital Subscriber Line) or T1 lines and faster connections. However, GPRS only enables speeds in the range of 115 kbps.

ii. EDGE: Enhanced Data Rate for GSM Evolution (EDGE) can simply be termed as a faster version of the GSM wireless service. EDGE technology enables data to be delivered at rates up to 384 kbps on broadband connections. The standard is based on the GSM standard and uses TDMA multiplexing technology. In essence, the EDGE may enable higher functionality, such as the downloading of music and videos over mobile devices.

iii. CDMA 2000: Code Division Multiple Access 2000 (CDMA 2000) is essentially a migration or upgrade of the CDMA standard discussed in the second-generation section. CDMA 2000 is also an "always-on" technology that offers transmission speeds around 100 kbps.

Network Systems: World Wide Web (WWW)

The invention of the WWW by Berners-Lee was a revolution in the use of the Internet. Users could now surf the web, that is, the *hyperlinks* among the millions of computers in the world, and obtain information easily. The WWW creates a space from which users can access information easily in any part of the world. This is done using only a web browser and simple web addresses. Browsers are used to connect to remote computers over the Internet and to request, retrieve, and display web pages on the local machine. The user can then click on hyperlinks on web pages to access further relevant information that may be on an entirely different continent. Berners-Lee developed the first web browser, called the World Wide Web browser. He also wrote the first browser program, which allowed users to access web pages throughout the world.

The WWW is revolutionary in that:

- No single organization is controlling the web.
- No single computer is controlling the web.
- Millions of computers are interconnected.

- It is an enormous marketplace of millions (billions) of users.
- The web is not located in one physical location.
- The web is a space and not a physical thing.

Analytics: Descriptive Process Analytics

Descriptive analytics is the preliminary stage of advanced analytics. Descriptive analytics summarizes what has happened or is happening, and characterizes the main features in business (Zwingmann 2022; Schniederjans et al. 2014; Kohtamäki 2017).

The main objectives and goals at this stage are:

1. answering the questions "what happened?" and "why did it happen?";
2. summarizing the main features and trends in business;
3. understanding what has happened or is happening in data and business;
4. generating descriptions of business operations, performance, dynamics, trends, and exceptional scenarios, with implications about possible driving factors and reasons;
5. presenting regular and periodic summaries and statistics of business concerns.

The main reporting and analytical approaches and methods at this stage include:

i. major effort on explicit analytics and standard reporting;
ii. statistical analysis of data indicators related to or reflecting business operations, performance, dynamics, trends, and exceptions;
iii. generating standard, ad hoc, and/or cubic (OLAP-based) reports as periodical summaries and statistics in relation to business;
iv. querying, drilling up/down;
v. factor analysis, correlation analysis, trends analysis and regression;
vi. identifying and generating alerts for business management and decision making.

The consequences and benefits of descriptive process analytics for business are:

- to summarize and describe hindsight about business;
- to understand routine and periodical business characteristics, trends, and evolution;
- to identify factors and correlations driving the routine and periodical normal development of business;
- to detect exceptional and risky events, occasions, areas, and scenarios and identify their implications beyond routine and regular development and trends.

Business reports (often standard analytical reports) generated by dashboards and automated processes are the means for carrying findings from analytics to management.

Conclusion

This chapter discussed digital transformation for efficient design blueprint in two parts. The first part on reframing for efficiency reviews the typical reference state at the commencement of the reframing for efficiency effort. This is in terms of activity-led enterprise operations, network business model (advanced planning systems (APSs), enterprise architecture (n-tier architecture), connecting mechanism (integration brokers), communications (2G mobile communications), network systems (Web 1.0), and analytics (descriptive process analytics). The second part on the means for the digital transformation of efficiency reviews the typical set of technologies like activity-based view (ABV) of enterprise operations, supply chain network and management, middleware architecture, LAN and WAN networks, 2.5G mobile communications, World Wide Web (WWW), and process analytics management.

This chapter highlights the specific powerful technologies that are associated with the digital transformation of efficiency competency.

PART II

Scalable Digital Transformation Model and Design Blueprint

CHAPTER 5

Scalable Digital Transformation Model

*This chapter presents an overview of the salient aspects of the enterprise scaling transformation model and design blueprint. The vision of **sentient enterprise** highlights aspects like "Enterprise as an Organism," scaling via resources, and smartization. E-business management highlights mass customization, volume growth, and system engineering performance. Distinctive artifacts for this digital transformation model include design thinking "Out of the New Box," services, and enterprise architecture.*

Vision of Sentient Enterprise

"Enterprise as an Organism"

The organism metaphor looks at organizations as wholes made up of inter-related parts. These parts function in such a way as to ensure the survival of the organization as an organism. For "enterprise as an organism," survival replaces goal-seeking as the driving force of the enterprise (Morgan 1986, 1997; Burrell and Morgan 1985). Organizations are open systems that must secure favorable interchanges with their environments, adapting to environmental disturbances as required. Managers influenced by this metaphor pay close attention to the demands of the environment and ensure that subsystems are meeting the needs of the organization. Critics argue that the organismic viewpoint forgets that individuals or groups in organizations may not share the organizations' overall purposes—they are not like the parts of the body in this respect. As a result, the metaphor hides conflict and internally generated change.

Scaling via Resources

Scalability is the ability to improve system performance by adding more resources to a single node or multiple nodes, such as the addition of CPUs, the use of multicore systems instead of single-core, or the addition of additional memory. On-demand scaling (and descaling) of computation is one of the critical needs of a computing platform (Mukherjee et al. 2024; Panda et al. 2022). Compute scaling can be either done at the infrastructure level or the platform level. At the infrastructure level, it is about increasing the capacity of the computing power, while at the platform level, the techniques are mainly to intelligently manage the different client requests in a manner that best utilizes the compute infrastructure without requiring the clients to do anything special during peaks in demand (Swaminathan and Meffert 2017; Gupta and Sharma 2004; Robertson 2002).

Scale-up or vertical scaling is about adding more resources to a single node or a single system to improve performance, such as the addition of CPUs, the use of multicore systems instead of single-core, or the addition of additional memory. Unless a system is virtualized, it is generally not possible to increase the capacity of a computer system dynamically without bringing down the system. The more powerful compute resource can now be effectively used by a virtualization layer to support more processes or more virtual machines (VMs), enabling scaling to many more clients. The advantage of scale-up systems is that the programming paradigm is simpler; unlike scale-out systems, it does not involve distributed programming (Kale 2019).

Scale-out or horizontal scaling, on the other hand, is about expanding the compute resources by adding a new computer system or node to a distributed application. A web server (like Apache) is a typical example of such a system. In fact, given that most cloud applications are service-enabled, they need to be developed to expand on demand using scaling-out techniques. The advantage of scale-out systems is that commodity hardware, such as disk and memory, can be used to deliver high performance. A scale-out system, such as interconnected compute nodes forming a cluster, can be more powerful than a traditional supercomputer, especially with faster interconnect technologies. Scale-out systems will essentially be distributed systems with shared high-performance disk storage used for common data (Fox and Hao 2018; Kumar et al. 2022).

Scale-out solutions have much better performance and price/performance over scale-up systems. This is because a search application essentially consists of independent parallel searches, which can easily be deployed on multiple processors. Scale-out techniques can be employed at the application level as well. For example, a typical web search service is scalable, where two client query requests can be processed completely as parallel threads (Kale 2020). The challenge in scale-out systems, however, is the complex management of the infrastructure, especially when the infrastructure caters to dynamic scaling of resources.

Scaling is the characteristic defining feature of a startup aspiring to become a unicorn (Kale 2024; Sisney 2021). Intangible assets differ from tangible assets because they are not what economists would term as "rivals in use," i.e., consumption by one individual customer does not deduct or reduce the amount left for another. Compared to most physical assets, once an intangible asset has been created or acquired, it can be used again and again at relatively very low costs. While rivalry might be the primary economic motive behind scalability, scalability can be used for convenience and conveying corresponding implications for requisites like delivery, traceability, security, fault tolerance, infrastructure, and so on. While network effects can be found among both tangible and intangible assets, big network effects are obtainable within intangible assets only. Consequently, intangible assets are significantly more scalable than tangible assets, and scalability becomes supercharged with network effects (Moro-Visconti 2022; Gorton 2022; Atchison 2020; Suteanu 2022; Bounfour and Miyagawa 2015).

The vision of *enterprise scaling* is implemented through enterprise architecture via elastic computing, that is, virtual machines (VMs), networks, and storage. Cloud computing and its advancements, like microservices, serverless computing, edge computing, etc., are discussed in Chapters 6 and 8. Cloud computing is detailed in the references (Comer 2021; Marinescu 2023; Kale 2015b). Distributed computing and parallel processing are discussed in (Kale 2020; Pacheco and Malensek 2022).

Smartization

Digitalization or smartization refers to the waves of changes that empower society through the increased utilization of digital technology (Gong et al. 2024; Carpo 2017). Businesses have been developing rapidly with the advent of advanced technologies such as the Internet of Things (IoT) and Industry 4.0. These technologies offer opportunities to increase efficiency, improve quality control, and expand decision-making capabilities. Therefore, many companies are looking for ways to implement smart technologies in their operations. However, the implementation of smart technologies is challenging; it requires a complex strategy that takes into account the unique needs and capabilities of each company. Technologies that can sense changes in their conditions and take measures to improve their functionality in new conditions offer huge benefits in terms of performance, efficiency, operating costs, and resilience. These technologies can be very useful for businesses because they can quickly respond to changes in the environment and improve their performance.

Automation with Limited Autonomy

Machine learning (ML) is part of AI, which focuses on developing methods and algorithms that allow a program to automatically learn and adapt to different input data without explicit programming. This means that the program can develop its solutions based on the information it has learned in the learning process. ML algorithms include elements of mathematical statistics and statistical analysis methods that work with precise data. Data analysis is also used to identify trends and patterns in data. The output of ML is an estimate or prediction that is based on calculations and accurate data. Algorithms can perform three basic tasks: classification, regression, or clustering.

These algorithms are divided into three categories according to the learning method:

- Learning with a teacher, or supervised learning
- Learning without a teacher or unsupervised learning
- Learning with a combination of supervised and unsupervised learning

Cyber-Physical-Social Systems (CPSS)

Integrating social networks into cyber-physical systems (CPS) results in a new paradigm called *cyber-physical-social systems* (CPSS) (Stoyanov et al. 2020). CPSS includes human-to-device communications and device-to-device communications, and creates continuous interaction of human-device relationships. Wireless sensor networks, big data, and AI are the supporting technologies of CPSS. A CPSS is viewed as the future industrial system that integrates computing, physical, and human resources to connect interactions among the cyber, physical, and social worlds.

Learning Organization via General AI (ML, DL, and Generative AI)

Learning organizations create, acquire, and transfer knowledge, and modify their behavior to reflect new knowledge and insights (Argote 2013). All organizations are Learning Organizations (LOs) to some degree, although not all organizations are equally effective LOs (Banasiewicz 2021). The only real and sustainable competitive advantage organizations have is the rate at which the organizations can learn faster than the competition via their employees empowered with software learning systems.

General AI systems (based on ML, DL, and Generative AI) are quite unlike the traditional AI systems in that they are statistical and probabilistic in perspective, and produce approximate results. But they have the advantage of producing comparatively quicker results with an accuracy quantified in terms of a *"loss function"* (Jung 2022; Zielesny 2016).

The advanced approach of *reinforcement learning* is discussed in Chapter 7, "Innovable Transformation Model."

Machine Learning

The challenge for most AI technologies is in the learning aspect. Intelligence at a human level is based on constant surveying of information, learning from that information, and adjusting decisions accordingly.

A basic approach to learning is to create the ability to reproduce regularities (Rebala et al. 2019; Geetha and Sendhilkumar 2023; Jo 2021). The results are known through laws of nature or expert knowledge and are used to teach the system. A hypothesis is a function that assigns the assumed output value to each input value. A learning algorithm attempts to find a hypothesis that makes predictions as accurate as possible.

The three main learning techniques are learning by example, learning by exploration, and blended learning. In learning by example, as a representative example, children learn by watching and copying others; they watch their parents, friends, and siblings do things and try to copy them. In learning by example, the task being copied or emulated is specific, and the child knows what she is copying. In learning by exploration, children learn by experience and observation—the child observes without knowing what she may find. This is markedly different from learning by example. In blended learning, children learn by a combination of learning by example and exploration. These three learning techniques are respectively called supervised, unsupervised, and semi-supervised learning.

1. Supervised Learning: It is defined by the use of labeled datasets to train the algorithms so that they can be trained to classify data or predict outcomes accurately. A cross-validation process is used here to ensure that the model avoids overfitting or underfitting. Supervised learning helps to solve a huge number of real-world problems, such as classifying spam and separating this from your inbox folder. Some popular methods used in supervised learning include logistic regression, linear regression, k-nearest neighbors, decision trees support vector machine (SVM), and more.

2. Unsupervised Learning: In unsupervised ML techniques, the users do not need to train the model. It allows the model to work on its own experience to achieve accuracy. There is no dataset to train the model, and it mainly deals with the unlabeled data. Unsupervised learning algorithms allow users to perform more complex processing tasks compared to supervised learning, although unsupervised learning can be more unpredictable compared with other natural learning methods. Unsupervised learning algorithms include clustering, anomaly detection, neural networks, etc.

3. Semi-supervised Learning: Semi-supervised learning is a blend of supervised and unsupervised learning. In this case, the machine is given a large dataset, in which only a few data points are labeled. The algorithm will use clustering techniques (unsupervised learning) to identify groups within the given dataset, and use the few labeled data points within each group to provide labels to other data points in the same cluster/group. One of the most prominent benefits of this technique is that it obviates the need to spend a lot of time and effort in labeling each data point, which is a highly effort-intensive and time-consuming manual process.

Figure 5.1 shows the taxonomy of machine learning methods.

Deep Learning

The real challenge to AI was to solve tasks that were easy for humans to perform but whose solutions were difficult to formulate through mathematical rules (Agarwal 2023; Drori 2023; Vasudevan et al. 2022). These are tasks that humans solve intuitively, such as speech or face recognition. Hans Moravec's paradox posits that machines can be made to learn difficult or complex tasks like playing chess or solving algebra equations, yet

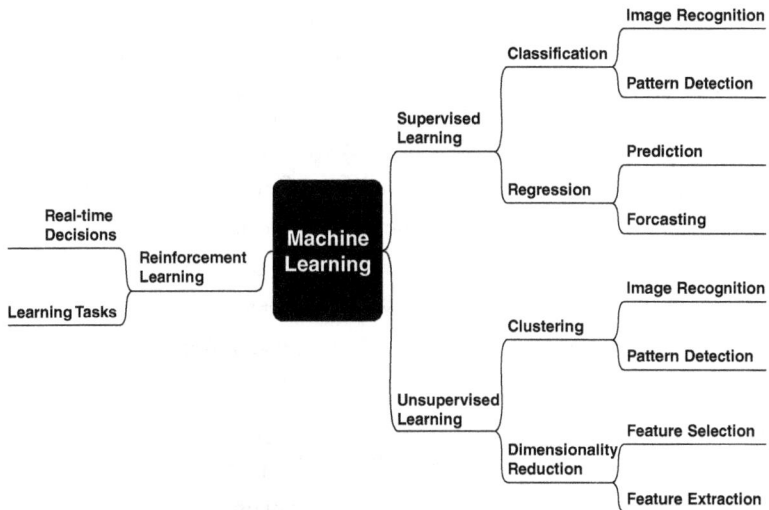

Figure 5.1 Machine learning methods

they can't replicate the capabilities of a toddler to recognize faces, walk across a room, or associate words with items they see. Thus, skills that are seemingly more difficult for humans to grasp, such as geometry or calculus, can be programmed more easily into a computer's repertoire of capabilities.

One possible cause for Moravec's paradox is evolution. Hans Moravec conjectured that the older the skill, the longer it will take to reverse engineer and recreate through software.

A computer-based solution for this type of task involves the ability of computers to learn from experience and to understand the world in terms of a hierarchy of concepts. Each concept is defined by its relationship to simpler concepts. By gathering knowledge from experience, this approach avoids the need for human operators to formally specify all the knowledge that the computer needs for its work. The hierarchy of concepts allows the computer to learn complicated concepts by assembling them from simpler ones. This is why this approach was called "deep learning" (DL).

DL is based on huge neural networks to learn complex patterns in large amounts of data. DL uses a series of hierarchical layers or a hierarchy of concepts to perform the process of ML. The artificial neural networks used in this process are built like the human brain, with neurons inter-connected like in a network. The first visible layer of the neural network processes raw data input, such as the individual pixels of an image. This first layer forwards its outputs to the next layer. This second layer pro-cesses the information from the previous layer and passes the result on to the next layer. The next layer receives the information from the second layer and processes it further. These layers are called hidden layers. The characteristics contained in each of these layers become progressively ab-stract. The model itself determines which concepts are useful for explain-ing the relationships in the observed data—this continues at all levels of the artificial neural network. The result is the output in the final visible layer.

DL applications are known to be limited in their explanatory capacity. In other words, a trained DL system cannot explain "how" it arrived at its predictions, even when they are essentially correct.

In conventional ML techniques, feature extraction is mainly done by humans, which is time-consuming and depends heavily on the knowledge base provided. The most important component of DL is the feature-extraction system or representation-learning system. The system captures spatiotemporal dependencies of data and represents it in a hierarchical artificial neural network by a feature-extraction process called *feature learning*. DL is a learning hierarchical representation wherein each level of the network learns to transform its input data into a more informative and composite representation based on the data regularities.

Generative AI and OpenAI GPT-3 & GPT-4

Generative AI does not use deep neural networks to cluster, classify, or make predictions on existing data; it uses those powerful neural network models to generate brand new content, from images to natural language, from music to video. Generative AI models can deal with different kinds of data, from natural language to audio or images.

For years, natural language processing (NLP) applications did not see much impact from the new DL revolution. Traditional sequence modeling architectures, such as recurrent neural networks (RNNs) and long short-term memory (LSTM), have been used for NLP applications. The sequential nature of such architectures had limited the possibilities to train on the same scale of data that showed value for computer vision after 2012. The main driver of that success was the convolutional neural network (CNN) architecture. The efficiency and parallelization of CNN allowed computer vision architectures to pre-train on enormous data, which has proved to be a key factor in their success.

In 2017, Google introduced the *transformer* architecture to process sequential data with much more parallelization (Kamath et al. 2022). Such an architecture enabled efficient training on much larger datasets than was possible before. This powered transformers to revolutionize the NLP field the same way CNN had done to computer vision. Transformers are now becoming the core part of many neural architectures employed in a wide range of applications such as NLP, speech recognition, time series, and computer vision. OpenAI uses transformers in their GPT2/GPT3/ GPT4, which has registered state-of-the-art performance levels in various NLP tasks (Thakur et al. 2024). DeepMind's AlphaStar program, which defeated a top professional StarCraft player, also uses the transformer architecture.

> A Generative AI system at its core consists of a large language model (LLM) and a large reasoning model (knowledge graph-enhanced RAG (Retrieval-Augmented Generation))(Kejriwal et al. 2025; Lane 2025).

Governance: Availability with Integrity

Regarding scaling, governance represents seamless functional availability— the probability that the system is capable of conducting its required function when it is called upon, given that it has failed or is undergoing a repair or an update action (Smallwood 2020).

Availability can be defined as the ability to guarantee non-loss of data and subsequent recovery of the system in a reasonable amount of time (Fox and Hao 2018). The availability of a system depends on the availability of the configuration of supporting blocks, such as local area networks (LANs), wide area networks (WANs), and routers, as well as the computer system itself, with its layers of software (SW). The outage of a disk, tape, or other pieces of hardware (HW) may cause an outage of one application or service, but does not affect the other.

E-Business Management

E-business has become an increasingly important aspect of the global economy, with more and more businesses turning to digital channels to reach customers and streamline their operations (Wirtz 2024; Jelassi and Martínez-López 2020; Chaffey et al. 2019; Overby and Audestad 2018, 2021). By using electronic means such as websites, mobile applications, and social media, businesses can offer customers the convenience of shopping anywhere and anytime. They can also collect valuable data on customer behavior and preferences (Papazoglou and Ribbers 2006; Harmon et al. 2001; Mithas 2016). E-business facilitates faster and more efficient communication between businesses and their partners, enabling them to collaborate more effectively and make quicker decisions. E-business also allows businesses to reduce costs by automating processes and eliminating the need for physical storefronts or offices.

E-businesses generate and store vast amounts of data on their customers, transactions, and other business activities. To manage this data effectively, e-businesses use digital systems such as customer relationship management (CRM) software and enterprise resource planning (ERP) systems. These systems enable e-businesses to store, manage, and analyze their data, providing valuable insights that can be used to make informed business decisions.

The expansion of the Internet has had many effects on e-business:

1. It has led to the emergence of a global marketplace that enables firms to connect with clients and partners worldwide. This has allowed new types of e-commerce, such as online marketplaces and digital storefronts, which enable firms to offer items and services to clients without a physical shop or sales staff.
2. New business models, such as the software-as-a-service (SaaS) model, have emerged due to the Internet's influence on e-business. This strategy enables enterprises of all sizes to engage in the digital economy by providing access to robust e-business tools and platforms without requiring substantial internal IT resources.
3. New means of communication and cooperation, including e-mail, instant messaging, and video conferencing, have revolutionized how organizations communicate with their consumers, partners, and suppliers. This has resulted in the rise of new types of e-business, such as e-service and e-procurement, which use digital technology to expedite corporate operations and enhance the customer experience.

E-business systems encompass a comprehensive range of activities, including marketing, advertising, customer service, and supply chain management. Each activity may require different digital tools and platforms, creating a more complex and challenging environment. However, the benefits of e-business systems often outweigh the complexity, as they can lead to greater efficiency, reduced costs, and improved customer experiences. E-commerce systems are generally more straightforward since they are focused on facilitating transactions between buyers and sellers. They typically involve a relatively small number of digital tools and platforms, such as an online store and a payment gateway. E-commerce allows businesses to reach a wider audience, expand their customer base, and increase revenue streams. With the rise of mobile commerce and the increasing use of social media platforms as shopping channels, the scope and potential of e-commerce are continuously expanding, creating new opportunities for businesses and consumers alike.

E-business has opened up numerous opportunities for organizations of all sizes, enabling them to reach a global audience, streamline operations, and provide better customer service. E-service has revolutionized how businesses handle customer support, providing a faster, more accessible way to assist clients around the clock. With e-service, businesses can offer immediate assistance to customers, regardless of location, through various digital channels. This helps companies save money by reducing the need for extensive customer support teams while still providing customers with a high level of service. Additionally, e-logistics has transformed how businesses manage their supply chain, making it more efficient and effective. Through digital platforms, companies can track inventory, monitor shipments, and manage logistics in real time, reducing delivery times and ensuring that products reach customers in a timely and cost-effective manner.

Thus, e-businesses offer a range of benefits that enable organizations to compete and thrive in the digital era:

- Increased efficiency: E-businesses enable simplifying operations, automating repetitive processes, and eliminating manual processes by using digital technologies, resulting in quicker and more efficient processes. This can help businesses increase productivity, reduce costs, and enhance their bottom line.

- Reduced expenses: E-businesses enable saving money on rent, electricity, and other costs associated with maintaining a physical presence by eliminating the need for storefronts.
- Wider reach: E-businesses enable companies to reach a larger audience without costly marketing activities, reducing the cost of customer acquisition.
- Enhanced customer engagement: E-businesses enable closer customer engagement for feedback, complaints, and problem resolutions by using mobile-based applications. E-businesses can provide services and sell products around the clock, enabling them to generate revenue even when their physical stores are closed. E-businesses can operate 24/7 without being limited by traditional business hours or geographical restrictions.

Overall, the development and expansion of the Internet have profoundly affected e-business, allowing organizations to access new markets, simplify operations, and develop new kinds of trade, communication, and cooperation.

Mass Customization

Manufacturing started with an artisan making a single product for a single customer, and, as such, was recognized as craft production. Manufacturing continued to evolve in the late 1800s during the Industrial Revolution, pioneering mass production at the beginning of the twentieth century. Later, the market demanded more and more variety, forcing manufacturing to move toward the paradigm of mass customization, which can be defined as the capability to produce personalized goods, with near mass production costs and efficiency. Thus, mass customization in a way is similar to producing goods and services to meet an individual customer's needs but with near mass production efficiency (Tseng and Piller 2003; Tsigkas 2013; Fogliatto and da Silveira 2011).

Mass customization was anticipated by Stan Davis in the book, *Future Perfect* in 1987: "The same large number of customers can be reached as in mass markets… and simultaneously they can be treated individually as in the customized markets of pre-industrial economies" page

169 (Davis 1987). Pine in 1993 introduced an industrial perspective on the newborn concept and defined mass customization as "providing tremendous variety and individual customization, at prices comparable to standard goods and services" to enable the production of products and services "with enough variety and customization that nearly everyone finds exactly what they want" page 15 (Pine and Davis 1993).

One of the keys to mass customization is the use of dynamic business networks within and among enterprises. These are formed out of a set of loosely coupled autonomous business process capabilities with a linkage system that allows them to be reconfigured instantly for any particular customer order. By engineering the flexibility of the processing units and coordinating the flow of resources (materials or services) between these units, the mass customizer can produce an almost infinite variety of base products or services, at a cost that is competitive when compared even with a mass producer. Whereas labor in the mass production design is organized to perform repetitive tasks according to a singular command and control system, the mass customizer organizes labor to routinely respond to an ever-changing set of rules and commands. The mass customizer organizes labor to work effectively in a dynamic network of relationships and to respond to work requirements defined by the dynamically changing customer needs. Although there is a great degree of centralization in both of these models, there is a fundamental difference like centralization: in the case of mass production, all decision-making is centralized, whereas in the case of the mass customizer, it is only the coordination and control that is centralized. The mass customizing enterprises centralize the allocation of work to different processing units to produce the customer's product or service order.

Mass customization production can be achieved with strategies such as the following:

a. Provide quick response throughout the value chain: Reducing the time needed along a firm's entire value chain is known as time-based competition. Speeding up new product development and reducing setup time in manufacturing significantly decreases variant product-specific costs. Shortening the order-to-delivery cycle in marketing also lowers complexity costs by reducing final goods inventory.

b. Create customizable products and services: This method involves producing goods that customers can easily adapt to individual needs in a "self-service" manner. It changes the focus of development and marketing, while production and delivery remain almost undisturbed. Office furniture that can be adjusted and computer applications that allow users to create their system environment provide examples of this widely employed method.

c. Provide point-of-delivery customization: As customers know best what they want, this method performs the final customizing step at the point of sale or delivery. For example, men's suits and eyeglasses are individualized to a customer's specific preferences right at the shop. This can be achieved for general products if a firm shifts the entire production process to the point of delivery; however, this would adversely impact the functioning of the whole enterprise. Hence, the method discussed here is more appropriate for products having (say) only one inherently customer-specific attribute on an otherwise relatively standardized commodity. In this way, the standard part can be manufactured centrally, while the customized characteristic can be produced at the point of sale.

d. Customize services around standardized products and services: A standardized product can be tailored by people in marketing and delivery before it reaches customers. For example, car rental companies add customized services such as express service and club memberships for frequent customers to their standard commodity service.

e. Modularize components to customize end-products and services: This is considered the most effective method of mass customizing products—modularize components that can be configured to a large number of product variants. Economies of scale are achieved through the components, while economies of scope and customization are gained by reusing the components to create a large stream of product variants.

Volume Growth: Value Appropriation Maximization via Long Tail Strategy

The Long Tail has significant implications for all users of the web. By removing the traditional barriers to content production and storage, the road is open for production by anyone; the web becomes a read/write space again, but this time on a massively greater scale with infinite room for endless niche markets. This mass production creates not only a vast amount of data but several possibilities that arise from the data that are exploited by savvy applications and businesses aware of its potential.

Research in the late 1990s revealed power-law distributions in the structure of the Internet and the interconnectedness of the web. A power-law distribution is a curve with a very small number of very high-yield events (like the number of words that have an enormously high probability of appearing in a randomly chosen sentence, like "the" or "to") and a very large number of events that have a very low probability of appearing (like the probability that the word "probability" or "baffel-gab" will appear in a randomly chosen sentence). The number of events with a very low probability creates a heavy or long tail as the probability decreases but never quite reaches zero.

"Wired" editor Chris Anderson argued that this distribution is an important property of the web, in particular, because the content and commodities available on the web are digital (Anderson 2006). A traditional business, constrained by storage capacity and costs, focuses on the high-frequency end of the power-law distribution to reap the greatest profit from every transaction. Anderson uses a music shop as an example. Thus, music shops will focus on providing popular albums because the faster they shift them, the less time the albums remain on the shelves, which in turn means the profit margin is greater. The more difficult-to-sell albums take up space and cost, especially the longer they idle on the shelves. Such a situation enforces the power-law distribution because it ensures that customers find it harder to buy less popular albums.

However, an online music shop has only virtual shelf space and can therefore virtually stock an infinite number of albums, including the least popular. It costs Amazon no more to virtually stock a highly popular album than it does to stock a niche product. As a result, the artificial barrier to users buying less popular albums is lifted, and the tail of the distribution grows. Although the number of events under the tail of the distribution is small compared to the high-frequency end, it is still a substantial number considering the total number of users of the web. Hence, there are significant advantages to businesses in supporting the tastes of those customers who make up the tail. According to Anderson, in traditional retail in 2005, new albums accounted for 63 percent of sales, but online that percentage was only 36 percent.

Performance: System Engineering

Regarding scaling, *performance* is the ability of a system to meet timing requirements. Performance can be measured in terms of throughput and latency for both interactive and embedded real-time systems, although throughput is usually more important in interactive systems, and latency is more important in embedded systems.

Numerous elements in a computer system can have a complementary or orthogonal effect on the performance. They can be classified under the headings of application design and coding, network links, online transaction processing (OLTP), and database management system (DBMS) or relational database management system (RDBMS), supporting software such as middleware, system software, and hardware (Kale 2019). Many of the processes or tasks involved in computational work are serial, and in such cases, the final performance of the computational work will depend on the performance of the elements in the execution chain. Some work can, of course, be run in parallel, such as scientific programs or parallel data paths provided to speed up data transmission or storage I/O, but for performance planning and capacity work, it is wise to take the worst case of everything operating serially and not in parallel.

The objective of achieving maximum performance can be accomplished by:

1. Optimizing the speed of doing things that have to be done—for example, executing program code and transferring data to or from storage across networks are things that have to be done.

2. Minimizing inhibitors to this aim—elimination or minimization of any delays (latency) in the execution of the application and the other activities that support the application. These delays are called waits or waiting times in queuing terms.

Response time is the elapsed time between a work request being submitted and the receipt of a response by the same submitter, normally measured as the last character sent by the user to the first character returned. It is possible to increase the throughput at the expense of response time, or vice versa. The setup of the system will, in theory, be done to satisfy the performance criteria in a service level agreement (SLA). These numbers, when used in an SLA, are essentially those that are reproducible, unlike (say) analytical queries, which may take seconds to hours to complete, depending on the parameters involved in a particular query. Numbers regarding and helping to quantify performance in systems are normally referred to by the generic term performance metrics.

Distinctive Artifacts

Design Thinking "Out of the New Box"

Traditionally, the two diametrically opposing approaches to problem-solving can be categorized as:

- deductive
- inductive

Design thinking weaves these two opposing methods together into abductive reasoning. Design thinking uses abductive reasoning to infer ever-improving solutions, up to the point where the outcome is considered good enough or can no longer be improved upon. The abductive reasoning framework starts with observations to seek a first-cut, simple, and intuitive solution. Oftentimes, the initial solution is either only a partial solution or only partially addresses the problem at hand. Often, the initial solution results in a rephrased problem statement. By subsequently analyzing the intuitive solution and gathering data to either validate or invalidate it, the initial solution is revised and improved upon (Johannesson and Perjons 2021; Wieringa 2014).

Design thinking is effective because:

a. Design thinking is customer-centric: Problem-solving starts with observing and understanding customers and their needs, their pain points, their expected benefits, and their minimal requirements. Insights are acquired by focusing on observing and listening to customers in their natural environment, avoiding any intermediate interference or filters that can distort the observations. Traditional analytical approaches rely on historical data, like surveys or past experiences, to understand customers and their needs. The rationale behind the data is often missed.

b. Design thinking is iterative: It incrementally addresses challenges, improving solutions step by step, considering what has previously been learned, and using resources (time and money) wisely. It allows for avoiding unfocused data gathering and analysis. Design thinking is based on the understanding that it is not possible to get the solution to a wicked problem right the first time. Design thinking relies on iteratively trying out different options and improving solutions over time by considering what has been learned, what worked, and what did not work.

c. Design thinking is based on prototyping and validating ideas: It ensures that the designed solutions work. It does not assume that there exists a single best solution, but rather uses prototyping to identify trade-offs, validate them, and retain those solutions that work. Stakeholders are actively involved in ideation, designing prototypes, and experimentation. Observations and insights are transformed into prototypes of ideas that can be validated with real customers. Each validation round leads to new observations and insights, which allow for improving upon previous prototypes.

In 2005, researchers at the newly founded d.School at Stanford University developed a five-step design-thinking process that has been at the heart of many subsequent research on design-thinking processes (Kale 2024):

i. Empathize: This first step is about understanding the problem at hand. Observations, interviews, and measurements are some of the key tools used to gain an objective, non-judgmental view of the challenge at hand. The key is empathy and customer centricity. Empathy is at the heart of a human-centered design process.

ii. Define: During the second step of the design-thinking process, the gained data is used to clearly define the problem at hand and describe the core challenge to solve in an objective way. The problem is defined in terms of customers and their needs, rather than the firm's internal goals.

iii. Ideate: During this step, new possible solutions are created by starting with a large number of ideas and narrowing them down by eliminating those ideas that are unacceptable in terms of cost, value, time, resources, etc. This step is about developing a wide range of solutions, i.e., to develop and visualize as many ideas, and as many different ideas, as possible. The entire process should be strictly separated between the generation and evaluation of ideas, so as not to restrict the creative flow at an early phase.

iv. Prototype: Prototyping is about transforming ideas into actionable concepts that can be shared, reviewed, and validated. Prototypes need not be perfect and are iteratively refined and improved until they can demonstrate value from a customer perspective. At this step, several prototypes are usually defined. Prototyping transfers ideas from the mind into the physical world. In later stages, the prototypes should be refined and allow careful investigation of specific issues.

v. Test: Before selecting a prototype as the problem's solution, they are tested and validated. To do so, experiments are designed and performed. Based on the outcomes of the experiments, the prototypes are iteratively refined until a validated working solution is found.

Testing offers the opportunity to receive qualitative feedback on the prototypical solutions, to make them better, to learn more about the users, and thus to deepen their empathy for them.

Services

Services represent a type of relationship-based interaction (activities) between at least one service provider and one service consumer to achieve a certain service goal or solution objective. The interaction between the service provider and service consumer can happen in real time, online, or offline (Kale 2024; Qui 2014; Ravindran et al. 2018; Crandall and Crandall 2008).

Services have an innate connection between scalability, connectivity, and population-oriented value creation (Hsu 2009).

Characteristics of Services

There are five differences between products and services.

a. Intangibility: Services are intangible; products such as cars, TVs, computers, clothing, and food items, can be seen and touched and can be used or consumed. Most services provide some personal value to the customers. The value may be in the form of satisfaction after watching a movie, seeing a doctor for an illness, eating at a restaurant, or listening to a live concert.

b. Perishability: Services are perishable; products can be produced ahead of time, stored, and then sold later to the customers. Perishability of services is one of the biggest challenges in managing capacity and demand for services. Empty seats in an airline have no value once the plane takes off, cricket game tickets are worthless after the game is over, and today's movie tickets are worthless tomorrow!

c. Proximity: Most services require closer proximity to the service provider and its customers. Products can be produced anywhere in the world and shipped over long distances to customers.

d. Inseparability: Most services are created and consumed at the same time; in other words, there is direct consumer interaction during service. On the other hand, consumer presence is not required when producing products. Inventory of finished goods separates the producer and customer. For example, you do not have to be present when your car is manufactured at the plant.

e. Variability: Most service providers provide the same service to several customers in the same way. Since services invariably involve interaction between the provider and the consumer, the provider's physical and psychological condition plays an important role in service delivery, and these conditions may not always be the same every day; even customers may have different perceptions of what they have received and, therefore, experience different levels of satisfaction. Moreover, the same person performing the same service may not deliver the same service at every performance.

Challenges Posed by Services

The unique characteristics of services—intangibility, perishability, proximity, and simultaneity—have posed special challenges in designing and controlling service systems.

a. Serviceized products or productized services: All the products customers buy cannot be classified strictly as goods or services; many are a combination of goods and services.

b. Co-creation: The introduction of self-service at gas stations, retail stores, airports, and other locations has resulted in customers interacting more actively with their services. Customers do all the work at "self-checkout" lanes.

c. Service quality: Because services are intangible and require customer interaction, it is difficult to measure the quality of service (QoS) while designing service systems.

d. Service demand and capacity management: While designing the capacity of manufacturing systems, inventory is used as a buffer to account for the variability in customer demand and supply. However, perishability (no inventory) and simultaneity (direct customer interaction) make capacity management very difficult in service systems. Tools, such as "revenue management," are specifically designed to address this challenge.

Automation and advances in digital technology have blurred some of the differences between goods and services. In the past, customers had to go physically to a bank, during normal business hours, to complete their financial transactions. With the introduction of ATMs, customers could do their transactions at select locations at any time. Then came online banking, which customers can use to complete their bank transactions 24/7 from home. Thus, "proximity" is no longer a difference. However, direct customer interaction (simultaneity) is still valid; the interaction is now between the customers and the bank's "surrogates"—ATMs and the bank's computers.

The *smartization* trend is toward an increasingly higher percentage of *digital* services and provisioning through Service as a Software (SaaS)!

Enterprise Architectures (EAs)

EA which is composed of business, information, application, and technical architecture, is critical for enabling the scaling competency of the organization (Kirischian 2016; Chalmers 2011; Ziemann 2022; Iyamu 2024; Musukutwa 2022; Kleppmann 2017; Proper et al. 2017; Escalona et al. 2014).

Business Architecture

The business architecture results from the implementation of business strategies and the definition of processes. This architecture dictates the functional requirements of business processes that determine the information systems that will operationally support the business. The core concept within the business architecture is the business process. A business process is a set of value-adding activities that operate over input entities, producing output entities. These activities are either orchestrated by a central controlling entity or choreographed—the actual coordination mechanism is only relevant while detailing how the process is enacted.

Although an organization always comprises multiple sets of coordinated activities, each may or may not be classified as an actual business process. What distinguishes an arbitrary set of coordinated activities from a business process is the fact that the process necessarily adds value to a customer, whether internal or external to the organization.

An activity is performed during a specific period. As a precondition for its enactment, all of the business roles must be fulfilled by specific entities. These entities will be engaged in playing their roles for the duration of the activity. The activity post-condition is that all of the roles would have been completed by the end of the specified period.

An activity describes the business roles required of the organizational entities for its operation. These roles include:

i. Actor role: An activity requires one actor, or a combination or team of actors to be executed. The actor represents a person, a machine or device, or an information system. An actor provides the services required for fulfilling the business role required by the activity.

ii. Resource role: A resource is used as input or output of an activity during its operation. A resource is usually created, used, transformed, or consumed during the operation of the activity.

iii. Observable state role: An observable state is a specific resource role that is used as a means to observe the status of an activity.

The major components for describing the business architecture are as follows:

- Business strategy: Key business requirements, processes, goals, strategies, key performance indicators (KPIs), business risks, and the business-operating model
- Business function: Key business services, processes, and capabilities that will be affected by the organizational architecture (OA) effort
- Business organization: The high-level nature of organizational structures, business roles (internal audiences, external customers, and partners), the decision-making process, and organizational budget information

Information Architecture

The information architecture describes what the organization needs to know to run its processes and operations as described in the business architecture. It is an abstraction of the information requirements of the organization and provides a high-level logical representation of all the key information elements that are used in the business, as well as the relationship between them. It defines a view of the business information that is independent of the application and technology architectures.

Business information is structured as a collection of informational entities. Entities describe various resources required by processes, including business, support, and management processes. An entity can result from the composition or specialization of other entities in the object-oriented sense. Entities have an identifier defined from a business perspective along with the associated set of roles with a related set of attributes; each role integrates its set of attributes into the entity. Thus, every entity has an overall set of attributes that results from the summation of attributes derived from each role the entity can play.

The principal components for describing information architecture are as follows:

- Information strategy: Information architecture principles, information governance and compliance requirements, canonical data models, industry data model support strategy, and dissemination patterns and reference models
- Information assets: A catalog of critical business data types and models (such as customer profile, purchase order, product data, and supply chain), relationships between such business data types, and all the processes and services that interact with these data

Application Architecture

The application architecture fulfills two major goals: supporting the business requirements and allowing efficient management of the organization's entities. To satisfy these goals, the application architecture should be derived top-down from the analysis of the business and information architectures.

The application architecture defines the applications required to enable the business architecture. This includes identifying how the applications interact with each other, how they will interact with other business integration elements, and how the application and data will be distributed throughout the organization. It typically includes descriptions of automated services that support the business processes, and of the interaction and interdependencies between an organization's application systems, plans for developing new applications, and revision of old applications based on the enterprise objectives.

The architecture of a business process support system is described using the structure of an information system (IS) block. An IS block is then defined as an organized collection of services, mechanisms, and operations designed to handle organizational information. Each block may state several attributes, such as availability, scalability (ability to scale up performance), and profile-based access (ability to identify who does what).

The application architecture defines the applications needed for data management and business support, regardless of the actual software used to implement systems. It functionally defines what application services are required to ensure entities and processes are supported in an acceptable time, format, and cost. Service is the aggregation of a set of operations provided by an architectural block. It can be seen as a generalization of the concept of web services. Service is of three types:

i. Business service: A set of operations provided by IS blocks supporting business processes.
ii. IS service: A set of operations provided by an IS block to other IS blocks. This is used to aggregate multiple IS blocks.
iii. IT service: A set of technological services provided by the specific application platforms.

The principal components for describing application architecture are as follows:

- Application strategy: The key application architecture principles (build vs. buy, hosted vs. in-house, open source vs. commercial grade, open standards vs. .NET, etc.), application governance, portfolio management, and a set of reference application architectures relevant to the customer

- Application processes: A series of application-specific processes that support the business processes in BA
- Application services: An inventory of the key application services exposed to internal and external applications that support the business services
- Logical components: An inventory of relevant product-agnostic enterprise application systems that is relevant to stated business objectives
- Physical components: Actual products that support the logical application components and their relationships to relevant components and services in information and technology architectures

The granularity of abstraction required by an enterprise depends on factors such as domain, scope, responsibilities, design and construction roles, and so on. Increasingly more detailed abstractions focus inwardly based on a frame of reference established by a higher abstraction. Each architecture in this example constrains the downstream architect, and although not shown here, detailed designers and implementers would be maximally constrained at the finest granularity of abstraction.

Technical Architecture

The technological architecture represents the technologies behind application implementation as well as the infrastructure and environment required for the deployment of the business process support systems.

The technological architecture addresses a large number of concepts since it must cope simultaneously with continuous technological evolutions and the need to provide different specialized technological perspectives, such as those centered on security and hardware. These concepts are abstracted as an IT block. An IT block is the infrastructure, application platform, and technological or software component that realizes or implements a set of IS blocks.

The principal components for describing technology architecture are as follows:

- Technology strategy: It comprises technology architecture principles; technology asset governance methodology; portfolio management strategy; and technology standards, and patterns. These assets and artifacts go a long way in strengthening and sustaining technology-driven business solutions.
- Technology services: An inventory of specific technology services and their relationships, and the business services, application services, information assets, and logical or physical technology components that realize such services.
- Logical components: The product-agnostic components that exist at the technology infrastructure tier to support each technology service.
- Physical components: The set of technology products that exists behind each logical technology component to implement the technology service.

Case Study: Digital Transformation at Amazon

Amazon is a multi-business organization (multi- "Out of the New Box") with multi-resources and multi-scaling characteristics across diverse industries from e-retailing to physical stores to video streaming, secure online computer processing/storage, and potentially into pharmaceuticals and health insurance. Amazon sells over 500 million products and employs about 700,000 people. Amazon has become the largest online retailer and the largest cloud service provider. Over 50 percent of online shoppers use Amazon; with its Amazon Prime offer, the company reaches 82 percent of U.S. households. Daily sales of more than $400 million have been achieved (Kreutzer 2022).

Amazon's multi-businesses are:

1. Amazon e-commerce marketplace: Amazon began as an online bookstore via Amazon.com in 1995, and today still sells books

there and also via other online platforms that it has acquired. It also now publishes books directly (Amazon Publishing). In 1999, Amazon.com expanded to offer other goods by third-party vendors. This was followed by offering fair-priced "private-label" goods that are sold exclusively on Amazon.com, either with an Amazon brand or with a third-party brand. Vendors selling on Amazon.com can choose to either handle delivery logistics and customer services themselves, or Amazon can handle them (Fulfillment by Amazon - FBA). Amazon charges a percent commission on all goods sold, and the commission is higher for private-label sales.

2. Fulfillment by Amazon (FBA): FBA is a representative Amazon service. Sellers can store their stock in Amazon's fulfillment center, and when an order is placed via Amazon.com, Amazon will pick, pack, and ship products to buyers and handle any customer service issues. Amazon charges a higher FBA fee on goods sold using this service.

3. Amazon Marketing Services (AMS): AMS monetizes the Amazon platform traffic by offering advertising to Amazon vendors. AMS can place advertisements for vendors' products on Amazon.com and create a frictionless path to purchase—customers click on the ads on the product page and complete a purchase. AMS offers a variety of pay-per-click marketing solutions for Amazon vendors.

4. Amazon Prime: In 2005, a paid customer loyalty program called Amazon Prime was launched. Prime represents a premium membership that offers benefits across the Amazon ecosystem. Prime members pay an annual subscription to access premium services such as free two-day delivery, streaming video and music (Amazon Prime Video), and so on. Prime is well-known for its media and games streaming service, for which Amazon also funds and creates content (films and television series). Only Prime subscribers can access it, and they also pay an additional fee to access premium content.

5. Kindle E-Reader: Amazon's successful e-reader, the Kindle, was launched in 2007 as a device with a non-glare screen for reading digital books.

6. Amazon Echo and Alexa Amazon: Customers can use voice-activated virtual assistant Alexa via the smart speaker Echo device

(that is connected to Wi-Fi) to perform tasks in their homes. For example, a person may ask Alexa to turn on the radio, play an audiobook, or provide weather, traffic, and other real-time information. The Echo device can also connect to other smart devices and so acts as a *command center*. Users can install third-party applications such as weather programs and audio features.

7. Amazon Web Services (AWS) AWS offers on-demand cloud computing services to companies and governments. Amazon AWS is now a world leader in cloud computing-based services, providing cloud-based infrastructure to hundreds of thousands of businesses in 190 countries. AWS allows users to use their browser to log in, configure, and use virtual systems offered by Amazon.

Conclusion

This chapter provided an overview of salient aspects of the scaling transformation model and design blueprint. The vision of *sentient enterprise* highlights aspects like "Enterprise as an Organism," scaling via resources, and smartization. E-business management highlights mass customization, volume growth, and system engineering performance. Distinctive artifacts for this transformation model include design thinking "Out of the New Box," services, and EA.

This chapter focuses on characteristics of the enterprise scaling transformation model or design blueprint, namely, the vision of "Enterprise as an Organism," scaling via resources, smartization, services, and EA.

CHAPTER 6

Scalable Design Blueprint

This chapter discusses digital transformation for scaling design blueprint in two parts. The first part, on reframing for scaling, reviews the typical reference state at the commencement of the reframing for scaling effort. This is in terms of resource-led enterprise operations, a network business model (platform businesses and network effects), enterprise architecture (web services architecture), connecting mechanism (enterprise service bus), communications (3G mobile communications), network system (Web 2.0), and analytics (predictive analytics). The second part, on means for the digital transformation of scaling, reviews typical technologies like resource-based view (RBV) of enterprise operations, e-business models, microservices architecture, Internet of Things (IoT), 4G mobile communications, social networks, and predictive resource analytics.

Reframing for Scaling

Resources-led Enterprise Operations

Business operations envisaged as per the resources-led view of operations strategy for an e-business and e-commerce system (Van Mieghem and Allon 2015; Gupta 2018) have the following aspects:

- Reimagining Organization Design
  - Innovation Networks
  - Talent Management
- Reimagining Customer Relationships (Szatvanyi 2022)
  - Customer Centricity
- Reimagining People Relationships (Kopelman 2020)
  - Team-Based Management
- Business Model Improvisation

Systems like SAP HANA 2.x for Cloud, SAP S/4HANA Enterprise Management (Digital Core), etc., can provide this functionality and services.

Network Business Model: Network Effects and Platform Businesses

Network effects are invariably leveraged to grow the firm and integrate them into products and services to transform them into platform businesses. The strength and direction of network effects drive major decisions and outcomes of platform businesses, including growth and profitability.

Network Effects

By network effects, the reference is to the value one set of users attaches to the other set of users in the platform. The number and quality of users on one side attract users on the other side. For instance, the number and quality of the right segment of browsers on a website attracts specific advertisers to the site. Network effects describe the simple but potentially very powerful idea that the more nodes, users, or connected points there are in a network, the more powerful that network becomes. So, like the telephone, the greater the number of users that are using a social network, the more valuable that network becomes to every user. Products that scale using network effects get better and better the more people use it, creating a virtuous circle of growth (Hess 2022; Perkin and Abraham 2021).

Metcalfe's Law originated in the 1980s as a way to express the concept that a network enabled by communications technologies becomes exponentially more valuable as more devices are connected to it. In the 1990s, assuming two-way communication, this was expressed as the value of a network being proportional to the square of the number of users connected to that system. A simple example of Metcalfe's Law might be the telephone system. If just two telephones existed, that would not be of much productive use. But as more telephones are added to the network, the number of people that can talk to each other using that technology increases, and consequently, the value of every telephone node increases as the number of connections rises.

Social networking applications like LinkedIn attract users to connect and communicate with similar users—their friends and colleagues. The more people like oneself are active on LinkedIn, the more likely that someone similar will be active on LinkedIn. Such network effects are called direct or same-side network effects. The more the readers, the more the advertisers are willing to advertise and pay, but not vice versa. Such network effects are referred to as positive cross-side or indirect network effects. The more space advertisements take in the newspaper, the less the readers are willing to read and pay for the newspaper. Such network effects are labeled negative cross-side network effects. A good example of negative same-side network effects would be a B2B exchange. The more direct competitors one finds in a B2B exchange, the less valuable it is for individual businesses to affiliate with such a platform.

> Network effects are not the same as popularity or word-of-mouth attraction of users that urges others to join and enjoy the same value. Network effects highlight the increase in value added by the business to the users as *more (or less) users* join and use the same.

Platform Businesses

Platforms typically operate in network markets. Network markets are characterized by four special features: complementarity, compatibility, and standards; consumption externalities; switching costs and lock-in; and significant scale economies in production (Srinivasan 2023). Platforms address the three classic information economics problems that traditional industries confront—information asymmetry, adverse selection, and moral hazard. Differences in the information available across the different contracting parties is termed as *information asymmetry*, e.g., used-car business. When the seller exploits this asymmetric information to bargain for higher prices at the cost of the buyer, this is termed as *adverse selection*. Post-contracting, a likelihood of a change in the behavior of one party that can have a material impact on the other party is termed as a *moral hazard*. When platforms intermediate between different sets of users, they address these traditional problems, enabling them to increase the efficiency of these markets.

Imagine a travel-support platform like BookMyTrip. In that platform, user reviews on the hotels and vacations bridge information asymmetry between service providers and clients; prior information about prices and packages published by the hotels helps ameliorate the adverse selection issues; and intermediating all payments and reviews through the intermediary (BookMyTrip) insures against moral hazards. In most markets characterized by such inefficiencies, platforms have contributed significantly to improving economic value for both transacting parties.

Six key decisions need to be undertaken by every platform business:

i. Platform businesses need to decide and articulate the specific sets of users that they cater to, and define/discover/develop network effects. Given the network effects and interdependencies, no one joins unless everyone joins!

ii. Platform businesses need to clearly articulate the combination of utilities that constitute their value architecture.

iii. Platform businesses need to clearly articulate which side(s), if at all, to subsidize and monetize, given the nature of interactions between users and the network effects.

iv. Platform businesses need to clearly articulate how they work with other complements and engender the evolution of the ecosystem. Conscious engagement with the ecosystem will shape the industry structures and standards as well.

v. Platform businesses need to clearly articulate how platforms compete with other firms and platforms, and vie for market dominance, shaping industry evolution and market shares.

Network effects and platform businesses are powerful concepts. By merely registering with requisite identity details and asset-related financial information, a web-based application of Amazon or Uber, or Airbnb enables an individual to become an instant customer, buyer, and consumer, or supplier, seller and provider of things, services, or experiences. Or, even both at the same time! Even for offerings that involve the use of an asset, the identity can be separated from or made independent of the particulars of the asset. Redefining the identity at a more generalized level, enables a combination of network(s) (effects) and optimization of products/ services/ experiences like booking for travel accessories (GetMyAccessories), road/ railway/ airline tickets (MakeMyTrip), and accommodation (BookMyRoom) depending on the timing of the travel (morning/ evening/ night) and priority/ convenience/ cost preferences.

Enterprise Architecture: Web Services Architecture

The cloud is a collection of technologies accessed via a web portal. Thus, the cloud is interfaced through a web server and other backend components. However, unlike the traditional web server where server-side scripts might be executed (Papazoglou 2008; Etzkorn 2017), the cloud offers processing services including productivity software (word processors, spreadsheets, etc.), accounting software, communications software (e.g., to support teleconferencing), games, and so forth. This adds additional layers to the necessary software that our web servers must run. In most cases, the execution of such software is offloaded to other computers. Remote access to a cloud processing service is often referred to as *cloud computing*. Another added component to the cloud is that of backend storage. Although the web server stores its website and perhaps backend databases, the cloud offers storage to the clients, which might utilize a storage area network. Using the cloud for storage is often referred to as *cloud storage*. Microsoft, Google, and Amazon can be examples of architectural stacks from different vendors.

The AWS architectural stack consists of three layers: global infrastructure, foundation services, and platform services:

i. Platform services are relational databases, data warehousing analytics, various forms of applications such as e-mail and streaming, management tools, and mobile services.

ii. Foundational services are more generic, comprising computing, storage, and networking.

iii. Infrastructure is the Internet-based implementation offering these services through, for instance, regional support and edge solutions.

Connecting Mechanism: Enterprise Service Bus (ESB)

An ESB is a set of infrastructure capabilities implemented by middleware technology that enable a service-oriented architecture (SOA) and alleviate disparity problems between applications running on heterogeneous platforms and using diverse data formats. The ESB supports service invocations, message, and event-based interactions with appropriate service levels and manageability. The ESB is designed to provide interoperability between larger-grained applications and other components via standard-based adapters and interfaces. The bus functions as both a transport and transformation facilitator to allow the distribution of these services over disparate systems and computing environments (Papazoglou 2008).

The ESB distributed processing infrastructure is aware of applications and services and uses content-based routing facilities to make informed decisions about how to communicate with them. In essence, the ESB provides docking stations for hosting services that can be assembled and orchestrated and are available for use by any other service on the bus. Once a service is deployed into a service container, it becomes an integral part of the ESB and can be used by any application or service connected to it. The service container hosts, manages, and dynamically deploys services, and binds them to external resources, for example, data sources, enterprise, and multiplatform applications, as shown in Figure 6.1.

Communications: 3G Mobile Communications with wCDMA, UMTS, and iMode

3G mobile communication systems support data rates of over 153.6 kbps. 3G systems provide the ability to transfer both voice data, such as a phone call and non-voice data, such as uploading and downloading information, e-mail exchange, and instant messaging. They provide a better quality of experience for the users and support multimedia data transfers, such as the transfer of audio, video, text, and pictures. 3G enables receiving wired Internet features and services at ISDN-like speeds over a mobile handset. Examples of 3G technology include the wideband CDMA (wCDMA) and Universal Mobile Telecommunication System (UMTS) (Jiang and Han 2024).

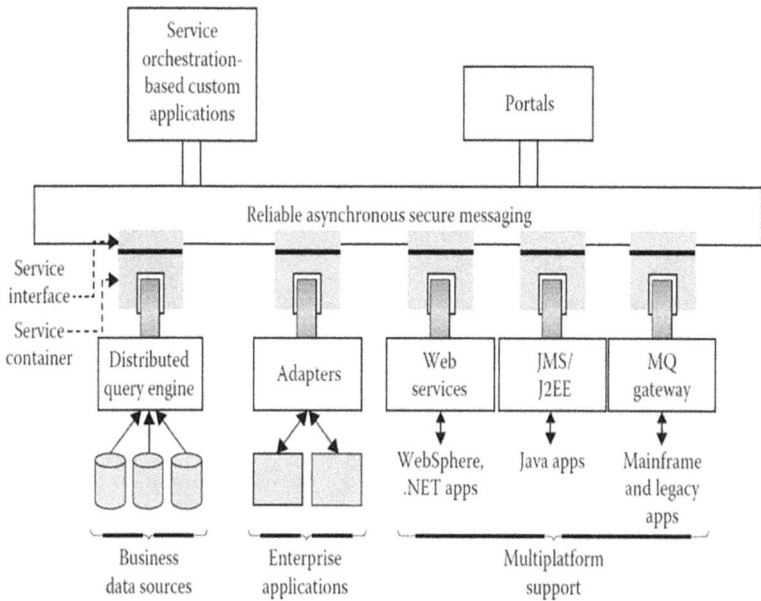

Figure 6.1 Enterprise Service Bus (ESB)

UMTS uses CDMA, which allows for greater capacity and improved spectrum efficiency.

i. Packet-switched core network: UMTS uses a packet-switched core network, which allows for more efficient use of network resources and faster data transfer rates.

ii. High-speed data transfer rates: In Release 99, UMTS supports high-speed data transfer rates up to 384 kbps. In Release 7, this maximal rate is raised to 28Mbps in DL and 11.5 Mbps in UL.

iii. Increased network capacity: UMTS provides increased network capacity through the use of wider frequency bands and more efficient use of available spectrum.

iv. Multimedia services: UMTS provides support for multimedia services such as video conferencing, streaming video, and high-speed Internet access.

v. Enhanced voice services: UMTS provides enhanced voice services such as better call quality, improved voice clarity, and reduced background noise.

vi. Increased security: UMTS provides increased security features, such as user authentication and encryption, to protect against unauthorized access and eavesdropping.

vii. Advanced roaming capabilities: UMTS supports advanced roaming capabilities, allowing users to access services and features seamlessly while roaming between different networks and countries.

viii. Support for location-based services (LBS): UMTS provides support for LBS, allowing operators to offer services based on the user's location, such as location-based advertising, tracking, and emergency services.

Network Systems: Web 2.0

Web 2.0 is a highly interactive and dynamic application platform that is more dynamic than its predecessor, Web 1.0. Web 2.0 has brought about the emergence of social media platforms such as Myspace, Facebook, Twitter, YouTube, Instagram, blogs, and wikis, with some reaching billions of users. This generation of the web is called the "social web era" and focuses on collaboration and data transmission at online platforms, such as social networking sites, blogs, wikis, and mashups, where social media dialogues enable interaction and collaboration. This new era of the web is characterized by the emergence of the next generation of web-related technologies and standards that separate the data exchange layer from the presentation layer, allowing web pages and web applications to change content dynamically without reloading the entire page (Avsar 2023). The increased ability to share ideas and access information from experts, coupled with the reduced costs of communication technologies, travel, and operations, has made many subjects more accessible and functional. Consequently, paradigm changes have occurred in several social areas, including education, trade, health, security, and tourism, after the emergence of Web 2.0.

Web 2.0, or service-oriented applications, lets people collaborate and share information online in seemingly new ways—examples include social networking sites such as myspace.com, media sharing sites such as YouTube.com, and collaborative authoring sites such as Wikipedia (Kale 2018b). Unlike traditional Hypertext Markup Language (HTML)

Table 6.1 Comparison between Web 1.0 and Web 2.0

Web 1.0 characteristics	Web 2.0 characteristics
Static Content	Dynamic Content
Producer-based information	Participatory-based information
Messages pushed to consumer	Messages pulled by consumer
Institutional control	Individual control
Top-down implementation	Bottom-up implementation
Users search and browse	Users publish and subscribe
Transaction-based interactions	Relationship-based interactions
Goal of mass adoption	Goal of niche adoption
Taxonomy	Folksonomy

web pages, *weblogs or blogs* allow the non-programmer to communicate regularly. Weblogs remove many constraints by providing a standard user interface that does not require customization. The biggest advancement made with weblogs is the permanence of the content, which has a unique Universal Resource Locator (URL). A wiki is a website that promotes the collaborative creation of content.

A comparison between Web 1.0 and Web 2.0 is presented in Table 6.1.

Analytics: Predictive Analytics

Predictive analytics is about using past data. The objective is to give the finest evaluation of what will happen shortly. The past data is given to a mathematical model that takes into account key patterns and trends in the data, followed by the application of the model to present data and forecast what will occur next. This analytics can be employed to decrease risks, enhance operations, and increase revenue (Zwingmann 2022; Schniederjans et al. 2014; Sinha and Park 2017). Thus, more organizations are now inclined to use predictive analytics as it can resolve complex problems and reveal new opportunities. Consumer behavior patterns, weather forecasting, predicting political events, and predicting the course of diseases in patients, to name a few. It is based on data and facts as well as information indicating that it is scientific and methodical and not based on instinct and rumor.

Predictive analytics helps organizations to sift through current and past data to discover trends, and predict events and situations that should happen at a particular time, based on provided factors. Moreover, organizations can detect risks and opportunities by finding and exploiting patterns present within the data. Models can be drawn, to learn associations between several behavior features. Such models allow the evaluation of promises or threats presented by a particular set of situations, managing informed decision making across several classes of procurement events and supply chains. Predictive analytic models support rational decision making, limiting the threat of biases in decisions, and predictive analytics to forecast consumer behavior by using behavior informatics and analytics methods improve business decision making.

Predictive analytics can prove beneficial to companies in targeting customers on the basis of their behavior. Companies may use these analytics to collect data on consumers followed by predicting future actions based on past behavior. This information obtained can then be used to make decisions that influence the business's bottom line and impact outcomes.

Means of Digital Transformation of Scaling

Resource-Based View (RBV) of Enterprise Operations

Business operations envisaged per the RBV of operations strategy (Briffaut 2015; Van Mieghem and Allon 2015) have the following aspects:

- Organizational Reconfiguration
- Customer Re-engagement
- Employee Re-engagement
- Business Model Reification

Digital transformation would involve upgrading to the latest functionality, modules, and e-business systems like SAP SuccessFactors, SAP Ariba (Spending) etc., SAP Leonardo (IoT/Edge Comp, Machine Learning (ML), Blockchain, Big Data, Analytics), SAP Cloud Platform, SAP Joule Gen AI Assistant, and so on (Das et al. 2025).

Network Business Model: e-Business Models

To stay competitive, organizations must assess various e-business models and revenue models and focus on those that are most suitable for their e-business. E-business models outline how organizations create, deliver, and capture value through electronic technologies (Wirtz 2024; Xu 2014). Examples include business-to-business (B2B), business-to-consumer (B2C), consumer-to-consumer (C2C), consumer-to-business (C2B), business-to-government (B2G), government-to-business (G2B), and mobile commerce models (Table 6.2).

There are several examples of businesses that employ these various e-business concepts. The business-to-business (B2B) model is also popular, with firms such as Alibaba.com, IBM.com, and Salesforce.com employing it to offer goods and services to other businesses. These organizations provide various tools and services to assist firms in streamlining their processes and improving their performance. Amazon.com employs the business-to-consumer (B2C) model to sell items and services directly to customers. Nike.com is another example of a B2C corporation, where consumers may buy sports shoes and gear online. Consumer-to-Consumer (C2C) firms such as eBay.com, Etsy.com, and Craigslist.org enable people to purchase and sell items and services directly to one another. Mobile commerce (m-commerce) is growing in popularity, with firms like Amazon and Uber providing mobile applications enabling people to buy items or services with only a few clicks.

E-business revenue models are the numerous ways an Internet firm produces revenue or makes money. A company's revenue model is determined by the sort of e-business it conducts, the industry in which it competes, the target audience, and the competitive environment. Revenue models for e-businesses describe how organizations generate revenue from their products or services. Common examples include subscription-based, pay-per-use, advertising-based, and transaction-based models. Selecting an appropriate revenue model is vital for an e-business's success, as each model presents unique benefits and challenges (Table 6.3).

Google, Facebook, Instagram, and Twitter rely on advertising for revenue. These businesses generate substantial revenue by providing their platforms to advertisers who wish to reach a large, engaged audience.

Table 6.2 e-Business models

e-Business Model	Advantages	Disadvantages
Business-to-Consumer (B2C) model	Large addressable market	Competition can be intense
	Direct customer feedback	High customer acquisition costs
	Opportunities for personalization	High levels of customer churn
Business-to-Business (B2B) model	High transaction values	Long sales cycle
	Repeat business opportunities	Complex decision-making processes
	Potential for long-term partnerships	Limited addressable market
Consumer-to-Consumer (C2C) model	Low overhead costs	Limited ability to control product quality
	Large addressable market	Limited ability to scale
	Reduced barriers to entry	Lack of trust among buyers and sellers
Consumer-to-Business (C2B) model	More efficient use of resources	Limited addressable market
	Increased access to specialised skills	Need for effective reputation management
	Reduced administrative costs	Need for effective branding
Business-to-Government (B2G) model	Large, stable customer base	Complex procurement processes
	Potential for long-term contracts	Intense competition for contracts
	Potential for repeat business	Need to comply with government regulations
Government-to-Business (G2B) model	Access to government contracts	Need to comply with government regulations
	Increased opportunities for revenue	Long procurement cycles
	Reduced competition	Complex bidding processes
Mobile Commerce (m-commerce) model	Increased convenience for customers	Limited screen-size makes browsing difficult
	More opportunities for personalization	Limited ability to showcase products
	Reduced overhead costs	Technical challenges related to mobile optimizations

Table 6.3 e-Business revenue models

Revenue Model	Advantages	Disadvantages
Advertising-based	Can generate significant revenue	Can be intrusive and annoying to users
	No direct cost to users	Revenue can be unpredictable
Subscription-based	Provides predictable revenue streams	May limit users to those willing to pay
	Users have an ongoing commitment to the product or service	Users may be hesitant to long-term subscriptions
Transaction-based	Revenue directly tied to sales	Revenue maybe variable and unpredictable
	Minimal overhead costs	May require significant marketing and advertising costs to drive traffic
Affiliate marketing	Low overhead costs	Revenue maybe unpredictable
	Revenue generated through third-party advertising	Dependence on third-party advertising resources
	No need to produce or maintain products	
Freemium	Can attract a large users base	Difficult to find the right balance between free and paid features
	Provides opportunities for revenue growth through premium offerings	May limit revenue potential
Commission-based	Generates revenue through partnerships and collaborations	Revenue maybe unpredictable
	Minimal overhead costs	Dependence on third-party business
Licensing	Provides predictable revenue streams	Limited growth potential
	Revenue not tied to sales volume	Dependence on a limited number of licensing agreements
Crowdfunding	Provides initial capital for startups	Limited revenue potential beyond the initial funding
	Validates demand for products or services	Success depends on market acceptance and enthusiasm

One of the benefits of the advertising-based revenue model is that it enables e-businesses to provide users with free content or services, which can help to attract and retain a large audience. Netflix, Spotify, Microsoft Office 365, and Amazon Prime are examples of companies that use the subscription-based revenue model. Payment processing companies like PayPal and Square, which generate revenue by charging transaction fees for each payment processed on their platform, are examples of e-businesses that use the transaction-based revenue model. Similarly, ride-sharing companies such as Uber and Lyft generate revenue by charging drivers transaction fees for each ride facilitated through their platforms. Amazon Associates, which enables e-businesses to earn a commission on Amazon product purchases, and Commission Junction, which gives access to a broad selection of affiliate programs across multiple sectors, are two examples of e-businesses that employ the affiliate marketing income model.

Users are expected to like the free version enough to see the value in subscribing to the premium version. Software, mobile applications, and gaming firms often adopt freemium models. Popular productivity tools such as Trello and Evernote, for example, provide free basic versions while charging a charge for more sophisticated features and capabilities. Similarly, famous gaming applications like Candy Crush give out a limited number of lives and features for free but charge a price for infinite lives and advanced capabilities. Amazon operates on a commission-based income model. Third-party vendors may sell their items on Amazon, and Amazon receives a percentage on each sale. The commission rate varies according to the product category, with some categories having more excellent commission rates than others.

Microsoft is one example of an e-business that employs the license revenue model. Microsoft offers many software products, including the Windows operating system and the Office suite, which it licenses to other firms for a price. Another example is Spotify, a music streaming business that obtains licenses from record companies and pays them a part of its earnings.

Partner Networks

Organizations in many industries become connected as large networks of *partners*. Partners (or alliances or joint ventures) are important tools for building and reinforcing the collective competitive advantage or *network power* (NP). Partners can be defined as enduring and formalized collaborative relationships between two or more firms that involve significant exchanges of information, resources, and *influence or decision power*; partner networks are conduits across which information, resources, and decisions flow, reflecting the company's NP. The traffic between partners includes the exchange of ideas, technologies, resources, people, and power. All of the alliances a company has with its partners represent the company's alliance portfolio. Organizations have different positions in partner networks. A firm's NP and, hence, success is majorly dependent on the configuration of the partner networks and the company's situational position within any of these networks.

A partnership can be defined as an ongoing relationship between firms that involves a commitment over an extended time period and a mutual sharing of information and the risks and rewards of the relationship. The characteristic features of alliances are as follows:

- Partners work closely together at all levels.
- There is openness and mutual trust.
- Senior managers and everyone in the organizations support the alliance.
- There is a shared business culture, goals, and objectives.
- There is long-term commitment.
- Information, expertise, planning, and systems are shared.
- There is flexibility and willingness to solve shared problems.
- There are continuous improvements in all aspects of operations.
- The joint development of products and processes occurs.
- There are guaranteed reliable and high-quality goods and services.
- An agreement is made on costs and profits to give fair and competitive pricing.
- There is increasing business between partners.

Table 6.4 details the motives for collaborations.

Enterprise Architecture: Microservices Architecture

The microservice architectural style is a lightweight subset of the service-oriented architecture (SOA); "the main difference between SOA and microservices is that the latter should be self-sufficient and deployable independently of each other while SOA tends to be implemented as a monolith." This architectural style is gaining acceptance as regards

Table 6.4 Motives for collaborations

Market development	Cost advantages	Knowledge development	External pressure
Developing joint market power	Realizing advantages of scale	Organizing joint innovation	Political pressure: "One face to Citizens"
Improving and increasing distribution power	Overcoming investing impediments	Gaining access to new technology	Legal obligation of consultation
Gaining access to new markets	Establishing joint supporting services	Using partner complimentary competencies	Moral appeals from society or politics
Protection against competition	More efficient and rationalized production	Learning from partners' skills and knowledge	
Chain integration through better chain coordination		Learning from partners' culture	
		New patents as well as access to patented knowledge	

overcoming the shortcomings of a monolithic architecture in which, rather than having the application logic within one deployable unit, applications are decomposed into services, each of which is deployable on a different platform, runs its own process, and communicate by means of lightweight mechanisms (Fernando 2023, 2021) (Table 6.4).

The main principles of microservices are (Fowler and Lewis 2013):

- Componentization via services: Software is broken up into multiple services that are independently replaceable and upgradable and communicate by means of inter-process communication facilities using an explicit component-published-interface.
- Organized around business capabilities: Microservices are implemented around business areas, in which services include a user interface, storage, and any external collaborations.
- Products not projects: Development teams own a product throughout its entire lifetime, taking full responsibility for the software in production.

- Smart endpoints and dumb pipes: Business logic, related business rules, and data reside in the services themselves rather than in centralized middleware. Simple messaging or a lightweight messaging bus is used to provide communication among microservices.
- Decentralized governance: Standardization on a single technology platform is avoided; the right technological stack for a job should be used, and each microservice manages its own decisions regarding tools, languages, and data storage.
- Decentralized data management: Decisions concerning both the conceptual model of the world and data storage will differ between microservices.
- Infrastructure automation: Automatic means to integrate and deploy in new environments.
- Evolutionary design: Services are independently replaced and upgraded, which is achieved by using service decomposition as a tool so as to enable application developers to control changes in software applications at the pace of business changes.

The microservices architecture has been widely adopted as an architectural style that enables the building of software applications with speed and safety. The microservices architecture fosters building a software system as a collection of independent autonomous services (developed, deployed, and scaled independently) that are loosely coupled. These services form a single software application by integrating all such services and other systems (Table 6.5).

The online retail software application can be transformed into a microservices architecture by breaking the monolithic application layer into independent- and business-functionality-oriented services.

Connecting Mechanism: Internet of Things (IoT)

With the advent of IoT, the physical world itself will become a connected information system. In the world of IoT, sensors and actuators embedded in physical objects are linked through wired and wireless networks that connect to the Internet (Rayes and Salam 2022; Solanki et al. 2019; Soldatos 2021). This information system churns out huge volumes of data

Table 6.5 Comparing monolith and microservices

Category	Monoliths	Microservices
Time to Market	Fast in the beginning, slower later as the codebase grows	Slower in the beginning because of the technical challenges that microservices have. Faster later.
Refactoring	Hard to do, as change can affect multiple places	Easier and safe because changes are contained inside the microservice
Deployment	The whole monolith has to be deployed, always	Can be deployed in small parts, only one service at a time
Scaling	Scaling means deploying the whole monolith	Scaling can be done only one service at a time
DevOps skills	Does not require much, as the number of technologies is limited	Lots of DevOps skills required because of multiple different technologies
Performance	No communicational overhead Technology stack might not support performance	Adds communicational overhead Technology choices may add possible performance gains
Understandability	Hard to understand as complexity is high. Lot of interacting parts	Easy to understand as codebase is strictly modular and services use SRP (Single Responsibility Principle)

that flow to computers for analysis. When objects can both sense the environment and communicate, they become tools for understanding the complexity of the real world and responding to it swiftly. To reap the full benefits, any successful solution to build context-aware data-intensive applications and services must be able to make this information transparent and available at a much higher frequency to substantially improve the decision making and prediction capabilities of the applications and services.

IoT refers to a network of interconnected things, objects, or devices on a massive scale connected to the Internet. These objects, being smart, sense their surroundings and gather and exchange data with other objects. Based on the gathered data, the objects make intelligent decisions to trigger an action or send the data to a server over the Internet and wait for its decision. Most common examples of nodes in IoT are sensors used in many areas from industrial process control, sensors used inside ovens and refrigerators, and RFID (radio-frequency identification) chips used as tags in many products of everyday use. Almost all of these smart devices have a short communication range and require very little power to operate. Bluetooth and IEEE ZigBee are the most common communication technologies used in this regard (Marcham 2021).

1. Sensing technologies: Radio-frequency identification (RFID) and Wireless Sensor Networks (WSN) are the two main building blocks of sensing and communication technologies for IoT. However, these technologies suffer from different constraints (e.g., energy limitation, reliability of wireless medium, security, privacy, etc.).
2. Compute technologies: The middleware is a software interface between the physical layer (i.e., hardware) and the application one. It provides the required abstraction to hide the heterogeneity and complexity of the underlying technologies involved in the lower layers. The service-based approaches lying on a cloud infrastructure open the door toward highly flexible and adaptive middleware for the IoT.
3. Actuate technologies: The Internet of Things enhances the passive objects around us with communication and processing capabilities to transform them into pervasive objects. Various equipment and devices (like individual robots, sensors, and smartphones) that can measure the world or interact with people in both the physical and digital worlds are treated uniformly.

It is important to highlight that this book does not discuss other foundational technologies like big data (Hadoop, NoSQL, Network Databases, In-Memory, etc.), statistics, analytics, cloud computing, mobile computing, web, and so on. This is not in any way indicative of their lesser significance. On the contrary, they are important prerequisites for all the concepts, technologies, and aspects discussed in this book (Kale 2015b, 2017b, 2018b, 2019; Mulder 2023; Sajja and Akerkar 2012; Rivera 2020; Kumar et al. 2022).

Internet of Things (IoT) Security

There is a critical requirement for a framework that can provide an operational guarantee for IoT applications (Bishwash and Addya 2021).

Starting from the topmost layer, the seven-layer security framework is as described below:

1. Interface layer: This is the highest layer at which users and different computing devices can interact with any smart system using cloud services or application software. This layer includes several interfaces for a variety of applications from small RFID applications to large, smart-city applications, which can be implemented using standard protocols.

   Responsibility: This layer provides information interpretation with the help of software cooperation between the cloud server and its applications. Actors at this layer are analytics and visualization tools, IoT support applications, websites, and cloud software, etc.

   Software vulnerabilities: Third-party failure, software bugs, unauthenticated access, and configuration errors may generate serious issues at this layer.

   Type of attacks: Malicious code injection, reprogramming attack, DDoS, reverse engineering, backdoor, and phishing attack

   Immunity against attacks: Security checks, Internet firewall, tamperproof design, lightweight cryptography algorithms, etc.

2. Data abstraction layer: Sensors generate voluminous amounts of repetitive data; thus, normalization, consolidation, filtering, and indexing can help in managing such data assisted by rules and algorithms, decision-making analyzers, and big data tools that can simplify the data further.

   Responsibility: Reformatting of data, preserving data for an authentic user, normalizing and indexing data for faster response

   Software vulnerabilities: Software vulnerability, redundant data, and sensitive information leakages

   Type of attacks: Excessive privilege, improper queries, and the malicious insider

   Immunity against attacks: Authentication mechanisms, access control policies, preparing statements, auditable processes, and effective logging

3. Service layer: The service layer is a kind of middleware that is an enabler of services and applications. It is designed to provide common application programming interfaces (APIs) and protocols.

Responsibility: Information storage, data processing, analytics services, integration of services, and event processing, etc. To enable any service with an application of IoT, the following components are used: service discovery, service composition, service APIs, and trust management. Actors at this layer are cloud services, back-end services, database and storage management, and data storage components.

Software vulnerabilities: Reliability of service, insecure cryptography, data protection, and Internet dependency

Security requirements: Authorization, service authentication, privacy protection, antireplay, and availability

Type of attacks: Data loss and modifications, VM escape, malicious VM creation, insecure VM migrations, and brute force attacks

Immunity against attacks: Backup and retention, trusted cloud computing, mirage, VNSS, and site scanner

4. Internet layer: At this communication or network layer, the data abstracted in previous layers can be shared remotely using Internet connectivity.

Responsibility: Routing of the packets, plugins, protocols, IP-based communication, network security implementation, and reliable delivery of packets

Software vulnerabilities: IP address spoofing, route spoofing, wireless access points, and vulnerable transmission media

Type of attacks: low-rate denial of service, traffic analysis attack, false routing, eavesdropping, and spoofing

Immunity against attacks: Hilbert Huang transforms, tools to analyze packets, biverification of the route, deterministic path loss model, and trust anchor interconnection loop

5. Data sensing and acquisition layer: This layer is used to collect data on a local server or a gateway to process and extract useful data. This is essential to get faster responses in real-time applications.

Responsibility: Collection and filtering of data, triggering the event, data aggregation, and gateway to the network

Software vulnerabilities: Insufficient validation, inadequate testing mechanism, and information leakage

Type of attacks: Malicious code, traffic monitoring, and inefficient logging

Immunity against attacks: Pretesting mechanism, encrypting the log file and pattern finding

6. Wireless sensor network layer: This layer enables the low-cost and low-power network that can collect information from heterogeneous sensors.

Responsibility: This network has two components—aggregation and base station. Aggregation point is used to collect information from nearby sensors. Then the information is integrated and sent to the base station to process the collected data.

Software vulnerabilities: Unencrypted information movement and unprotected communication channels

Type of attacks: Injecting false data in WSN, impersonating, unauthorized access, overloading the WSN, and monitoring and eavesdropping

Immunity against attacks: limiting the administration control rate, access control, secure routing, and strong and proper authentication techniques

7. Perception layer: This is the lowest layer that consists of several physical devices like sensors, actuators, microcontrollers, RFID tags, embedded systems, micro-operating systems, RFID readers, etc. Data are captured or sensed by different sensors and shared between the components by using a network.

Responsibility: Deployment of the nodes, heterogeneity of devices, cost, size, and energy consumption by end nodes

Software vulnerabilities: Availability and accessibility of the hardware components

Type of attacks: Natural calamities (such as earthquakes, floods, storms, etc.) and environmental threats (such as fire, chemical accident, etc.) can destroy the whole infrastructure of the system. An attacker can easily deploy an attack to a sensory node and can also modify the data collected from the sensors.

Immunity against attacks: Device authentication, trusted devices, physical protection, and tamperproof design using Hash-based techniques, intrusion detection systems, and granular segmentation

Communications: 4G Mobile Communications

4G is a fully IP-based integrated system, and the Internet work is accomplished by the union of wired and wireless networks including computers, consumer electronics, communication technology, and the capability to provide 100 Mbps and 1 Gbps, respectively, in outdoor and indoor environments with better quality of service (QoS) and improved security, facilitating any kind of services anytime, anywhere, at affordable cost, and single billing (Jiang and Han 2024).

MIMO allows the exploitation of spatial dimensions as an additional degree of freedom for wireless communications, achieving high spectral efficiency. In environments with rich scattering, the theoretical spectral efficiency scales linearly with the minimum number of transmission and receiver antennas.

MIMO can offer three kinds of technical benefits:

i. Spatial multiplexing: This is the transmission of multiple data streams simultaneously at the same frequency using multiple spatial layers created by multiple antennas. As a result, higher spectral efficiency is obtained.

ii. Spatial diversity: Use of independent propagation paths enabled by multiple antennas improves the reliability of the signal transmission against the effect of multiple fading.

iii. Array gain: Concentrating the transmitted energy of an antenna array in particular directions improves the received power of desired signals or suppresses co-channel interference.

Network Systems: Social Networks

Popular social networks like Facebook, Google+, LinkedIn, and Twitter are familiar worldwide. Social networks differ from most other types of networks, including technological and biological networks, in two important ways. First, they have non-trivial clustering or network transitivity, and second, they show positive correlations between the degrees of adjacent vertices. Social networks are often divided into groups or communities; this division can account for the observed clustering.

Furthermore, group structure in networks can also account for degree correlations. Hence, assortative mixing in such networks with a variation in the sizes of the groups provides the predicted level of interaction and compares well with that which is observed in real-world networks (Kale 2018b). Social Network Analysis (SNA) is used to understand the social structure that exists among entities in an organization. The defining feature of SNA is its focus on the structure of relationships, ranging from casual acquaintances to close bonds. This is in contrast with other areas of the social sciences where the focus is often on the attributes of agents rather than on the relations between them. SNA is focused on uncovering the patterning of people's interactions.

A definition of social networks is merely based on their structure: "A social network is an organized set of people that consists of two kinds of elements: human beings and the connections between them." The online social network in that case is the tool or the platform that facilitates the development and maintenance of this relationship, which may stem from different needs of the participants. The two basic elements of social networks are links and nodes. Links are connections, or ties, between individuals or groups, and nodes are the individuals or groups involved in the network. A node's importance in a social network refers to its *centrality*. Central nodes have the potential to exert influence over less central nodes.

> Using a network perspective, Mark Granovetter put forward the theory of the "strength-of-weak-ties." Granovetter found in one study that more numerous weak ties can be important in seeking information and innovation. Because cliques have a tendency to have more homogeneous opinions and common traits, individuals in the same cliques would also know more or less what the other members know. To gain new information and opinion, people often look beyond the clique to their other friends and acquaintances.

Analytics: Predictive Resource Analytics

Predictive analytics is a key element of advanced analytics, which involves making predictions about unknown future events, occasions, or outcomes (Zwingmann 2022; Schniederjans et al. 2014).

The main objectives and goals at this stage are:

1. answering the questions "What could/is likely to happen?" and "Why could/will it happen?";
2. generating a reasonable estimation of the trends and future directions of business;
3. predicting what will happen and why it will happen in business;
4. estimating the future development of business operations, performance, dynamics, and exceptional scenarios, with implications about possible driving factors and reasons;
5. identifying probable future risks and exceptions.

The main analytical and learning approaches and methods at this stage include:

i. forecasting, in particular, focusing on regression analysis techniques (including linear/logistic regression, time series analysis, regression trees, and multivariate regression);
ii. statistical prediction and forecasting of future business operations, performance, dynamics, trends, and exceptions;
iii. ML, AI, and data/text mining techniques for predictive modeling (classification methods such as neural networks, support vector machines, Naive Bayes and nearest neighbor-based methods; pattern-based methods; computational intelligence (CI) methods such as fuzzy set and evolutionary computing; trend prediction methods; and geospatial predictive modeling).

Predictive analytics may bring benefits and impact to businesses such as:

- identifying insights about the future;
- understanding the likelihood of future business trends and evolution;
- identifying probable factors that will drive the future development of the business;
- predicting exceptional and risky events, occasions, and scenarios, and determining possible driving factors.

Predictors, patterns, scoring, and other findings are created for and presented through dashboards and analytical reports to business managers and decision-makers to understand projected future trends and directions, and the reasons behind them. Analytical reports are delivered to predict trends and exceptions, and to explain the underlying factors.

Conclusion

This chapter discussed digital transformation for scaling design blueprint in two parts. The first part, on reframing for scaling, reviews the typical reference state at the commencement of the reframing for scaling effort. This is in terms of resource-led enterprise operations, network business model (platform businesses and network effects), EA (web services architecture), connecting mechanism (ESB), communications (3G mobile communications), network systems (Web 2.0), and analytics (predictive analytics). The second part, on means for the digital transformation of scaling, reviews the typical set of technologies like RBV of enterprise operations, e-business models, microservices architecture, Internet of Things (IoT), 4G mobile communications, social networks, and predictive resource analytics.

This chapter highlights the specific powerful technologies that are associated with the digital transformation of scaling competency.

PART III

Innovable Digital Transformation Model and Design Blueprint

CHAPTER 7

Innovable Digital Transformation Model

*This chapter presents an overview of the salient aspects of the innovation transformation model and design blueprint. The vision of **cognitive enterprise** highlights aspects like "Enterprise as a Brain," innovation via agile innovation, and metamorphosis. Entrepreneurial management highlights mass innovation, business growth, and agile system performance. Distinctive artifacts for this digital transformation model include creative thinking "Beyond the Box," experiences, and business models.*

Vision of Cognitive Enterprise

"Enterprise as a Brain"

The brain metaphor, deriving directly from cybernetics, emphasizes active learning rather than the rather passive adaptability that characterizes the organismic view. This leads to attention being focused on decision-making, information processing, and control (Morgan 1986, 1997; Burrell and Morgan 1985). The organization, having decided on its purposes, must be designed as a complex system to respond to environmental disturbances relevant to those purposes. In turbulent environments, this necessitates decentralized control because not all the information necessary to cope with change can be processed at the top of the organization. The organization must manage single-loop learning, correcting deviations from prescribed goals; it also needs to be capable of double-loop learning, changing the nature of its purposes if these become unattainable as the environment shifts. The brain metaphor is criticized for the lack of consideration it gives to individuals and their motivations, to power and conflict, and to how purposes are derived.

Innovation via Agile Innovation

Innovations are the basis for the competitiveness and, hence, accelerated growth of companies. Everything, starting from new promising ideas to new products and from new business concepts to industry-shaping success stories, is easily labeled as innovation (Kraner 2018). To be referred to as an innovation, a new idea must be implemented or applied. In product innovation, for example, it is not enough to discover penicillin, but also to develop a market-ready product. The same also applies to process innovations (for example, the introduction of the "drive-in" in 1971 or cashless payment by smartphone using near-field communication technology). Even in the case of conceptual innovations (for example, novel organizational structures), innovation can only be considered as such when these have been implemented or applied.

Innovation can be categorized depending on

- technology (e.g., radio networks)
- product (e.g., a mobile phone)
- service (e.g., location-based services)
- marketing/culture (e.g., smartphone represents lifestyle)
- organization and process (e.g., automated service procedures)
- business model/strategy (e.g., mobile-based payments)

Innovation has been described in detail via a two-dimensional matrix (Henderson and Clark 1990) in Figure 7.1.

		Components / Core Concepts	
		Reinforced / improved	Overturned/ changed in major way
System Linkages / Architecture	Unchanged	Incremental innovation	Modular innovation
	Changed	Architectural innovation	Radical innovation

Figure 7.1 Innovation matrix

a. Incremental innovation: The architecture of a system remains unchanged but the component parts can be improved in performance and, thus, they can be stated to have been reinforced or made better than before in one or more characteristic features.

b. Modular innovation: The architecture of a system remains unchanged but the component parts of a system may involve drastic changes. In other words, the interrelationships between the component parts remain unchanged but the component parts themselves may be changed in a major way. In automobiles, the best example of such innovation is the introduction of automobiles powered by electricity.

c. Architectural innovation: While the component parts remain the same as before, the relationship between the component parts gets changed or improved for better performance. For instance, early washing machines comprised two drums, one for washing the clothes and the second for spin drying the washed clothes. The clothes had to be transferred from the wash drum to the drying drum manually; these were semi-automatic twin-tub washing machines. Subsequently, while keeping the component parts the same, the architecture was changed to combine the washing and drying functions in the same drum. Now, after the washing is complete, the same wash drum—after being drained of water—spins at high speeds for centrifugal drying of the washed clothes. These are the fully automatic washing machines that are the most common type in use today, in various models.

d. Radical innovation: Both the architecture as well as the component parts that comprise the system change at the same time. The introduction of the automobile over the earlier standard animal-drawn carriage or cart is an excellent example of radical innovation. The new vehicle involved a total change of several components, along with the introduction of a few altogether new ones. The former were the replacement of the animal with an internal combustion engine to deliver motive power, and the change of the steering mechanism from a system of leather reins—to force the animal to turn to either side—with a rack and pinion steering system that changed the angle of the wheels for direction control. New systems added included the mechanical starting system and engine control system through pedals for acceleration, braking, a clutch mechanism, and a system of gears for transition between different modes of movement. The interaction between these very different and new components was very different from the interaction between the earlier components, and thus, the architecture also had to be changed. Radical innovations usually lead to a different way of doing things.

> The vision of *enterprise innovation* is implemented through enterprise business models defined via metaverse, Web 3.0, and blockchain (Shin 2023; Cheng 2023; Rojas and Martínez-Cano 2025; Marr 2021).

Metamorphosis

Metamorphosis refers to the adaptations and adoptions that firms make to thrive in an increasingly digital world (Gong et al. 2024; Carpo 2023). Unlike adaptation, which is about changes of degree, adoption represents a metamorphosis—a qualitative change in kind. Unlike adaptation, adoption entails several nonlinear processes that require a creative mind as opposed to a designing mind. Metamorphosis is the result of prerequisite lean and agile transformations combined with information, communication, technology (ICT)-assisted transformation processes that are more akin to the "metamorphosis" of a caterpillar into a butterfly.

Automation with Autonomy

The term *automation* is the umbrella term that includes several phases of automation, beginning with driver-assistance systems. The term *autonomous* describes the final stage of automation, the situation in which a system takes over all steering, accelerating, and braking maneuvers. In this phase, a person is out of the loop, and (say) the autonomous car can act alone at all times and in all traffic situations. Vehicles that have reached this stage can be described as autonomous, driverless, or self-driving (Sjafrie 2020; Vongbunyong and Chen 2015).

Figure 7.2 shows the maturity levels of autonomous driving. Level 0 is the starting point—there is no automation and the driver steers,

0	1	2	3	4	5
No Automation	Driver Assistance	Partial Automation	Conditional Automation	High Automation	Full Automation

THE HUMAN MONITORS THE DRIVING ENVIRONMENT   THE AUTOMATED SYSTEM MONITORS THE DRIVING ENVIRONMENT

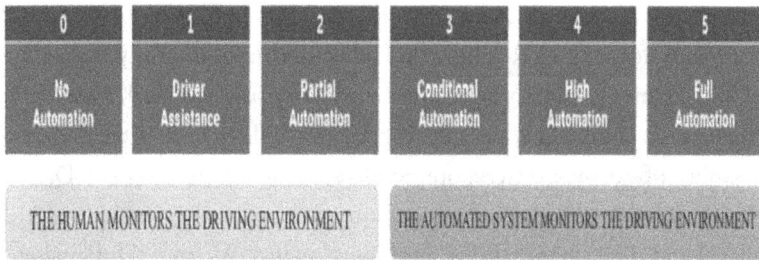

Figure 7.2 Maturity levels of autonomous driving

accelerates, and chooses to apply the brakes on the vehicle without any system support. With Levels 1 and 2, the system takes over more and more of these driving tasks. However, the driver is obliged to permanently monitor the system, the traffic, and the surroundings, and must be able to take over the driving function at any time. Level 3 means that the driver no longer has to continuously monitor the activity, because the system indicates to him or her when it is necessary to take control of the vehicle. With Level 4, the system masters all driving functions in normal operation and in defined surroundings, but the driver can overrule the system's decisions. With Level 5, the driver is totally out of the loop, and the car is autonomous, driverless, or self-driving.

Cyber-Physical-Cognitive Systems (CPCS)

CPCS represents the highest level of cognitive modeling of complex systems (Gorelova 2020; Bermúdez 2023). Cognitive modeling of complex systems is designed to describe the structure and behavior of a complex system in the face of uncertainty.

The recent surge in VR technology blurs the lines between the physical and digital worlds. The concept of a cognitive triad, where humans, AI, and digital twins collaborate within VR, potentially paves the way for a future *digital reality* that seamlessly blends the physical and digital worlds (Horváth et al. 2024). Cognitive Virtual Reality (cVR) investigates the next phases of IT evolution characterized by a transition from digital environments based on 2D graphical user interfaces (e.g., windows, images, 2D widgets) to 3D spaces which represent a higher-level integration of virtual, augmented, and mixed reality (VR/AR/MR) systems, human spatial cognition, the 2D digital world (i.e., Web 2.0, Web 3.0), and AI. A primary focus of cVR is how this transition simultaneously makes use of and augments human capabilities, including psychological, social, and cognitive capabilities, especially capabilities linked to a deeper understanding of geometric, temporal, and semantic relationships. A Digital Reality (DR) is a high-level integration of virtual reality (including AR, virtual and digital simulations, and digital twins), AI, and 2D digital environments, which creates a highly contextual reality for humans in which previously disparate realms of human experience are brought together.

Learning Organization via Agentic AI

Human learning in intelligent systems results in the best of both worlds (Albert et al. 2022; Hurwitz et al. 2020).

Reinforcement Learning (RL)

Reinforcement Learning (RL) is a superset of ML in which the algorithm is based on a feedback system rather than trained on some data. It is a method to train the ML models based on some sequence of performance by the agent (Huang 2025; Biswas and Talukdar 2025). This trial-and-error-based learning method rewards the desired behaviors and punishes the undesired ones (Elakkiya and Subramaniyaswamy 2024; Powell 2022; Dimitrakakis and Ortner 2022).

The various building blocks for this algorithm are:

Agent: It has to perform all the functions and decisions that will train the model.
State: It is fostered by the agents to know the environment.
Reward: It is a function to teach the right behavior.
Environment: There are some different conditions that may arise, and the agent has to deal with them.
Value Function: It is a function to decide the best action that an agent can take
Action: It is taken by the agent depending on the environment.

Reinforcement learning is the most generalized approach to general AI (including ML and DL). This stance is markedly different from that

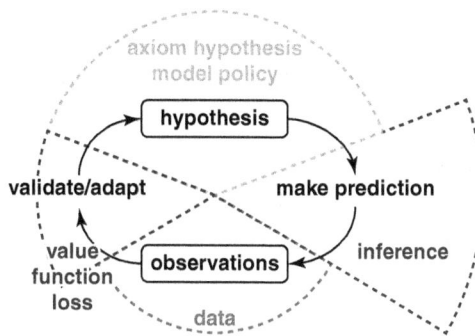

Figure 7.3 Reinforcement learning schema

of most books on ML and DL; why RL is a superset of ML and DL would require a whole book to explain. Figure 7.3 describes the simplified version of the reinforcement learning schema analogous to the scientific method.

For general AI, domain-specific functionality or context used to be addressed by symbolic AI's comparatively stable Knowledge Graphs (KGs). As AI agents become the building blocks of applications, the future of software engineering is shifting from designing APIs to orchestrating collaborative intelligent agents with emerging standards such as the Model Context Protocol (MCP) and Agent-to-Agent (A2A) communication, redefining how systems communicate, collaborate, and scale. MCP provides a standardized way for AI models to interact with external tools, enabling real-time data access, tool integration, and reasoning across services. A2A enables structured collaboration between agents across platforms, clouds, and organizations, using shared goals, secure state management, and observable actions.

Reinforcement Learning (RL), and its derivatives like ML and DL, consolidate the emergence and ascendency of *data* as the fourth discovery paradigm following the three paradigms of theoretical, experimental, and computational (simulational) discovery (Gray 2007; Berthold et al. 2020; Bean 2021; Pentland et al. 2021). Discussing and explaining this would require yet another book.

Digital Twins with Multi-Agent Systems (MAS)

Modeling and simulation have become the cornerstones of engineering and science for the last few decades. A large amount of R&D work has been directed toward computational methods for improving modeling. Such computer models are useful for system design and serve to mitigate the high costs of experiments and testing. However, there is a need to track the evolution of systems with time for diagnostics, prognostics, and life management (Ganguli et al. 2023). Degradation models of systems coupled with data emanating from sensors placed on the system allow the construction of digital twins, which permit tracking of a physical system in real time. The digital twin is an adaptive computer model (of the physical twin) that resides in the cloud.

A digital twin is essentially a virtual representation of a physical object, process, or system. But it is much more than a mere digital replica—it is about creating a symbiotic relationship between physical entities and their virtual counterparts. This harmony allows the emulation of a wide range of scenarios right in the digital space, venturing into possibilities that simply would not exist otherwise (Crespi et al. 2023). The power lies not only in monitoring and analyzing but also in predicting future behaviors and outcomes. This capability opens up a whole new level of hindsight, insights, and foresight for various industries, from manufacturing to healthcare, urban planning, and beyond. Previously, engineers relied on computer-aided design (CAD) and similar technologies to create static models for analysis and design. However, digital twins push these boundaries further by integrating real-time data, allowing continuous updates and iterative learning based on real-world inputs. Consequently, digital twins become dynamic and living models that adapt as the physical object evolves. This concept leverages a myriad of technologies, including the Internet of Things (IoT), AI, and data analytics, to furnish a robust framework for understanding reality like never before.

An agent-based system may contain one or more agents. There are cases in which a single-agent solution is appropriate. However, the multi-agent case—where the system is designed and implemented as several interacting agents—is arguably more widespread and more interesting from a software engineering standpoint (Poole and Macworth 2017). Multi-agent systems (MAS) can be defined as a collection of possibly heterogeneous computational agents, each with their problem-solving capabilities, and which can interact to reach an overall goal. MAS is ideally suited to representing problems that have multiple problem-solving methods, multiple perspectives, and/or multiple problem-solving entities. Such systems have the traditional advantages of distributed and concurrent problem-solving but have the additional advantage of sophisticated patterns of interaction (Shehory and Sturm 2014; Cao 2015).

Examples of common types of interactions include:

- Coordination (working together toward a common aim)
- Cooperation (organizing problem-solving activities so that harmful interactions are avoided or beneficial interactions are exploited)
- Collaboration (coming to an agreement that is acceptable to all parties involved)

If a problem domain is particularly complex, large, or unpredictable, the only way it can reasonably be addressed is to develop several functionally specific and modular agents that are specialized at solving a particular problem aspect. In MAS, applications are designed and developed in terms of autonomous software agents that can flexibly achieve their objectives by interacting with one another in terms of high-level protocols and languages.

Governance: Triple-Entry Accounting via Blockchain

Triple-entry accounting (TEA) is described as an enhancement to conventional DEA where the accounting entries are cryptographically sealed by a third entity (the blockchain; Kale 2024). Blockchain technology may represent the next step for accounting; instead of keeping separate records based on transaction receipts, companies can write their transactions directly into a joint register, creating an interlocking system of enduring accounting records. As all entries are distributed and cryptographically sealed, falsifying or destroying them to conceal activity is practically impossible (Dai and Vasarhelyi 2017).

The companies would benefit in numerous ways. Standardization would allow auditors to verify a large portion of the most important data supporting the financial statements automatically (Appelbaum and

Nehmer 2017). The efforts, time, and, hence, costs necessary to conduct an audit would decline considerably. Auditors could spend freed-up time on areas where they can add more value, for example, very complex transactions or internal control mechanisms.

Entrepreneurial Management

Entrepreneurship is not a state of being but of becoming entrepreneurial, i.e., it is a process. The entrepreneurship process is characterized by proactiveness, innovativeness, and risk-taking (Passiante 2020; Hisrich and Ramadani. 2017). Becoming entrepreneurial is relevant to organizations of all types (traditional or startup) and sizes (large and small enterprises); this process fundamentally involves the creation of value and embracing the irreducible uncertainty that lies at the heart of all prospective business opportunities. The entrepreneurship process primarily entails the discovery, evaluation, and exploitation of business opportunities continually.

The process of discovering new business opportunities involves an assessment of the current products, services, or offerings in the target market and their improvement from the customer's perspective via digitalization or digital transformation. Furthermore, it involves understanding the current business model that creates and delivers value for the customer, as well as considering reconfigurations of the business model for delivering additional or enhanced value for the customer. Evaluation of the business opportunities entails assessment of the potential market size for this opportunity as well as their ability to deliver the necessary value of this offering based on the resources available or accessible to them, including factors such as risk, finance, and others. Opportunity exploitation entails arranging for finance, resources (human, consumables, etc.), and activities (procurement, production, and sales and distribution, etc.), including the availability of infrastructure and facilities that are essential for the successful creation and delivery of value to the customer.

Mass Innovation

The more customized a product, the more customers are willing to pay a higher price because the product closely reflects their requirements. As customer benefit increases, the price elasticity of demand decreases, which enables the producer to harvest the consumer surplus. The know-how necessary to maintain such a market position is an invaluable asset, but it requires continuous investments (Bensaou 2022). Further costs are incurred by the large product variety, by increasing complexity throughout the value chain, by highly qualified personnel, and so on. This cost disadvantage can only be balanced by a higher price. Some of these negative cost effects can be balanced by the economies of scope that can be realized due to synergies while producing several products simultaneously. If those products have something in common (e.g., fabrication tools, R&D resources, etc.), the shared activities and assets can be "spread" across a group of products resulting in comparatively lower costs of production.

Pine and Gilmore described customer experience as the highest level of corporate development in their pioneering book *The Experience Economy* (Pine and Gilmore 2011). The development of the "experience economy" or customer experience as a central corporate KPI can be seen as a logical outcome of four forces, namely, competition, brand economics, society, and technology (Clatworthy 2019). In the current times of interchangeable services, customers no longer use the price-quality ratio for their purchase decision but rather the (anticipated) price-experience ratio. In other words, customers tend to sum up in their minds the (positive and negative) experiences, like preferred color or music, they have or are likely to have before, during, and after purchasing (say) a company service at a certain price, rather than merely paying attention to the quality of the service. This implies a change of perspective for companies—from product and service orientation to a focus on the psychology of the customer.

Business Growth: Market Share Maximization via Blue Ocean Strategy

Every market was new once, and the key to the success of a company is to find a new market that it can own. A study of successful and less successful companies shows that some markets are overcrowded and this limits everyone's growth. W. Chan Kim and R. Mauborgne observed that companies tend to engage in head-to-head competition in their search for growth, and this leads to a bloodbath—a red ocean. They suggest that an alternative and more profitable strategy for growth comes from tapping new opportunities in the *comparatively* "blue ocean" (Table 7.1). They argue that a blue ocean strategy allows the simultaneous pursuit of

Table 7.1 Comparing red ocean and blue ocean strategy

Red ocean	Blue ocean
Industry boundaries are defined and accepted, and the competitive rules of the game are known. Therefore, prospects for growth and profit are reduced and dimmed.	A consistent pattern of strategic thinking behind the creation of new markets and industries where demand is created rather than fought for, and the rules are irrelevant.
Red Ocean represents all the industries in existence today. Red Ocean strategy accepts the constraints of the game—and pursues either differentiation or low-cost strategy. A majority of new ventures are known to target Red Ocean.	Blue Ocean provides companies with guidelines on how to escape from intense competition from the same marketplace where there are limited customers with increasing number of competitors, by creating a *new* market place, where there is less competition, if any.
Commoditization of products/service offerings. Cut-throat competition for the existing market and demand.	Superlative business performance by creating a leap in value for customers. Innovative technological capabilities alone do not necessarily create the Blue Ocean.

differentiation and low cost (Chan Kim and Mauborgne 2004). Newer market spaces or blue oceans can be created by value innovation while at the same time driving down costs.

The authors suggest asking four searching questions about customers and the marketplace that could point to a new blue ocean:

- Reduce: Which factors offered to customers should be reduced well below industry standards?
- Eliminate: Which factors offered to customers are taken for granted and should be eliminated?
- Create: Which factors offered to customers should be created because they have never been offered and will be valued?
- Raise: Which factors offered to customers should be raised well above the industry standard?

Performance: Agile System

Agility is the ability to be responsive to unexpected change. Agility is an unplanned and unscheduled adaptation to unforeseen and unexpected external circumstances. This is in contrast to flexibility, which is a scheduled or planned adaptation to unforeseen yet expected external circumstances. The difficult challenges facing businesses today require enterprises to transition into agile structures that can respond to new market opportunities quickly with a minimum of new investment and risk. As enterprises have experienced the need to be simultaneously efficient, flexible, responsive, and adaptive, they have transitioned into *agile businesses* with small, autonomous teams that work concurrently and reconfigure quickly, and adopt highly decentralized management that recognizes its knowledge base and manages it effectively.

The traits of an agile business include flexibility of management practices and resources, organizational structures that support collaboration and learning, a high-performance culture, and rapid decision making and execution. They have innovative business models, are consumer-oriented, digitally enabled, have greater vertical integration, and have more convergence of industries. They extend the depth and breadth of their offerings to include external partners in the development and distribution of products and services that extend across boundaries, often with both cooperation and competition among the partners. It is about thinking like a startup, understanding the implications of technology for business growth, and creating the right human dynamic. Agile systems reimagine an organization as a collection of high-performing teams, each with a clear purpose and the skills it needs.

Maintaining an agile enterprise is not a matter of searching for the strategy but continuously strategizing; not a matter of specifying an organizational design but committing to a process of organizing; and not about generating value but continuously improving the efficiency and effectiveness of the value generation process. It is a search for a series of temporary configurations that create short-term advantages. In turbulent environments, enterprises that string together a series of temporary but adequate competitive advantages will outperform enterprises that stick with one advantage for an extended period. The key issue for the Built_to_Change enterprise is orchestration, or coordinating the multiple changing subsystems to produce high levels of current enterprise performance.

Agility can be wielded overtly as a business strategy as well as inherently as a sustainable-existence competency. An enterprise's change proficiency may exist in one or more dimensions of change. Change proficiency can be understood to be co-determined by four dimensions:

- Time: A measure of elapsed time to complete a change (fairly objective)
- Cost: A measure of monetary cost incurred in a change (somewhat objective)
- Quality: A measure of prediction quality in meeting change time, cost, and specification targets robustly (somewhat subjective)
- Range: A measure of the latitude of possible change, typically defined and determined by mission or charter (fairly subjective)

Distinctive Artifact

Creative Thinking "Beyond the Box"

Creativity is best encouraged if we embrace different paradigms as well as different metaphors. Although metaphors provide various viewpoints on problem situations, they do not demand that radically different, incompatible alternative perspectives are always explored. Paradigms demand that because they rest on assumptions that are mutually incompatible with those of other paradigms. Without adding paradigm creativity to metaphor creativity, it would be too easy to choose a set of metaphors that fit too well together and correspond with existing cherished beliefs. On the contrary, exploring different (social) paradigms ensures that mutually confronting alternative theoretical positions are always analyzed for consideration (Martin 2009; Riel and Martin 2017).

Morgan worked on different metaphors or images of organization that proved insightful to managers (Morgan 1986, 1997). At first, organizations were thought of as being "machines," and attention was focused on fitting well-designed jobs into appropriate structures to ensure efficient goal-seeking (scientific management, bureaucracy theory, administrative management; see Chapter 3, Section "Enterprise as a Machine"). Later, they were studied as "organisms": complex systems in close interrelationship with their environments and with subsystems meeting their survival needs (see Chapter 5, Section "Enterprise as an Organism"). With the advent of cybernetics, it became possible to see organizations as "brains" or information-processing systems, and, as a result, interest developed in decision making, learning, and decentralized control (see Section "Enterprise as a Brain").

As stated above, another way to look at the problems is to view them from the perspectives offered by different sociological paradigms. The four most commonly recognized paradigms in social theory are as follows:

a. Functionalists want to ensure that everything in the system is functioning well to promote efficiency, adaptation, and survival. An understanding can be gained of how systems work by using scientific methods and techniques to probe the nature of the parts of the system, the interrelationships between them, and the relationship between the system and its environment. The expertise it provides puts executives more in control of their operations and organizations, and enables them to eliminate inefficiency and disorder.

b. Interpretives want to ensure that social systems like organizations result from the purposes people adopt that stem from the interpretations they make of the situations in which they find themselves. This paradigm wants to understand the different meanings people bring to collaborative activity, resulting in shared purposeful activity.

c. Emancipatory wants to ensure that social systems like organizations liberate oppressed individuals and groups from all forms of discrimination, whether based on class, status, sex, race, disability, sexual orientation, age, etc. This paradigm is suspicious of authority and tries to reveal forms of power and domination that it sees as being illegitimately employed. It wants to criticize the status quo and wants to encourage a radical reformation of the current social order.

d. Postmodernists want to ensure that social systems like organizations challenge any attempts to provide all-encompassing comprehensive explanations of how organizations function. This paradigm posits that organizations are far too complex to be understood by using any single paradigm per se. It also insists that much can be learned by bringing conflict to the surface, claiming a space for disregarded opinions, and encouraging variety and diversity.

Experiences

With the advent of the experience economy, impactful customer experiences have now become a part of customer expectations. This change in customer sentiment implies a need for all companies to discover new ways of engaging with their customers. Companies that can recognize this shift and adapt in time, as a result of providing strong, engaging experiences, will be able to benefit from the positive effects of higher perceived value, satisfaction, loyalty, word of mouth, and revenue growth (Kale 2024).

Experience can be defined as the overall perception of a company's offering, including cognitive, emotional, physical, sensorial, spiritual, and social responses to interactions throughout the engagement with the offering. Correspondingly, this overall perception of the offering itself is reframed as the experience offering (Pine and Gilmore 2011; Clatworthy 2019; Hulten 2018).

In the earlier stages of economic development, the production of products was more or less related to needs. The consumers wanted commodities, goods, and services to satisfy their survival—which the manufacturing sector provided; later, the need expanded to the need for materialism, knowledge, and solving problems—which the service sector provided. Customers are now looking for more than mere products or services—now they want to have an interesting life, experience new aspects of life or new places, be entertained, and learn enjoyably. These are all fulfilled by experiences.

> Experiences are the result of attention and emotion management. The latter gives rise to the phenomenon of choices and preferences.

Two experience creation projects are rarely alike, which means that all experience projects to a certain extent, are innovations, as an innovation is defined as a new combination of things that come to the market. Most of them are incremental innovations, as only a few innovations are truly radical.

Characteristics of Experiences

There are five differences between services and experiences (Kale 2024):

a. Intangibility: Experiences are intangible like services; services may utilize products; experiences may utilize products and services.
b. Perishability: Experiences are perishable like services, but continue for an extended finite duration. Experiences can be launched on demand, can be invoked, or can be triggered by an event.
c. Customizability or adoptability: Most experiences can be customized or adopted as per customer inclination, preferences, or choices, which may render it more complex and costlier, respectively.
d. Composability: Most experiences are composed of sub-experiences, service(s), and product(s). Cricket games may incorporate an introduction to players of your choice, an ongoing open food court, as well as sales of sports merchandise.
e. Replicability: Experiences are replicable like services; services are rendered by processes, but experiences are rendered by projects.

> The *metamorphosis* trend is toward an increasingly higher percentage of *digital* experiences and provisioning through Experience as a Software (EaaS)!

Business Models

The business model requires much more than just selecting and integrating new technologies. It also requires a fresh view of the customer and user experiences, putting the traditional business logic to the test, and is usually connected with a cultural change in the organization. Metamorphosis or radical digital transformation depends more on the business model than on technology (Osterwalder and Pigneur 2010; Ronteau et al. 2023; Linz 2021, 2017; Johnson 2018; Amit and Zott 2021; Wirtz 2020, 2019; Sehgal 2024; Tesch 2017; Escalona et al. 2014).

A business model innovation (BMI) happens when a company modifies or improves one or several elements of its business model (Amit and Zott 2021; Molenaar 2022; Munter 2021; Fleisch et al. 2014; Chhajed and Lowe 2008) (Table 7.2).

Table 7.2 Elements of a business model

Meta-component	Business Model Building Block	Description
Value proposition	Value propositions	Gives an overall view of company's bundle of products, services, and experiences
Value delivery	Customer segments	An organization serves one or several customer segments
	Channels	Value propositions are delivered to customers through communication, distribution, and sales channels
	Customer relationships	Customer relations are established and maintained within each customer segment
Value creation	Key resources	Key resources are the assets required to offer and deliver the previously described elements
	Key activities	Numerous key activities performed by key resources
	Key partnerships	Some activities are outsourced and some resources are acquired from outside the organization
Value capture	Revenue stream	Revenue streams result from value propositions successfully delivered to customers
	Cost structure	The business model elements result in the cost structure

The business model itself is a useful lens for understanding a company's underlying logic because it describes what value is provided, how this value is created and delivered, and how profits can be generated therefrom (Figure 7.4).

a. Customer Segments: A customer segment refers to various classes of consumers or organizations that an enterprise looks out to serve.

b. Value Proposition: A value proposition embraces all those activities of the firm that are designed to create value for its customers.

c. Channels: Channels are the processes through which a business communicates with and attains its consumer segments carry out its value proposition. Channels may comprise the company's

Key Partnerships	Key Activities	Value Proposition	Customer Relationships	Customer Segments
• Strengthened company ties inside the supply chain • Strengthened data integrity • Facilitation of payments • Shared networks • Elimination of lengthy processes	• Transform business process • Peer-to-peer networks	• Verifiability • Access new products or services • Faster transactions • Less expensive transactions • Smart contracts, fewer middle layers	• Greater transparency • Self-service • Automation • No middlemen	• Reach new customers • Reach new customer segments
	Key Resources Access via peer-to-peer networks, Improvements in: • Verification • Documentation • Audits		**Channels** • New channels • New APIs, SDKs	

Cost Structure	Revenue Streams
• Reduced search costs • Reduced negotiation costs • Reduced IT costs • Reduced transaction costs • Increased costs of IT/software, development personnel	• Recurring revenues • Transaction revenues • Services revenues • Crowdfunding

Figure 7.4 Business model canvas

website, sales force, or stores of the company's wholesalers or partners.

d. Customer Relationship: An organization's customer relationship building block explains the variety of relationships it has with specific segments of its customers. Several categories of relationships exist, such as dedicated and personal assistance, automated and self-services, creating communities, etc. A company might build these relationships for a variety of reasons, such as to gain and keep consumers or to boost sales.

e. Revenue Streams: Revenue streams are the processes through which revenue is obtained from customers. Once the key target market segments have been identified, attention should be given to estimating what anticipated annual revenue might be obtained from each one. Important considerations are how price-sensitive the market is and how much the customer is willing to pay.

f. Cost Structures: Cost structures are the financial costs necessary to establish and maintain a business model. Overhead costs need to be reduced to allow the venture to break even as quickly as possible. Also of importance are any variable costs that will impact the firm's gross profit.

g. Key Resources and Key Activities: Key resources are those resources or assets that are critical to fabricating a business model. These resources are the ones that define a value proposition, market outreach, nurture relationships with customers, and generate revenue. Resources can be financial, human, intellectual, or physical. An organization's key activities include all those undertakings that are essential to deliver value, which means all those processes that result in the metamorphosis of resources and assets into value.

h. Key Partnership: Partnerships can take the form of joint ventures, strategic alliances, or purchase and supplier relationships to secure authentic supply.

Business model innovation is a powerful concept, and companies that are adversely affected by its impact, more often than not, do not even survive to testify to its devastating effectiveness. Circuit City failed to take note and effectively respond to Amazon's online category killer strategy, which focused on dominating a particular product category by offering a wide selection of products, competitive prices, and a convenient shopping experience. Circuit City was not alone; many other respected brands succumbed to the same fate. They were all slowly treading the path followed by Circuit City, Blockbuster Video, Borders, Toys "R" Us, and numerous others by not adapting effectively to the challenges and opportunities of *business model transformation or, more generally, digital transformation.*

Figure 7.5 shows Amazon's business model CANVAS which highlights Amazon's value creation and captures aspects of its business (Voigt et al. 2017).

Intangibles are the *core component* of modern competitive advantage that expresses the leverage of a business over its competitors. An intangible is a non-monetary asset that manifests itself by its economic properties. It does not have physical substance but grants rights and economic benefits to its owner.

According to Michael Porter, firms can achieve a competitive edge with a cost or differentiation advantage. Intangibles play a crucial role in both strategies—bringing cost savings (with know-how, patents, etc.), enabling differentiation (using brands, etc.), and fostering a structural shift in business models (Moro-Visconti 2022; Kaplan and Norton 2004; Jahani 2024; Amit and Zott 2021).

This traditional value driver has been amplified by a new generation of Internet-related intangibles, driven by the growth of the experience economy and the digital explosion.

Key Partner	Key Activities	Value Proposition	Customer Relationships	Customer Segments
Wholesalers and distributors	Fulfillment	Global online retail (electronics, media, Self-service household goods, apparel)	Self-service	Global consumer market
Logistics partners	IT infrastructure & software development		Customized online profiles and recommendation system	Third-party vendors and retailers
Third-party vendors and retailers	Merchandising own product portfolio	Additional services (e.g., Amazon Prime)	Long-term customer binding through effortless shopping experience	
	Developing and extending the reach of its international websites	Convenient shopping with attractive pricing		
	Key Resources		**Channels**	
	IT infrastructure & software		Language/-country-specific websites	
	Fulfillment infrastructure		Mobile app	
	Amazon brand affiliates			

Cost Structure

Cost-driven

Cost of sales, fulfillment costs and costs for technology and content

Revenue Streams

Long-tail revenue streams stemming from the immense product offer

Sales margins of product and service sales as well as monthly subscriptions (e.g., for the Prime service)

Service fees from third-party vendors

Figure 7.5 Amazon's business model canvas (Voigt et al. 2017)

Case Study: Digital Transformation at Netflix

Netflix had to adapt its business model effectively continuously, and twice even radically ("Beyond the Box") (Linz 2021). By 2018, Netflix was the world's leading Internet entertainment service with over 139 million paid memberships in over 190 countries delivering more than 2 billion hours of television shows and movies per month, including original TV series, documentaries, and feature films across a wide variety of genres and languages to their customers. Members can watch as much as they want, anytime, anywhere, on any Internet-connected screen. Members can play, pause, and resume watching, all without commercials or commitments.

Netflix started by offering a video-direct-by-mail rental service in the United States. In April 1998, the company launched a website offering customers the opportunity to rent or purchase videos. Customers could select videos online, and Netflix would mail them for a seven-day, in-home rental. Netflix charged U.S. $4 per DVD rental plus U.S. $2 for postage. Customers had to return the DVDs in Netflix's prepaid and pre-addressed envelopes.

The first radical transformation happened in two steps (Linz et al. 2017). The first step was taken in 1999 with the introduction of the subscription-based business model, which increased the inclusiveness of the transaction significantly, and the second step was taken in 2007 with the ability to distribute content through the Internet, enabled by the new video streaming technology. Netflix's goal was to be a global Internet television network offering legal access to a rich base of movies, documentaries, and television series, without commercials, and with unlimited viewing on any Internet-connected screen for a monthly fee. This means the company does not stream all video types. It is focused on movies and television series, and therefore does not compete with companies such as Amazon, Apple, Sony, and Google on the entire spectrum of entertainment. Some of the content is exclusive, available only on Netflix. The business model is based on fixed costs and scale effects—the more members Netflix has, the less influence the fixed costs have in terms of buying content, and the better the company's bargaining power in terms of reducing these costs.

The second radical transformation was the subsequent decision in 2013 to invest in original content. Through this move of backward integration, Netflix added to its dominant platform business model as a distributor, and a new product business model as a movie maker. It used the data it got from its distributor business model to invest in a well-targeted way in standardized entertainment products.

Netflix has had to take advantage of the swift pace of technological change to follow changing customer needs (Voigt et al. 2017). It has had to go beyond its original capabilities and reinvent itself tirelessly. This challenge will remain in the future, and new capabilities will be needed, such as the competence to market and brand its content.

Conclusion

This chapter provided an overview of the salient aspects of the innovation transformation model and design blueprint. The vision of **cognitive enterprise** highlights aspects like "Enterprise as a Brain," innovation via agile innovation, and metamorphosis. Entrepreneurial management highlights mass innovation, business growth, and agile system performance. Distinctive artifacts for this transformation model include creative thinking "Beyond the Box," experiences, and business models.

This chapter focuses on characteristics of the enterprise innovation transformation model or design blueprint, namely, the vision of "Enterprise as a Brain," innovation via agile innovation, metamorphosis, experiences, and business models.

CHAPTER 8

Innovable Design Blueprint

This chapter discusses digital transformation for innovable design in two parts. The first part, on reframing for innovation, reviews the typical reference state at the commencement of the reframing for innovation effort. This is in terms of market-led enterprise operations, network business model (Industry 4.0), enterprise architecture (serverless architecture), connecting mechanism (software-defined networks), communications (5G mobile communications), network systems (Web 3.0), and analytics (predictive experience analytics). The second part, on means for the digital transformation of innovation, reviews the typical technologies like market-based view (MBV) of enterprise operations, Industry 5.0, edge computing architecture, Internet of Everything (IoE), 6G mobile communications, metaverse, and prescriptive experience analytics.

Reframing for Innovation

Market-led Enterprise Operations

Business operations envisaged per the market-led view of operations strategy (Van Mieghem and Allon 2015; Basu and Muylle 2023) have the following aspects:

    i. Organizational Innovation
    ii. Customer Innovation (Peppers and Rogers 2017; Teixeira 2019)
   iii. People Innovation (Machado and Davim 2024a)
   iv. Business Model Innovation (Machado and Davim 2024b)

Systems like SAP C/4HANA (Customer Experience), SAP Success-Factors, SAP Ariba (Spending), Web 3.0, Blockchain, etc., can provide this functionality and services (Banda et al. 2022; Shin 2023; Marr 2023; Duffey 2023; Mangrulkar and Chavan 2024).

Network Business Model: Industry 4.0

Until the last few decades, the business of the global economy was, essentially, manufacturing. The focus on goods rather than services led to a product-focused, mass-market marketing strategy, resulting in a high cost of acquiring new customers and a low cost for customers switching to other brands. There has always been a focus on customer needs, but with the advent of computers, there has been a shift away from producing goods or providing services, toward discovering and meeting the needs of the individual customer (Misra et al. 2021; Kale 2024). Don Peppers and Martha Rogers pioneered the concept of one-to-one marketing made possible by the advent of computer-assisted database marketing. Businesses with highly diversified customer needs and highly differentiated customer valuations were expected to benefit from one-to-one customized marketing. The one-to-one paradigm has extended inward onto the production systems via Industry 4.0.

In the eighteenth century, the first Industrial Revolution, Industry 1.0, was characterized by mechanical production powered by water and steam. The Industrial Revolution in the twentieth century, Industry 2.0, introduced mass production, based on the division of labor and powered by electrical energy. In the 1970s, Industry 3.0 was set in motion by embedded electronics and IT for further automation of production. Industry 4.0 (especially in Europe; Industrial Internet in the United States), reflects the rise of a basket of new digitally-enabled industrial technologies, i.e., digital manufacturing that enables the realization of the manufacturing of individual products in a batch size of one while maintaining the economic conditions of mass production, i.e., mass customization.

Industry 4.0 Principles

The Industry 4.0 principles are as follows:

1. Agility means the system's flexibility to adapt to changing requirements by replacing or improving the separated modules based on standardized software and hardware interfaces.

2. Integrated business processes are the link between physical systems and software platforms by enabling communication and coordination mechanisms assisted by corporate data management services and connected networks.
3. Virtualization enables monitoring of the entire system, new system adaptation, and system changes using simulation tools or AR.
4. Decentralization or self-decision making of the machines relies on learning from previous events and actions.
5. Interoperability implies the communication of CPS components with each other using the Industrial Internet and regular standardization processes to create a smart factory.
6. Service orientation is the satisfaction of customer requirements adaptation to the entire system using a perspective of integrating both internal and external subsystems.
7. Real-time data management: Real-time data management is the tracing and tracking of the system through online monitoring to prevent failures when they occur.

Industry 4.0 Enabling Technologies

a. *Manufacturing Technologies*
   i. Internet of Things (IoT): The IoT is the broad connection of devices that can interact with each other and share data to a larger network, where the shared data can be leveraged to extract value.
   ii. Additive Manufacturing: Additive manufacturing is a set of emerging technologies that produce three-dimensional objects directly from digital models through an additive process, particularly by storing and joining the products with proper polymers, ceramics, or metals. The machines use the transmitted descriptions as blueprints to form the item by adding material layers. The layers, which are measured in microns, are added consecutively until a three-dimensional object emerges.
   iii. Robotics: Flexible and adaptive robots combined with AI techniques provide easier manufacturing of different products by enabling recognition of parts and sub-components of each part.

This decomposition enables a decrease in production costs, and a reduction in production time and wait times in production operations.

b. *Assisting Technologies*

   i. Artificial Intelligence (AI): AI is the branch of computer science that enables machines to mimic human behavior, such as learning or problem-solving. Some of the most significant application areas within AI are solution search at combinatorial problems, knowledge-based systems or expert systems, NLP, pattern recognition, robotics, ML, interference functions, and automatic programming.

   ii. Computational Intelligence (CI): CI solves problems based on connections trained from example data. The principal notion in CI is that precision and certainty carry a cost, and that computation, reasoning, and decision making should exploit (wherever possible) the tolerance for imprecision, uncertainty, approximate reasoning, and partial truth for obtaining low-cost solutions. Artificial Neural Networks, Genetic Algorithms, Fuzzy Systems, Evolutionary Programming, Artificial Life, etc., are included in CI.

   iii. Machine Learning (ML): ML can be defined as a type of AI in which a machine is capable of learning and adapting itself to any change in data without being explicitly programmed. More specifically, ML uses data mining techniques and other learning algorithms to build models of what is happening behind some data so that it can predict future outcomes. DL is an offshoot of ML that tries to emulate the function of the inner layers of the human brain to create knowledge from multiple layers of information processing.

c. *Supporting Technologies*

   i. Mechatronics: Mechatronics is the synergistic integration of mechanical engineering with electronics and intelligent computer control in the design and manufacturing of industrial products and processes.

   ii. Cyber-Physical Systems (CPS): Many manufacturing processes rely on CPS as part of manufacturing. CPS comprise interacting digital, analog, physical, and human components engineered for function through integrated physics and logic.

iii. Embedded Computing: In contrast to general-purpose computing systems, embedded systems (ES) usually provide a specific function. To fulfill this purpose, ES consists of hardware and software components specifically designed for the information-processing requirements of the device. In addition, embedded systems have to be designed to be cost- and energy-efficient. As a result, ES is typically constrained regarding its hardware capacities, for instance, processing capabilities, energy consumption, memory, and other hardware characteristics.

d. *Auxiliary Technologies*

i. Big Data: Big data can be defined as volumes of data available in varying degrees of complexity, generated at different velocities and varying degrees of ambiguity that cannot be processed using traditional technologies, processing methods, algorithms, or commercial off-the-shelf solutions. An important characteristic of big data computing systems is the inherent scalability of the underlying hardware and software architecture. Big data computing systems can typically be scaled linearly to accommodate virtually any amount of data, or to meet time-critical performance requirements by adding additional processing nodes to a system configuration to achieve billions of records per second processing rates (BORPS).

ii. Cloud Computing: Cloud computing is a model for enabling convenient, on-demand network access to a shared pool of configurable computing resources (e.g., networks, servers, storage, applications, and services) that can be rapidly provisioned and released with minimal management effort or service provider interaction (Comer 2021; Marinescu 2023; Kale 2015b). This cloud model promotes availability and is composed of five essential characteristics (on-demand self-service, broad network access, resource pooling, rapid elasticity, and measured service), three delivery models (Infrastructure as a Service (IaaS), Platform as a Service (PaaS) and Software as a Service (SaaS)), and four deployment models (public, private, hybrid, and community cloud).

    iii. Parallel Computing: Parallel Computing means solving a computing problem in less time by breaking it down into parts and computing those parts simultaneously. Parallel computers provide more computing resources and memory to tackle problems that cannot be solved in a reasonable time by a single processor core (Kale 2020; Pacheco and Malensek 2022). They differ from sequential computers in that multiple processing elements can execute instructions in parallel, as directed by the parallel program. We can think of a sequential computer, as described by the von Neumann architecture, as executing a stream of instructions that access a stream of data. Parallel computers work with multiple streams of instructions and/or data.

e. *Tools and Techniques*

    i. Modeling and Simulation: Modeling and simulation (M&S) refers to the overall process of developing a model and then simulating that model to gather data concerning the performance of a system. M&S depends on computational science for the simulation of complex, large-scale phenomena. M&S uses models and simulations to develop data as a basis for making managerial, technical, and training decisions. For large, complex systems that have measures of uncertainty or variability, M&S might be the only feasible method of analysis of the system.

    ii. Virtual Reality: Virtual reality is composed of an interactive computer simulation that senses the user's state and operation, and replaces or augments sensory feedback information to one or more senses in a way that the user gets a sense of being immersed in the simulation (virtual environment). We can thus identify four basic elements of VR: the virtual environment, virtual presence, sensory feedback (as a response to the user's actions), and interactivity.

    iii. Data Science: Data science encompasses a set of principles, problem definitions, algorithms, and processes for extracting non-obvious and useful patterns from large datasets by analyzing data.

Enterprise Architecture: Serverless Systems

Serverless is a means to create software that will run on a server fully managed by a cloud provider and should only be paid for actual utilization, not idle time or availability. The word "serverless" is a bit of a misnomer as there are servers involved in storing and running the code. It is called serverless because the developers no longer need to manage, update, or maintain the underlying servers, operating systems, or software. Redundancy, load balancing, networking, and, to some extent, security are also largely managed, guaranteed, and monitored by the cloud provider and dedicated 24/7 operations team. Serverless is *paid only* when used as a service (Krishnamurthi et al. 2023; Smart 2023).

Microservices can work together to meet an application's full set of requirements. In a serverless solution, there would be a microservice for transactions. This is the only microservice with access to the transactions database, which is exclusively for storing transactions. Other parts of a solution must go via this microservice to interact with transaction data, and all such requests can be more easily monitored, authorized, and audited in this one location. With serverless, the front-end and backend are entirely separate and running on different managed services, potentially even developed using different programming languages and by different teams. Multiple front-end interfaces running in a browser, mobile application, or desktop can all use the same backend, regardless of differences in the programming language, methodology, or even development team. To facilitate communication, serverless backends are typically an API.

Driven by the need to further simplify the infrastructure requirements for developers, serverless emerged as an architecture when AWS launched Lambda in 2014. Lambda is essentially a temporary container but with near-instant deployment. AWS entirely manages its deployment and all underlying technologies as part of the service. This was a key milestone in the history of serverless, automating and reducing the speed of deployment while guaranteeing the scalability and availability of the code. Developers could focus entirely on their code and service configuration. Outside of some configuration parameters, the infrastructure and hardware components involved in hosting software are now mostly invisible.

Lambda can be considered a new industry evolution called Function-as-a-Service (FaaS). Microservice-as-a-Service would be technically correct though this is not a commonly used term. A FaaS platform will store a developer's code, which will be run when a specified event occurs and shut down when the code finishes executing. This is also called event-driven, where the flow of the program is determined by different events such as a request for some data or a file being uploaded. This approach encourages fast and agile software development and can provide all the benefits of the cloud while addressing the underutilization of resources and increasing cost-effectiveness.

> Highly Scalable and Fast Scaling: Most serverless solutions have scaling built in, are fully automated, and often with no default limits. The services can scale from 100 to 100,000 users in seconds without any changes needed to the code or configuration, but this can cause problems if not considered during budget estimates and development.

Connecting Mechanism: Software-Defined Networks (SDN)

Existing traditional technologies cannot handle the vast and ever-changing network requirements. What is required is an intelligent network infrastructure like an SDN which can cater to the needs of a distributed and vast network, and handle the heterogeneity of the network devices and applications without deteriorating the network performance (Gupta et al. 2024; Nayyar et al. 2022; Awasthi et al. 2022; Duan and Toy 2017).

With the emergence of the Internet of Things (IoT), the number of devices connected to the Internet has grown exponentially and is expected to grow more soon. Because of users' changing demands due to the variety of online services, the devices connected to the Internet are heterogeneous. These heterogeneous devices are connected to networks and distributed globally all over the world covering the remote terrains as well. Every minute new users are connected to the Internet, and existing users either keep on changing the devices or might switch to a different network. With the advent of new applications, network traffic is increasing day by day—thereby increasing the network load and changing the characteristics of the existing network. Traffic characteristics like traffic congestion, bandwidth, delay, etc. are continuously changing, thereby demanding the reconfiguration of the network every single time to handle such changes. Therefore, the network needs to be modified continuously to serve such applications.

Users get connected to the network and use its services if they have subscribed to the network service, which is made available by a service provider. If each one of the service providers deploys separate networks to cater to the changing needs of the users and the network, then it would be too costly even for the service providers. This suggests that there can be a single network infrastructure, and multiple service providers can lease the resources depending on the requirements of the users. However, to support critical applications and requirements, the shared infrastructure must allow service providers to reserve resources for crucial situations. Consequently, there must be a provision of isolating part of the network and resources when it is allocated to any service provider. This is accomplished jointly by Software-Defined Networks (SDN) and Network Function Virtualization (NFV).

Software-Defined Networks (SDN)

The architecture of SDN has a decoupling property whereby the network is decoupled for controlling the forwarded data using direct programming. The advantages of this decoupling are as follows:

- SDN offers greater control.
- There is an improvement in the performance of the network.
- There is an enhanced configuration of the network and operation.
- The programmatically configured forwarded rules help in traffic steering.

The general architecture of SDN comprises of:

a. Application layer: This layer mainly consists of application software that communicates with the control layer; thus, the main focus is on network services.
b. Control layer: It is a fundamental layer of the SDN. It contains an SDN controller whose function is to control requests from the

application layer, along with managing network devices using the standard protocol.

c. Data plane layer: It contains physical switches, packet switches, and network devices that support interfaces.

d. Interfaces: Northbound APIs combined with SDN controllers enable various control mechanisms for SDN networks. The southbound API helps applications to control the forwarding devices by flexible programming. The communication interface between the controller layer and devices of the data plane is constructed by southbound API.

e. SDN controller: It is an extensible software that provides a framework for different user communications to communicate with the controller to allow automatic configuration of devices in a network. It is a logically centralized entity composed of:

   ○ Northbound agent
   ○ SDN control logic
   ○ Control to Data Plane Interface (CDPI) driver

Network Function Virtualization (NFV)

NFV architecture is composed of two planes:

a. Management plane: It comprises various virtual network functions (VNFs).

b. Data and control plane: It comprises VMs.

With the help of the above planes, the NFV architecture is created, whose main function is:

• Controlling and maintaining a firewall and virtual routing
• Monitoring and controlling traffic

VNF architecture is composed of the following components:

a. Physical hardware: This hardware layer is a bare metal machine and is used for hosting resources like CPU, storage, memory, I/O, etc.

b. Virtual hypervisor layer: This is the virtual software layer that runs on top of the physical hardware component. The hypervisor is responsible for managing all the underlying resources.

c. Virtual machine (VM): The software performs approximately all the functionalities of the physical platform and depicts a similar architecture to that of physical hardware. A VM uses only a small fraction of physical hardware. In this way, one physical hardware can host multiple VMs. The number of VMs hosted by a bare metal depends on the physical hardware capability and resource requirements of each VM.

> The management of resource allocation and de-allocation for VNF can be done with the help of any software controller, like an SDN controller in SDN. With the SDN controller, VNF-enabled devices can also be controlled, thereby raising the potential of using both kinds of architecture simultaneously.

SDN by using an SDN controller gives agility to routers, switches, etc. (generic forwarding devices), while NFV gives agility to network applications by the virtualized server. Despite the differences between SDN and NFV, they are closely related as SDN provides programming-enabled network connectivity to VNFs for traffic steering. NFV helps SDN controllers to run over the cloud, thus providing dynamic controller migration. For instance, in cloud computing-based IoT (cloud IoT) the challenges faced by cloud IoT, like delayed delivery, incorporation of traditional techniques in the cloud, etc., are solved by integration of SDN with cloud IoT (SDN-IoT).

Software-Defined Networks (SDN) Security

By using the property of the central view of data used by the SDN controller and its ability to reprogram data in the data plane, many security issues are taken care of. To deploy various security concerns without losing scalability, SDN networks are often combined with different technologies; one popular network is a combination of SDN with NFV (Network Function Visualization).

Communications: 5G Mobile Communications

5G aimed to broaden the scope of mobile communications. It extends beyond humans and includes objects, expanding from consumer applications to vertical industries, encompassing both public and private networks. This expansion resulted in a significant increase in potential mobile subscriptions, connecting not only billions of people but also enabling connectivity among machines and things. The disruptive nature of 5G opened up a variety of applications, such as Industry 4.0, VR, the IoT, and autonomous driving. In summary, new-generation International Mobile Telecommunications (IMT) systems need to support innovative use cases that require extremely high data rates, a massive number of connected devices, and low-latency high-reliability applications. 5G is essential for fulfilling the diverse requirements of various applications, offering additional capabilities that go beyond 4G mobile cellular networks (Jiang and Han 2024).

Unlike legacy networks, these demanded strict latency and reliability, especially in critical areas like healthcare, security, logistics, automotive applications, and mission-critical control. Additionally, 5G supports a wide range of data rates, from multiple gigabits per second to ensuring high availability and reliability at tens of megabits per second. It also enables scalable and flexible networks to accommodate numerous devices while minimizing complexity and extending battery life. The value of 5G services and applications became evident in facilitating remote surgical procedures, online education, remote work arrangements, autonomous vehicles, unmanned deliveries, robotic assistance, intelligent healthcare systems, and automated manufacturing processes.

While the 5G system integrated numerous techniques, the key advancements that stand out are:

1. Massive MIMO
2. mmWave
3. NOMA
4. Polar codes
5. Network function virtualization
6. Software-defined networks
7. Network slicing

Table 8.1 Comparison between Web 3.0 and Web 2.0

Category	Web 2.0	Web 3.0
Structure	• Owned by one entity • Maximization of shareholder value drives all decisions	• Community-based typically with a decentralized, autonomous framework for leadership • Use votes on major changes
Data storage	• Centralized	• Decentralized
Platform format	• Personal computer (PC) • Hardware for creating and using virtual and augmented realities (VR and AR) • Mobile/app	• Hardware for creating VR and AR experiences on a PC • Corresponding mobile/app version
Payments Infrastructure	• Traditional methods of payments (such as credit/debit cards)	• Bitcoin wallet
Digital Assets Ownership	• Leased on the same marketplace platform as the asset	• Tokens that cannot be exchanged for other assets (NFT)
Content creators	• Developers	• Community/developers

Network Systems: Web 3.0

The ultimate goal of Web 3.0 is to support machine-facilitated global information exchange in a scalable, adaptable, extensible manner, so that information on the web can be used for more effective discovery, automation, integration, and reuse across various applications (Avsar 2023). The three key ingredients to help achieve these goals are semantic markup, ontology, and intelligent software agents (Table 8.1).

Web 2.0 applications present information in natural language which humans can process easily; but computers can't manipulate natural language information on the web meaningfully. Enabling semantics in Web 3.0 radically changes the nature of the web—from a place where information is merely displayed to one where it is interpreted, exchanged, and processed.

Tim Berners-Lee, the founder of the World Wide Web, gave an interesting explanation of Web 1.0 to Web 3.0. Web 1.0 was the "readable" phase of the web, where we see limited interaction between users. Web 2.0 is the "interactive" phase of the web, where users can interact with sites and each other. Web 3.0 is the "executable" phase of the web, where computers can interpret information as humans do and then generate personalized content for users.

Analytics: Prescriptive Analytics

Prescriptive analytics relates to both predictive and descriptive analytics, but it stresses on actionable insights in place of data observation. Descriptive analytics provides BI insights into what has occurred; predictive analytics focuses on predicting possible results; and prescriptive analytics aims to discover the best result among a variety of options (Zwingmann 2022; Schniederjans et al. 2014). The field also empowers companies to make decisions based on optimizing the outcome of future events or threats, and offers a prototype to learn them. It is a statistical technique used to draw decisions and produce recommendations based on the computational results of algorithmic prototypes.

Prescriptive analytics analyzes the raw data to make good decisions in businesses. It especially factors in information about probable scenarios or circumstances, previous performance, present performance, and available resources, and suggests a strategy or plan. This kind of analytics can be used to make decisions on any time horizon. Prescriptive analytics is not restricted to predicting future outcomes only. It not only predicts why it will occur and what will occur, but also when it will occur.

When used effectively, it can help companies make decisions based on examined facts. It can simulate the likelihood of various outcomes and show the probability of each, helping organizations to gauge the level of risk and uncertainty they face than they could be relying on averages. Organizations get to know the likelihood of worst-case scenarios and plan accordingly.

Means of Digital Transformation for Innovation

Market-Based View (MBV) of Enterprise Operations

Business operations envisaged per the MBV of operations strategy (Van Mieghem and Allon 2015) have the following aspects:

- Organization Redesign
- Customer Experience Redesign
- People Workplace Redesign
- Business Model Transformation

Digital transformation would involve upgrading to the latest functionality, modules, and systems like metaverse, augmented reality (AR), virtual reality (VR), and tools (Cheng 2023; Rojas and Martínez-Cano 2025; Marr 2021).

Network Business Model: Industry 5.0

Industry 5.0 will integrate humans and machines to exploit human mental ability and creativity even better and to improve process performance by integrating processes with smart systems. Industry 5.0 integrates intelligent automation, gadgets, and systems in the workplace to increase cooperation along with collaboration between people, processes, robots, and shop floor machines. It assists highly skilled employees to lead smart devices and robots to work far better. Industry 5.0 is not just providing consumers the product they desire today, but also accomplishes tasks that surpass new elevations and are much more purposeful than they have been in more than a century.

Connecting the virtual and physical worlds is the main criterion for the manufacturers to examine data, keep track of the manufacturing process, handle risks, and reduce downtime, all achieved by simulations with the advent of digital twins. With the current innovations in large data handling and AI systems, it is currently possible to create a lot more sensible models depicting various operating circumstances and also characteristics of a process. While representing unpredictability in the process, digital twins offer an immense possibility by enabling reduced wastefulness by collaborating with the system. Industry 5.0 will bring unmatched challenges in the field of human-machine interaction as it will certainly place machines extremely close to the day-to-day life of any human.

Enterprise Architecture: Edge Computing Architecture

Edge computing seems simple: by moving to compute resources as close as possible to their end-users, theoretically, the latency between a user and their application can be reduced, the cost of data transport can be minimized, and these two factors combined will make new use cases

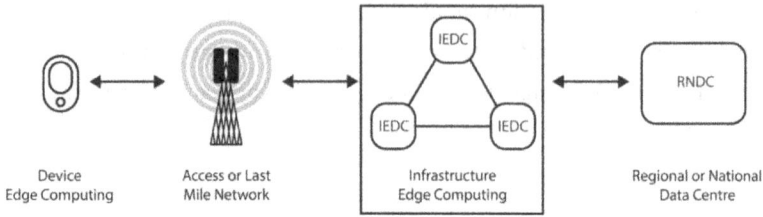

Figure 8.1 Edge computing

practical (Marcham 2021). Part of the challenge in defining edge computing is that by its very nature, the concept of an edge is contextual:
An edge is at the boundary of something and often delineates the specific place where two things meet. These two things may be physical, as
pieces of hardware; they may be logical, as pieces of software; or they
may be more abstract, such as ownership, intent, or a business model
(Figure 8.1).

The last-mile network is the clearest point of physical separation
between end-user devices and the data center infrastructure which supports them. The last-mile network refers to the transmission medium and
communications equipment that connects a user device to the network
of a network operator who is providing wide area network (WAN) or
metropolitan area network (MAN) service to one or more user devices,
whether large or small, fixed position or mobile. The last-mile network
is the clearest point of physical separation between end-user devices and
the data center infrastructure which supports them. In this context, the
last-mile network refers to the transmission medium and communications equipment that connects a user device to the network of a network
operator who is providing wide area network (WAN; or, metropolitan
area network [MAN]) service to one or more user devices, whether large
or small, fixed position or mobile.

The infrastructure edge refers to the collection of edge data center
infrastructure which is located on the infrastructure side of the last-mile
network. These facilities typically take the form of micromodular data
centers (MMDCs) which are deployed as close as possible to the last-mile
network and, therefore, as close as possible to the users of that network
who are located on the device edge.

Although it is typically deployed in a small number of large data centers today, the cloud itself is not a physical place. It is a logical entity that can utilize compute, storage, and network resources that are distributed across a variety of locations as long as those locations are capable of supporting the same type of elastic resource allocation as their hyperscale data center counterparts.

The device edge refers to the collection of devices that are located on the device side of the last-mile network. Common examples of these entities include smartphones, tablets, home computers, and game consoles; it also includes autonomous vehicles, industrial robotics systems, and devices that function as smart locks, water sensors, or connected thermostats or things that can provide many other Internet of Things (IoT) functionalities. Whether or not a device is part of the device edge is not driven by the size, cost, or computational capabilities of that device, but on which side of the last-mile network it operates. These devices may communicate directly with the infrastructure edge using the last-mile network or may use an intermediary device on the device edge, such as a gateway, to do so. An example of each type of device is a smartphone that has an integrated Long-Term Evolution (LTE) modem and so can communicate directly with the LTE last-mile network itself, and a device which instead has only local range Wi-Fi network connectivity that is used to connect to a gateway which itself has last-mile network access.

Connecting Mechanism: Internet of Everything (IoE)

The term "Internet of Everything" (IoE) was first used by Cisco in 2013. The integration of fog and edge computing results in decentralized processing capacity, providing increased computing power for these kinds of hybrid IoE networks. The primary aim of IoE is to connect anything with the Internet, with enough information provided at the right time; in this digitally driven modern era, IoE is a much broader system than IoT. It is considered to be a superset of IoT along with its variants like the Internet of Drones and Internet of Healthcare (Aujla et al. 2022).

It evolves from things in IoT to four pillars called:

1. People: IoE is responsible for making connections among people in a more effective and relevant manner.
2. Process: It consists of an efficient collection of processes that converts the collected information into the appropriate actions. It delivers accurate information to the person or object concerned at the appropriate time.
3. Data: The data is generated during interaction with objects and people in multiple forms. There is a requirement of efficient processing and handling of data that could further support the decision-making process and knowledge generation.
4. Things: These are physical objects having sensing and processing capabilities connected to the Internet. These could also be termed smart objects.

For instance, smart vehicle management and smart healthcare-based IoE systems are helping to connect roads with hospitals for real-time monitoring to save lives. It integrates the people with objects and intelligent processes more efficiently and effectively, such as connecting homes for more comfortable living, connecting food and people in SCM, and connecting the elderly population and their monitoring with healthcare experts. In general, applications of IoE have touched several different domains such as healthcare, digital transformation, home automation, energy conservation, security, information exchange and communication, and environmental monitoring.

Some relevant applications are:

• Smart Healthcare: In healthcare support, IoE has significant applications ranging from in-hospital support to smart wearable devices. There are IoE-based techniques available for diagnostic purposes for various diseases. It also has applications to assist patients with their regular activities, like assisting Alzheimer patients. There are also trackers like smart watches to keep track of routine health-related parameters like blood pressure and distance covered.

- Smart Home: There are a number of IoE-based household things on the market. These devices make a home connected to the Internet. They can operate autonomously according to the environment like an air conditioner that will automatically turn on/off based on set temperature. Other than this, basic electronic things in the house like a fan, fridge, washing machine, TV, and lights can operate autonomously.
- Smart City: The IoE has huge potential to develop infrastructure in a more organized and efficient manner. Applications are available to upgrade a city to a smart city. These applications could help in smart garbage collection, smart parking systems, and smart streetlights.
- Smart Vehicular Technology: There are vehicles equipped with sensors and connected to the Internet, making the drive safer and more comfortable. There are also vehicles in the development stage that can run on roads without driver support. The vehicles can use numerous sensors that can help them in judging road conditions and traffic.
- Smart Industry: IoE has brought about a revolutionary change in industries like manufacturing, food and logistics, and packaging. It has brought a new era of sensor-fitted robots that can replace humans in factories. They can work more efficiently and accurately than human beings. IoE-based systems are also used for the delivery of logistics in less time like drones.
- Smart Agriculture: This is one of the major applications of IoE for agriculture-dependent countries. It helps the farmers to regularly check their soil moisture and other parameters digitally. It also helps in developing the latest equipment that can help farmers grow and sell their crops more easily.

Communications: 6G Mobile Communications

6G is expected to support disruptive applications such as virtual reality (VR), augmented reality (AR), and mixed reality (MR), which fall under the umbrella term of extended reality (XR), the Internet of Everything, Industry 4.0, connected and autonomous vehicles, as well as yet-to-be-conceived use cases like the metaverse, holographic-type telepresence, the tactile Internet, digital twins, full immersiveness, multi-sense experiences, and blockchain technology (Jiang and Han 2024).

The role of IMT-2030 in the future will be to establish intelligent connections between numerous devices, processes, and humans, forming a global information grid. This advancement will create fresh opportunities across various industries and sectors. Given their distinct development cycles, a wide array of potential advancements and vertical transformations will continue to unfold in the post-2030 era.

Areas of application are as follows:

1. Holographic-Type Communication (HTC): Holographic displays represent the next step in enhancing the multimedia experience by projecting 3D images from one or multiple sources to multiple destinations, providing an immersive and lifelike encounter for users. The network's interactive holographic capability demands extremely high data rates and exceptionally low latency.

2. Tactile Internet: Tactile Internet ensures an exceptionally low E2E latency, meeting the demanding 1 millisecond or even faster reaction time, which approaches the limits of human perception. This, combined with high reliability, availability, security, and at times, high throughput, leads to the emergence of disruptive real-time applications. These advancements play a crucial role in enabling real-time monitoring and remote control for Industry 4.0 and Smart Grid. Human operators can remotely monitor machines using VR or holographic devices while being assisted by tactile sensors that may involve actuation and kinesthetic feedback for better control.

3. Extended Reality: For an ideal immersion experience, the quality of video with higher resolution, higher frame rate, more color depth, and high dynamic range is required, leading to a bandwidth demand of over 1.6 Gbps per device. One of the key challenges in supporting interactive XR experiences over cellular networks is the synchronized transport of multimodal flows (e.g., visual media, audio, and haptics) to and from various devices in a collaborative group engaging with the same XR application.

4. Digital Twin: A digital twin is a virtual representation of a physical object, system, or process, meticulously crafted using real-time and historical data to mirror its real-world counterpart's behaviors, characteristics, and conditions. This cutting-edge technology has garnered significant attention in the context of the IoT, Industry 4.0, and advanced manufacturing, offering businesses and organizations unprecedented insights into their physical assets and processes. With the ability to simulate, analyze, and monitor these objects or systems in a virtual environment, digital twins are poised to revolutionize industries and drive innovation in ways previously unimaginable.

5. Pervasive Intelligence: The widespread adoption of mobile smart devices and the emergence of connected technologies like robots, smart cars, drones, and VR glasses have paved the way for a surge in over-the-air intelligent services. These services heavily rely on traditional computation-intensive AI techniques such as computer vision, Simultaneous Localization and Mapping (SLAM), face and speech recognition, NLP, and motion control. However, due to the limited computing, storage, and connectivity resources of mobile devices, the full potential of these intelligent tasks can be realized only with the advent of 6G networks.

6. Internet of Everything (IoE): IoE encompasses a wide array of scenarios, including real-time monitoring of diverse elements such as buildings, cities, the environment, transportation systems, roads, critical infrastructure, and water and power networks, among others.

7. Multi-sense Experience: While humans possess five senses—sight, hearing, touch, smell, and taste—to perceive the external environment, current communication technologies primarily focus on optical (text, image, and video) and acoustic (audio, voice, and music) media.

8. Multidimensional Sensing: Leveraging wireless signals for sensing, positioning, and imaging will unlock a realm of possibilities in various fields. This technology will enable high-precision positioning, ultra-high-resolution imaging, mapping, and environment reconstruction, as well as advanced gesture and motion recognition

capabilities. These applications will require sensing systems with high resolution, exceptional accuracy, and efficient detection rates to deliver optimal performance and accuracy.

9. Intelligent Transportation and Logistics: Automatic and connected vehicles represent a transformative technological shift in the transportation landscape. The integration of vehicle-to-vehicle (V2V) and vehicle-to-infrastructure (V2I) communication and coordination, alongside autonomous transport capabilities, holds immense potential for reducing road accidents and traffic congestion. To achieve this, incredibly low latencies in the order of a few milliseconds will be crucial for enabling collision avoidance and supporting remote driving functionalities.

6G AI-Native Architecture Framework

Autonomous networks also use AI, but they are not AI-native networks. An AI-native implementation leverages a data-driven and knowledge-based ecosystem, where data/knowledge is consumed and produced to realize new AI-based functionality or augment and replace static, rule-based mechanisms with learning and adaptive AI when needed (Roy 2025) (Table 8.2).

Network Systems: Metaverse

As the next iteration of the Internet and web, the metaverse is designed to bring the digital and physical realms together. A metaverse is a shared

Table 8.2 Autonomous versus AI-native network

Feature	Autonomous network	AI-native network
Level of Automation	Minimum human intervention (zero touch)	Built from the ground-up with AI in mind
AI Applications	Monitoring and automation	Machine learning (ML) and deep learning (DL)
Performance	Improved performance and reliability	Potential for even greater performance and reliability
Adaptability	Adaptable to new and emerging applications	Even more adaptable to new and emerging applications

Table 8.3 Comparison of generations of communication technologies

Specifications	1G	2G	3G	4G	5G	6G
Year	1980–1990	1990–2000	2000–2010	2010–2020	2020–2030	2030–2040
Core network	PSTN	PSTN	Packet N/W	Internet	IoT	IoE
Services	Voice	Text	Photos	Video	3D VR/AR	Tacttil OFDMA
Multiplexing	FDMA	FDMA/TDMA	CDMA	OFDMA	OFDMA	Smart OFDMA plus IM
Architecture	SISO	SISO	SISO	MIMO	Massive MIMO	Intelligent Surface
Data transfer rate	2.4 kb/sec	144 kb/sec	2 Mb/sec	1 Gb/sec	34.6 Gb/sec	100 Gb/sec
Maximum Frequency	894 MHz	1900 MHz	2100 MHz	6 GHz	90 GHz	10 THz

Table 8.3 compares different generations of communication technologies. Here is a brief on the different generations of communication technologies (Koivusalo 2023; Verma and Zhang 2020):

i. 1G—Voice Calls: During the age of 1G communication technology, phones were heavy and bulky in size. They had big antennas with huge batteries, and the network reception was sketchy. The analog system-based 1G wireless communication enabled the exchange of information between two devices which were supported only with poor-quality voice call features. One of the key challenges of 1G communication technology was its fixed geographical area since it lacked roaming support by the network.

ii. 2G—Text: 2G communication technology facilitated better quality of voice calls as compared to 1G. The analog system based on 1G of wireless transmission was substituted by a more sophisticated digital technology known as Global System for Mobile (GSM) communication. In addition, it also supported new services, such as short/multimedia message service which is abbreviated as SMS and MMS, respectively.

iii. 3G—Era of Applications: The 3G communication technology was introduced with high-speed Internet services, laying the foundation for the development of smartphones equipped with a diverse range of applications. It also enabled the concept of online radio services, mobile television, e-mails on phones, etc.

iv. 4G—Internet Calling: The incorporation of the LTE (Long-Term Evolution) system significantly improved the data rate allowing synchronous transmission of both data and voice. VoLTE (Voice over LTE) or Internet calling is one of the fundamental improvements of the 4G communication network. It also facilitated the Voice over Wi-Fi (VoWi-Fi) feature which allowed one to make voice calls in either low-network areas or even in no-network-coverage areas.

v. 5G—IoT: 5G technology is still in the process of being fully rolled out globally, and it is likely to take a few years for it to be widely available and adopted. As compared to all the existing communication technologies, the advantage of the recently launched 5G technology is low latency with higher throughput features, which makes the network ideal with automation features and a connected ecosystem.

vi. 6G—IoE: The transition from 5G to 6G is not an immediate concern. It is expected that by the year 2030, 6G will bring a drastic evolution in communication mediums as it will enable the newly introduced intelligent Internet of Everything (IoE) concept. 6G is forecasted to bring high and sophisticated quality of service (QoS), for example, holographic communication and VR. The concept of the IoE is making progress in enhancing people's lives by enhancing the IoT and creating connections among individuals, processes, information, and devices. The advent of 6G technology will make communication instantaneous with low latency, thereby creating a seamless connection between the digital and physical world.

digital and online space inhabited by digital twins of people, places, and things that interact in real time. Metaverse uses new technologies such as digital twins, 5G, industrial IoT, and VR/AR/XR to deliver an immersive and multisensory user experience (Cheng 2023).

As an evolution of social technologies, the metaverse allows digital representations of people (avatars) to interact with each other in real time across multiple virtual locations, in various settings. A metaverse is a network of 3D virtual worlds where an individual can communicate, collaborate, explore, and create with other people (who are not in the same physical space) as if they were in the same physical world.

The metaverse layered architecture can be organized into seven layers (Radoff 2021) (Figure 8.2):

1. Experience: learning, gaming, shopping, working
2. Discovery: avatar, virtual stores, advertising networks
3. Creator economy: e-commerce, design tools, asset market
4. Spatial computing: virtual reality (VR), augmented reality (AR), extended reality (XR), multitasking
5. Decentralization: AI agents, blockchain, edge computing
6. Human interface: smart watch, smartphone, smart glasses, display device (mounted on the head), acoustic device
7. Infrastructure: Wi-Fi, data center, cloud, CPUs, GPUs, 5G, 6G

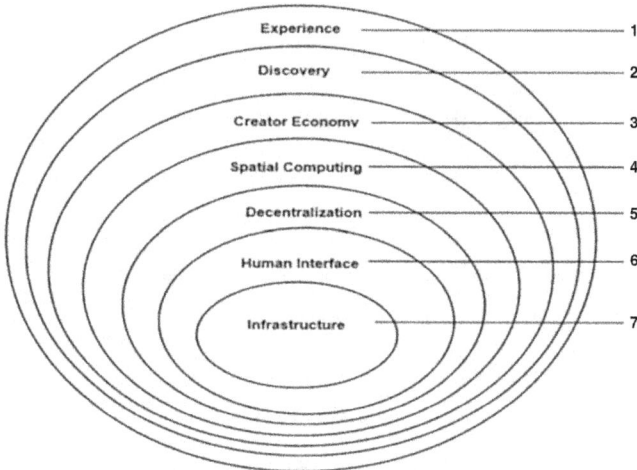

Figure 8.2 Layers of metaverse

Major companies focused on the metaverse are Meta (Facebook), Apple, Microsoft, NVIDIA, and Alphabet (Google).

Analytics: Prescriptive Experience Analytics

Prescriptive analytics is the most advanced stage of advanced analytics (Zwingmann 2022; Schniederjans et al. 2014). It suggests the optimal actions to take in decision-making.

The main objectives and goals at this stage are:

1. to answer the questions "What should happen?" and "Why should it happen?";
2. to estimate possible impact, i.e., "What would be the impact if an action is taken?"
3. to recommend the possible next-best action if a particular action has already been taken, or something untoward happens.

Prescriptive analytics contributes directly to business decision making, and is thus more beneficial for problem-solving and business impact. It achieves this by, for example:

- enabling the immediate application of analytical results by recommending optimal actions to be taken on business change;
- estimating the effect of one option over another, and recommending the better option for prioritized actions;
- promoting outcome-driven analytics and transforming actionable analytics and learning for effective problem-solving and better business outcomes.

Prescriptive decision-making strategies, business rules, proposed actions, and recommendations are subsequently disseminated to decision-makers to take corresponding action.

Conclusion

This chapter discussed digital transformation for innovable design blueprint in two parts. The first part, on reframing for innovation, reviews the typical reference state at the commencement of the reframing for innovation effort. This is in terms of market-led enterprise operations, network business model (Industry 4.0), EA (serverless architecture), connecting mechanism (SDN), communications (5G mobile communications), network systems (Web 3.0), and analytics (predictive experience analytics). The second part, on means for a digital transformation of innovation, reviews the typical set of technologies like market-based view (MBV) of enterprise operations, Industry 5.0, edge computing architecture, Internet of Everything (IoE), 6G mobile communications, metaverse, and prescriptive experience analytics.

This chapter highlights the more open, generalized, and sophisticated technologies that are associated with the digital transformation of business model innovation (BMI) competency.

Epilogue

This book is focused primarily on proposing a Built_to_Change strategy management fundamental framework for a business-driven digital transformation (BDDT) to select the appropriate digital transformation models and design blueprints suitable for the organizational priorities. Subsequently, the chosen strategy would need to be implemented. This epilogue gives a sketch of what such an exercise may entail and an estimate of the efforts required for implementing a particular digital transformation model.

> This book makes a reference to the SAP platforms and products mainly because they constitute 70-percent of the installed base of ERP systems across the world.

Implementing an Efficient Transformation Model

An efficient transformation model corresponds to a top-down strategy. It corresponds to the digitization of data and business processes. In these VUCA times, the average permissible time frame for implementing an efficient design blueprint is 1 year. An efficient design blueprint is generally a prerequisite for a scalable design blueprint.

Per the business division, the transformation team for implementing an efficient design blueprint is three scores each of functional and IT middle-level managers (including the Development Operations DevOps team; 72 Full-Time-Equivalents [FTEs]); these could be company employees or external consultants with requisite prior experience. Additionally, a team of three scores of *key functional users* would have to be trained on the TO BE system to undertake key user testing (with test documentation), end-user documentation, and eventually, end-user training as a part of the enterprise-wide rollout (36 FTEs). Key users have to be company employees only, as the implementation success completely depends on their satisfaction and buy-in. Only then can the key users be fully committed, involved, and enthusiastic in training the end-users successfully. Satisfied and committed key users are the real ambassadors of the implementation's success.

To recapitulate, the efficient transformation model essential for ensuring an agile enterprise would necessitate an elapsed time of 1 year and a manpower effort of 108 × 12= 1296 FTEs manmonths; and with contingencies, about 130 manyears.

Implementing a Scalable Transformation Model

A scalable transformation model corresponds to a bottom-up strategy.

It corresponds to digitalization, i.e., smartization of a *digital enterprise* (microservices architecture & Internet of Things (IoT) infrastructure) and *digital business* (E-business & E-commerce system).

In these VUCA times, the average time frame permissible for implementing a scalable design blueprint is half a year. Per e-business system, the transformation team for *vanilla* implementation of a scalable design blueprint is two scores each of functional and IT middle-level managers (including the Development Security Operations DevSecOps team) (48 Full-Time-Equivalents FTEs). Additionally, a team of two scores of TO BE *key functional users* and two scores of TO BE external consumer users would have to be trained on the TO BE e-business system to undertake key user testing (with test documentation), end-user documentation, and eventually, end-user training as a part of the enterprise-wide rollout (48 FTEs). Key users have to be company employees only, as the implementation's success completely depends on their satisfaction and buy-in. Only then can the key users be fully committed, involved, and enthusiastic in training the end-users successfully. Satisfied and committed key users are the real ambassadors of the implementation's success.

As efficient design blueprint is generally a prerequisite to scalable design; implementing the efficient transformation model would entail an elapsed time of 1 year and a total manpower effort of 1296 FTEs manmonths.

To recapitulate, the scalable transformation model essential for ensuring an agile enterprise, per e-business system, would necessitate an elapsed time of one-and-a-half years, and a manpower effort of (96 × 6) + 1296 = 1872 FTEs manmonths; and with contingencies, about 188 manyears.

Implementing an Innovable Transformation Model

An innovable transformation model corresponds to a lateral strategy since it enables the coexistence of multiple business models across the organization. The *innovator's dilemma* dictates continuance with many of these business models, in their originating project(s) or division(s), till such time that the digitally transformed business model(s) or design blueprint(s) is tested and proven in the market and taken a firm foothold in their originating project(s) or division(s).

An innovable transformation model corresponds to a digital meta-morphosis to a digital company, that is, of a *digital enterprise* (SDN and edge computing) and a *digital business* (business model with customer-, partner-, and employee specificity). In these VUCA times, since the stakes are high, the average time frame permissible for implementing an innovable design blueprint is half a year. Per the business model, the transformation team for implementing an innovable design blueprint is a two scores of senior managers and executive-level personnel from both business and IT (48 Full-Time-Equivalents FTEs).

Additionally, a team of two scores of TO BE *key functional users* and two scores of consumer users would have to be trained for the envisaged TO BE business model to eventually undertake prospective key users training (48 FTEs). Key users have to be company employees only, as the implementation success completely depends on their satisfaction and buy-in. Only then can the key users be fully committed, involved, and enthusiastic in eventually training the end-users successfully. Satisfied and committed key users are the real ambassadors of the implementation's success.

As a scalable design blueprint is generally a prerequisite to innovable design blueprint, implementing a scalable transformation model entails an elapsed time of one-and-a-half years and a manpower effort of 1872 FTEs manmonths.

To recapitulate, the innovable transformation model essential for ensuring an agile enterprise would necessitate, per business model, an elapsed time of two years and a manpower effort of $(96 \times 6) + 1872 = 2448$ FTEs manmonths; and with contingencies, about 245 manyears.

1. The above generic estimates are for a generalized company; these need to be ascertained for the specifics of a real company. The specific requirements of a company are dependent on the type of business, from manufacturing to service businesses. The specifics of the digital transformation effort for such a company are dependent on the industry sector and particular characteristics of that company.

2. The above estimates are only for the digital transformation service efforts; they do not include estimates for hardware, application & systems software, networking software, etc., both for on-premise and cloud-based solutions and services. Neither do they include estimates for conducting a parallel run and go-live phase. The above estimates do not include the equipment, facilities and services for business continuity and disaster recovery.

3. The above estimates presume the approach of vanilla implementation (i.e., without any customizations of industry-standard processes and procedures) of the enterprise, e-business, and cyber-physical systems. With customizations, no estimates are tenable.

4. The above estimates do not include the time and effort required for compilation/ preparation/ uploading of master/ transaction test data in accounts, customers/ suppliers, sales/ purchases, inventory, and manufacturing areas.

References

Agarwal, C. C. 2023. *Neural Networks and Deep Learning: A Textbook*. 2nd ed. Springer.

Albert, M. V., L. Lin, M. J. Spector, and L. S. Dunn, eds. 2022. *Bridging Human Intelligence and Artificial Intelligence*. Springer.

Alekseev, A. P. 2020. "Conceptual Approach to Designing Efficient Cyber-Physical Systems in the Presence of Uncertainty." In *Cyber-Physical Systems: Advances in Design & Modelling*, edited by A. G. Kravets, A. A. Bolshakov, and M. V. Shcherbakov. Springer.

Amit R., and C. Zott. 2021. Business Model Innovation Strategy: Transformational Concepts and Tools for Entrepreneurial Leaders. Wiley.

Anderson, C. 2006. *The Long Tail: Why the Future of Business is Selling Less of More*. Hyperion.

Appelbaum, D., and R. Nehmer. 2017. *Designing and Auditing Accounting Systems Based on Blockchain and Distributed Ledger Principles*. Feliciano School of Business.

Argote, L. 2013. *Organizational Learning: Creating, Retaining and Transferring Knowledge*. 2nd ed. Springer.

Atchison, L. 2020. *Architecting for Scale: How to Maintain High Availability and Manage Risk in the Cloud*. 2nd ed. O'Reilly Media.

Aujla, G. S., S. Garg, K. Kaur, and B. Siqdar. 2022. *Software Defined Internet of Everything*. Springer.

Avsar, B. 2023. "Historical Process and Theoretical Foundations of Metaverse Starting from Web 1.0." In *Metaverse: Technologies, Opportunities and Threat*, edited by F. S. Esen, H. Tinmaz, and M. Singh. Springer.

Awasthi, C., I. Sehgal, P. K. Pal, and P. K. Mishra. 2022. "Software-Defined Networks (SDN) for Cloud-Based Internet of Things." In *Transforming Management with AI, Big-Data, and IoT*, edited by F. Al-Turjman, S. P. Yadav, M. Kumar, V. Yadav, and T. Stephan. Springer.

Banasiewicz, A. 2021. *Organizational Learning in the Age of Data*. Springer.

Banda, S., S. Chandra, C. A. Gooi. 2022. *SAP Business Technology Platform: An Introduction*. Rheinwerk.

Barney, J. B. 1991. "Firm Resources and Sustained Competitive Advantage." *Journal of Management* 17: 99–120.

Barney, J. B. 1997. *Gaining and Sustaining Competitive Advantage*. Addison-Wesley.

Barney, J. B. 2002. *Gaining and Sustaining Competitive Advantage*. Prentice Hall.

Basu, A., and S. Muylle. 2023. *Competitive Digital Innovation: Transforming Products, Processes and Business Models to Win in the Digital Economy*. Palgrave Macmillan

Bean, R. 2021. *Fail Fast, Learn Faster : Lessons in Data-driven Leadership in an Age of Disruption, Big Data, and AI*. Wiley.

Bensaou, B. M. 2022. *Built to Innovate: Essential Practices to Wire Innovation into Your Company's DNA*. McGraw-Hill.

Bermúdez, J. L. 2023. *Cognitive Science: An Introduction to the Science of the Mind*. 4th ed. Cambridge University Press.

Berthold, M.R., C. Borgelt, H. Hoppner, F. Klawoonn, and R. Silipo. 2020. *Guide to Intelligent Data Science: How to Intelligently Make Use of Real Data*. 2nd ed. Springer.

Bessen, J. 2022. *The New Goliaths: How Corporations Use Software to Dominate Industries, Kill Innovation and Undermine Regulation*. Yale University Press.

Bishwash, S. K., and S. K. Addya. 2021. *Cloud Network Management: An IoT Based Framework*. CRC Press.

Biswas, A., and W. Talukdar. 2025. *Building Agentic AI Systems: Create Intelligent, Autonomous AI Agents that Can Reason, Plan, and Adapt*. Packt Publishing.

Bounfour, A., and T. Miyagawa, eds. 2015. *Intangibles, Market Failure and Innovation Performance*. Springer.

Briffaut, Jean-Pierre. 2015. *E-Enabled Operations Management*. Wiley.

Brown, B. R. 2023. *Engineering Intelligent Systems: Systems Engineering and Design with Artificial Intelligence, Visual Modeling, and Systems Thinking*. Wiley.

Burrell, G., and G. Morgan. 1985 . *Sociological Paradigms and Organizational Analysis*. Routledge.

Bushmann, F., R. Meunier, H. Rohnert, P. Sommerlad, and M. Stal. 1996. *Pattern-Oriented Software Architecture Volume 1: A System of Patterns*. Wiley.

Callan, G. 2024. *Digital Business Strategy: How to Design, Build, and Future-Proof a Business in the Digiyal Age*. De Gruyter.

Cantamessa, M., and F. Montagna. 2023. *Management of Innovation and Product Development: Integrating Business and Technological Perspectives*. 2nd ed. Springer.

Cantor, B., ed. 2020a. "Hook's Law: Elasticity." In *The Equation of Materials*. The Oxford University Press.

Cantor B., ed. 2020b. "The Burgers Vector: Plasticity." In *The Equation of Materials*. The Oxford University Press.

Cao, L. 2015. *Metasynthetic Computing and Engineering of Complex Systems*. Springer-Verlag

Carpo, M. ed. 2013. *The Digital Turn in Architecture 1992-2012*. Wiley.

Carpo, M. 2017. *The Second Digital Turn: Design Beyond Intelligence*. The MIT Press.

Carpo, M. 2023. *Beyond Digital: Design and Automation at the End of Modernity.* The MIT Press.

Carrijo, P., B. Alturas, and I. Pedrosa. 2023. "Similarities and Differences between Digital Transformation Maturity Models: A Literature Review." In *Intelligent Systems in Digital Transformation: Theory and Applications*, edited by C. Kahraman and E. Haktanir. Springer.

Chaffey, D., T. Hemphill, and D. Edmundson-Bird. 2019. *Digital Business and E-Commerce Management.* 7th ed. Pearson.

Chalmers, D. 2011. *Sensing and Systems in Pervasive Computing: Engineering Context Aware Systems.* Springer.

Chan Kim, W., and R. Mauborgne. 2004. *Blue Ocean Strategy: How to Create Uncontested Market Space and Make the Competition Irrelevant.* HBS Publishing.

Chhajed, D. and T.J. Lowe. eds. 2008. *Building Intuition Insights: From Basic Operations Management Models and Principles.* Springer.

Cheng, S. 2023. *Metaverse: Concept, Content and Context.* Springer.

Chu, R., 2017. "Business Model Revolution: Four Cases of the Fastest-Growing, Disruptive Companies of the Twenty-First Century." In *Revolution of Innovation Management Volume 2 Internationalism and Business Model*, edited by A. Brem and E. Vairdot. Palgrave Macmillan.

Clatworthy, S. D. 2019. *The Experience-centric Organisation: How to Win Through Customer Experience.* O'Reilly Media.

Comer, D. E. 2021. *The Cloud Computing Book: The Future of Computing Explained.* CRC Press.

Crandall, R. E., and W. R. Crandall. 2008. *New Methods of Competing in the Global Marketplace: Critical Success Factors from Service and Manufacturing.* CRC Press.

Creaspi, N., A. T. Drobot, and R. Minerva, eds. 2024. *The Digital Twin.* Springer.

Cuatrecasas, P. 2019. *Go Tech or Go Extinct: How Acquiring Tech Disruptors is the Key to Survival and Growth for Established Companies.* Berkeley Street Press.

Dai, J., and M. A. Vasarhelyi. 2017. "Toward Blockchain-Based Accounting and Assurance." *Journal of Information Systems* 31 (3): 5–21.

Das, A., P. Klee, and J. Reichel. 2025. *Enterprise Architecture with SAP: Planning, Management, and Transformation.* Rheinwerk.

Davis, R., and E. Brabänder. 2007. *ARIS Design Platform: Getting Started with BPM.* Springer.

Davis, S. 1987. *Future Perfect.* Basic Books.

Dimitrakakis, C., and R. Ortner. 2022. *Decision Making Under Uncertainty and Reinforcement Learning: Theory and Algorithms.* Springer.

Drori, I. 2023. *The Science of Deep Learning.* Cambridge University Press.

Duan, Q., and M. Toy. 2017. *Virtualized Software-Defined Networks and Services.* Artech House.

Duffey, C. 2023. *Decoding the Metaverse: Expand Your Business Using Web3.* Kogan Page.

Duncan, R. 1976. "The Ambidextrous Organization: Designing Dual Structures for Innovation." In *The Management of Organization*, edited by R. H. Killman, L. R. Pondy, and D. Sleven. North Holland.

Elakkiya, R., and V. Subramaniyaswamy. 2024. *Cognitive Analytics and Reinforcement Learning: Theories, Techniques and Applications.* Wiley.

Erder, M., P. Pureur, and E. Woods. 2021. *Continuous Architecture in Practice: Software Architecture in the Age of Agility and DevOps.* Addison-Wesley.

Escalona, M. J., G. Aragón, H. Linger, M. Lang, C. Barry, and C. Schneider, eds. *Information System Development: Improving Enterprise Communication.* Cham: Springer, 2014.

Evans, N. D. 2017. *Mastering Digital Business: How Powerful Combinations of Disruptive technologies are enabling the next wave of digital transformation.* BCS Learning & Development.

Etzkorn, L. H. 2017. *Introduction to Middleware: Web Services, Object Components, and Cloud Computing.* CRC Press.

Fantina, R., A. Storozhuk, and K. Goyal. 2022. *Introducing Robotic Process Automation to Your Organization: A Guide for Business Leaders.* Apress.

Fernando, C. 2021. *Designing Microservices Platforms with NATS: A Modern Approach to Designing and Implementing Scalable Microservices Platforms with NATS Messaging.* Apress.

Fernando, C. 2023. *Solution Architecture Patterns for Enterprise: A Guide to Building Enterprise Software Systems.* Apress.

Fleisch, E., M. Weinberger, and F. Wortmann. 2014. *Geschäftsmodelle im Internet der Dinge [Business models in the Internet of Things].* https://www .iot-lab.ch/wp-content/uploads/2014/09/GM-im-IOT_Bosch-Lab-White -Paper.pdf

Fogliatto, F. C., and G. J. C. da Silveira. 2011. *Mass Customization: Engineering and Managing Global Operations.* Springer.

Fowler, M., and J. Lewis. 2013. "Microservices: A Definition of This New Architectural Term." http://martinfowler.com/articles/microservices.html.

Fox, R., and W. Hao. 2018. *Internet Infrastructure: Networking, Web Services, and Cloud Computing.* CRC Press.

Frankenberger, K., H. Mayer, A. Reiter, and M. Schmidt. 2021. *The Digital Transformer's Dilemma: How to Energize Your Core Business While Building Disruptive Products and Services.* Wiley.

Gamma, E., R. Helm, R. Johnson, J. Vlissides, and G. Booch. 1994. *Design Patterns: Elements of Reusable Object-Oriented Software.* Addison-Wesley.

Ganguli, R., S. Adhikari, S. Chakraborty, and M. Ganguli. 2023. *Digital Twin: A Dynamic System and Computing Perspective*. CRC Press.

Geetha, T. V., and S. Sendhilkumar. 2023. *Machine Learning: Concepts, Techniques and Applications*. CRC Press.

Giachetti, R. E. 2010. *Design of Enterprise Systems: Theory, Architecture and Methods*. CRC Press.

Gilliam, D. and S. Taylor-Jones, 2005. *The Quantum Leap: The Manufacturing Strategy for Business; based on the Original Work by J. R. Costanza*. J. Ross.

Gobillot, E. 2007. *The Connected Leader: Creating Agile Organizations for People, Performance and Profit*. Kogan Page.

Gong, C., X. Parisot, and D. Reis. 2024. "The Evolution of Digital Transformation." In *Digital Disruption and Transformation: Case Studies, Approaches and Tools*, edited by D. Schallmo, A. Baiyere, F. Gertsen, C. A. F. Rosenstand, and C. A. Williams. Springer.

Gorelova, G. V. 2020. "Intellectual Cognitive Technologies for Cyber-Physical Systems." In *Cyber-Physical Systems and Control*, edited by D. G. Arseniev, L. Overmeyer, H. Kälviäinen, and B. Katalinić. Springer.

Gorton, I. 2022. *Foundation of Scalable Systems: Designing Distributed Architectures*. O'Reilly Media.

Gray, J. 2007. Gray, J. (2007). *EScience—A transformed scientific method*. http://research.microsoft.com/en-us/um/people/gray/talks/NRC-CSTB _eScience.ppt

Gupta, D. D., A. Dahiya, and E. Benkhelifa. 2024. *SDN and NFV: A New Dimension to Virtualization*. World Scientific.

Gupta, J. N. D., and S. K. Sharma. 2004. *Intelligent Enterprises of the 21st Century*. IGI Global.

Gupta, S. 2018. *Driving Digital Strategy: A Guide to Reimagining Your Business*. Harvard Business Review Press.

Hannan, M. T., and J. Freeman. 1984. "Structural Inertia and Organizational Change." *American Sociological Review* 49 (2): 149–164.

Harmon, P., M. Rosen, and M. Guttman. 2001. *Developing E-Business Systems & Architectures—A Manager's Guide*. Academic Press.

Henderson, R. M., and K. B. Clark. 1990. "Architectural Innovation: The Reconfiguration of Existing Product Technologies and the Failure of Established Firms." *Administrative Science Quarterly* 35 (1): 9–30.

Hess, T. 2022. *Managing the Digital Transformation: A Guide to Successful Organization Change*. Springer.

Hirooka, M. 2006. *Innovation Dynamism and Economic Growth: A Nonlinear Perspective*. Edward Elgar.

Hisrich, R. D., and V. Ramadani. 2017. *Effective Entrepreneurial Management: Strategy, Planning, Risk Management, and Organization*. Springer.

Hoe, L. S. 2023. *Digital Transformation: Strategy, Execution, and Technology.* CRC Press.

Holbeche, L. 2023. *The Agile Organization: How to Build an Engaged, Innovative and Resilient Business.* 3rd ed. Kogan Page.

Horváth, I., B. Berki, A. Sudár, Á. Csapó, and P. Baranyi. 2024. *Cognitive Aspects of Virtual Reality.* Springer.

Hsu, C. 2009. *Service Science: Design for Scaling and Transformation.* World Scientific.

Huang, K. 2025. *Agentic AI: Theories and Practices.* Springer.

Hulten, G. 2018. *Building Intelligent Systems: A Guide to Machine Learning Engineering.* Apress.

Hurwitz, J., H. Morris, C. Sidner, and D. Kirsch. 2020. *Augmented Intelligence: The Business Power of Human-Machine Collaboration.* CRC Press.

Hussey, D. 1998. *Strategic Management: From theory to implementation.* Butterworth-Heinemann.

Iyamu, T. 2024. *The Concept of Enterprise Architecture from Theory to Practice.* CRC Press.

Jahani, J. 2024. *Data Driven Decisions: Systems Engineering to Understand Corporate Value and Intangible Assets.* Wiley.

Jelassi, T., and F. J. Martínez-López. 2020. *Strategies for e-Business: Concepts and Cases on Value Creation and Digital Business Transformation.* 4th ed. Springer.

Jiang, W., and B. Han. 2024. *Cellular Communication Networks and Standards: The Evolution from 1G to 6G.* Springer.

Jo, T. 2021. *Machine Learning Foundations: Supervised, Unsupervised, and Advanced Learning.* Springer.

Johannesson, P., and E. Perjons. 2021. *An Introduction to Design Science.* 2nd ed. Springer.

Johnson, M. W. 2018. *Reinvent Your Business Model: How to Seize the White Space for Transformative Growth.* Harvard Business Review Press.

Jung, A. 2022. *Machine Learning: The Basics.* Springer.

Kale, V. 2015a. *Inverting the Paradox of Excellence: How Companies Use Variations for Business Excellence and How Enterprise Variations Are Enabled by SAP.* CRC Press.

Kale, V. 2015b. *Guide to Cloud Computing for Business and Technology Managers: From Distributed Computing to Cloudware Applications.* CRC Press.

Kale, V. 2016. *Enhancing Enterprise Intelligence: Leveraging ERP, CRM, SCM, PLM, BPM, and BI.* CRC Press.

Kale, V. 2017a. *Agile Network Businesses: Collaboration, Coordination, and Competitive Advantage.* CRC Press.

Kale, V. 2017b. *Big Data Computing: A Guide for Business and Technology Managers.* CRC Press.

Kale, V. 2018a. *Enterprise Performance Intelligence and Decision Patterns.* CRC Press.

Kale, V. 2018b. *Creating Smart Enterprises: Leveraging Cloud, Big Data, Web, Social Media, Mobile and IoT Technologies.* CRC Press.

Kale, V. 2018c. *Enterprise Process Management Systems: Engineering Process-centric Enterprise Systems using BPMN 2.0.* CRC Press

Kale, V. 2019. *Digital Transformation of Enterprise Architecture.* CRC Press.

Kale, V. 2020. *Parallel Computing Architectures and APIs: IoT Big Data Stream Processing.* CRC Press.

Kale, V. 2024. *Unleashing the Startup Unicorn: Breaking Through Constraints to the Entrepreneurial Spirit.* Business Expert Press.

Kaliraj, P., and T. Devi. 2022. *Artificial Intelligence: Theory, Models and Applications.* CRC Press.

Kamath, U., K. L. Graham, and W. Emara. 2022. *Transformers for Machine Learning: A Deep Dive.* CRC Press.

Kane, G. C., A. N. Phillips, J. R. Copulsky, and G. R. Andrus. 2019. *The Technology Fallacy: How People Are the Real Key to Digital Transformation.* The MIT Press.

Kaplan, R.S. and D.P. Norton. 2004. *Strategy Maps: Converting Intangible Assets into Tangible Assets.* Harvard Business School Publishing.

Karwal, Dheeraj. *The Automated Enterprise: Digital Reinvention through Intelligent Automation.* Independent Publication, 2020.

Kejriwal, M., C. A. Knoblock and P. Szekely. 2025. *Knowledge Graphs: Fundamentals, Techniques, and Applications.* The MIT Press.

Kersten, M. 2018. *Project to Product: How to Survive and Thrive in the Age of Digital Disruption with the Flow Framework.* IT Revolution.

Kirischian, L. 2016. *Reconfigurable Computing Systems Engineering: Virtualization of Computing Architecture.* CRC Press.

Kirschner, M. W., and J. C. Gerhart. 2005. *The Plausibility of Life: Resolving Darwin's Dilemma.* Yale University Press.

Klein, T. D. 2010. *Built for Change: Essential Traits of Transformative Companies.* Praeger.

Kleppmann, M. 2017. *Designing Data-Intensive Applications: The Big Ideas Behind Reliable, Scalable, and Maintainable Systems.* O'Reilly.

Kohtamäki, Marko, ed. *Real-time Strategy and Business Intelligence: Digitizing Practices and Systems.* London: Palgrave Macmillan, 2017.

Koivusalo, E. 2023. *Converged Communications: Evolution from Telephony to 5G Mobile Internet.* Wiley.

Kopelman, R. E. 2020. *Improving Organizational Performance: The Cube One Framework.* Routledge.

Kraner, J. 2018. *Innovation in High Reliability Ambidextrous Organizations: Analytical Solutions toward Increasing Innovative Activity.* Springer.

Kreutzer, R.T. 2022. *Toolbox Digital Business: Leadership, Business Models, Technologies and Change.* Springer.

Krishnamurthi, R., A. Kumar, S. S. Gill, and R. Buyya. 2023. *Serverless Computing: Principles and Paradigms*. Springer.

Kudriavtceva, A. 2020. "Cyber-Physical System as the Development of Automation Processes at All Stages of the Life Cycle of the Enterprise Through the Introduction of Digital Technologies." In *Cyber-Physical Systems and Control*, edited by D. G. Arseniev, L. Overmeyer, H. Kälviäinen, and B. Katalinić. Springer.

Kumar, J., A. K. Singh, A. Mohan, and R. Buyya. 2022. *Machine Learning for Cloud Management*. CRC Press.

Laguna, M., and J. Marklund. 2025. *Business Process Analytics: Modeling, Simulation and Design*. 4th ed. CRC Press.

Lane, M. 2025. Knowledge Graphs RAG: A Practical Guide to Designing and Implementing Graph-Based Systems. Amazon Digital Services LLC.

Lankhorst, M., ed. 2012. *Agile Service Development: Combining Adaptive Methods and Flexible Solutions*. Springer.

Lardi, K. 2023. *The Human Side of Digital Business Transformation*. Wiley.

Lawler III, E. E., and C. G. Worley. 2006. *Built to Change: How to Achieve Sustained Organization Effectiveness*. Jossey-Bass.

Lawless, W.F., R. Mittu, D.A. Sofge, T. Shortell and T.A. McDermott. 2021. *Systems Engineering and Artificial Intelligence*. Springer.

Lin, H. 2018. *Adoptive Management Innovation*. Springer.

Linz, C., G. Muller-Stewens, and A. Zimmermann. 2017. *Radical Business Model Transformation: Gaining the Competitive Edge in a Disruptive World*. 1st ed. Kogan Page.

Linz, C., G. Muller-Stewens, and A. Zimmermann. 2021. *Radical Business Model Transformation: How Leading Organization Have Successfully Adopted to Disruption*. 2nd ed. Kogan Page.

Machado, C., and J. P. Davim, eds. 2024a. *Building the Future with Human Resource Management*. Springer.

Machado, C., and J. P. Davim, eds. 2024b. *Smart Engineering Management*. Springer.

Mack, S. D. 2024. *The DevSecOps Playbook: Deliver Continuous Security at Speed*. Wiley.

Mangrulkar, R. S., and P. V. Chavan. 2024. *Blockchain Essentials: Core Concepts and Implementations*. Apress.

Marcham, A. 2021. *Understanding Infrastructure Edge Computing: Concepts, Technologies and Considerations*. Wiley.

Marinescu, D. C. 2023. *Cloud Computing: Theory and Practice*. 3rd ed. Elsevier.

Marr, B. 2021. *Extended Reality in Practice: 100+ Amazing Ways Virtual, Augmented and Mixed Reality are Changing Business and Society*. Wiley.

Marr, B. 2023. *The Future Internet: How the Metaverse, Web 3.0, and Blockchain Will Transform Business and Society*. Wiley.

Martin, J. 1995. *The Great Transition: Using the Seven Disciplines of Enterprise Engineering to Align People, Technology, and Strategy*. AMACOM.

Martin, R. 2009. *The Opposable Mind: How Successful Leaders Win Through Integrative* Thinking. Harvard Business Review Press

Mead, T. 2018. *Bioinspiration in Business and Management: Innovation for Sustainability*. Business Expert Press.

Miles, R. 2016. *Antifragile Software: Building Adaptable Software with Microservices*. LeanPub.

Misra, S., C. Roy, and A. Mukherjee. 2021. *Introduction to Industrial Internet of Things and Industry 4.0*. CRC Press.

Mitchell, D., and C. Coles. 2003. *The Ultimate Competitive Advantage: Secrets of Continually Developing a More Profitable Business Model*. Berrett-Koehler Publishers.

Mithas, S. 2016. *Digital Intelligence: What Every Smart Manager Must Have for Success in an Information Age*. Portfolio.

Modig, N., and P. Ahalstrom. 2013. *This Is Lean: Resolving the Efficiency Paradox*. Rheologica.

Molenaar, C. 2022. *Demand-Driven Business Strategy: Digital Transformation and Business Model Innovation*. Routledge.

Molotnikov, V., and A. Molotnikova. 2021. *Theory of Elasticity and Plasticity: A Textbook of Solid Body Mechanics*. Springer.

Morgan, G. 1986. *Images of Organization*. Sage Publications.

Morgan, G. 1997. *Images of Organization*. 2nd ed. Sage Publications.

Moro-Visconti, R. 2022. *The Valuation of Digital Intangibles: Technology, Marketing and Metaverse*. 2nd ed. Palgrave Macmillan.

Mukherjee, A., D. De, and R. Buyya. 2024. *Resource Management in Distributed Systems*. Springer.

Mulder, J. 2023. *Multi-Cloud Strategy for Cloud Architects: Learn How to Adopt and Manage Public Clouds by Leveraging BaseOps, FinOps, and DevSecOps*. 2nd ed. Packt Publishing.

Munter, M. T. 2021. "Disruption and Dynamics of Competitive Advantage—A Short Survey on Empirical Patterns of Entrepreneurial Innovation and Firm Dynamics in the Light of Technological Regimes." In *Entrepreneurial Connectivity*, edited by V. Ratten. Springer.

Musukutwa, S. C. 2022. *SAP Enterprise Architecture: A Blueprint for Executing Digital Transformation*. Apress.

Myerson, J. M. 2005. *The Complete Book of Middleware*. CRC Press.

Nayyar, A., B. Singla, and P. Nagrath, eds. 2022. *Software Defined Networks: Architecture and Applications*. Wiley.

O'Reilly III, C. A., and M. L. Tushman. 2004a. Winning Through Innovation: A Practical Guide to Leading Organizational Change and Renewal. Harvard Business Review Press.

O'Reilly III, C. A., and M. L. Tushman. 2004b. "The Ambidextrous Organization." *Harvard Business Review* 82: 74–81.

O'Reilly III, C. A., and M. L. Tushman. 2021. *Lead and Disrupt: How to Solve the Innovator's Dilemma*. 2nd ed. Stanford Business Books.

Osterwalder, A., and Y. Pigneur. 2010. *Business Model Generation: A Handbook for Visionaries, Game Changers, and Challengers*. Wiley.

Overby, H., and J. A. Audestad. 2018. *Digital Economics: How Information and Communication Technology is Shaping Markets, Businesses, and Innovation*. CreateSpace Independent Publishing Platform.

Overby, H., and J. A. Audestad. 2021. *Introduction to Digital Economics: Foundations, Business Models and Case Studies*. 2nd ed. Springer.

Ozbayrac, G. 2022. *Enterprise Agility: A Practical Guide to Agile Business Management*. CRC Press.

Pacheco, P. S., and M. Malensek. 2022. *An Introduction to Parallel Programming*. 2nd ed. Elsevier.

Panda, D. K., X. Lu, and D. Shankar. 2022. *High-Performance Big Data Computing*. The MIT Press.

Papazoglou, M. P. 2008. *Web Services: Principles and Technology*. Pearson.

Papazoglou, M. P., and P. Ribbers. 2006. *e-Business. Organizational and Technical Foundations*. Wiley.

Passiante, G., ed. 2020. *Innovative Entrepreneurship in Action: From High-Tech to Digital Entrepreneurship*. Springer.

Pentland, A., A. Lipton and T. Hardjono. 2021. *Building the New Economy: Data as Capital*. MIT Connection Science & Engineering.

Peppers, D., and M. Rogers, 2017. *Managing Customer Experience and Relationships: A Strategic Framework*. Wiley.

Perkin, P., and P. Abraham. 2021. *Building the Agile Business Through Digital Transformation*. 2nd ed. Kogan Page.

Pfenning, D. W., and K. S. Pfenning. 2012. *Evolution's Wedge: Competition and the Origins of Diversity*. University of California Press.

Pine B.J. 1992. *Mass Customization: The New Frontier in Business Competition*. Harvard Business School Press.

Pine B.J., and J. H. Gilmore. 2011. *The Experience Economy*. Harvard Business School Publishing.

Pismen, L. *Morphogenesis Deconstructed: An Integrated View of the Generation of Forms*. Cham: Springer, 2020.

Poole, D. L., and A. K. Macworth. 2023. *Artificial Intelligence: Foundations of Computational Agents*. 3rd ed. Cambridge University Press.

Porter, M. E. 1980. *Competitive Advantage*. Free Press.

Porter, M. E. 1985. *Competitive Advantage*. Free Press.

Powell, W. B. 2022. *Reinforcement Learning and Stochastic Optimization: A Unified Framework for Sequential Decisions*. Wiley.

Priyadarshini, R., R. M. Mehra, A. Sehgal, and P. J. Singh. 2023. *Artificial Intelligence: Applications and Innovations*. CRC Press.

Proper, H. A., R. Winter. S. Aier, and S. de Kinderen, eds. 2017. *Architectural Coordination of Enterprise Transformation*. Springer.

Protzman, C., F. Whiton, and D. Protzman. 2019. *Implementing Lean: Twice the Output with Half the Input!* Routledge.

Qui, R. G. 2014. *Service Science: The Foundations of Service Engineering and Management*. Wiley.

Radoff, J. 2021. *The Metaverse Value-Chain*. Medium.

Radziwill, N. M. 2020. *Connected, Intelligent, Automated: The Definitive Guide to Digital Transformation and Quality 4.0*. Quality Press.

Ravindran, A. R., P. M. Griffin, and V. V. Prabhu. 2018. *Service Systems Engineering and Management*. CRC Press.

Rayes, A., and S. Salam. 2022. *Internet of Things from Hype to Reality: The Road to Digitization*. 3rd ed. Springer.

Rebala, G., A. Ravi, and S. Churiwala. 2019. *An Introduction to Machine Learning*. Springer.

Riel, J., and R.L. Martin. 2017. Creating Great Choices: A Leader's Guide to Integrative Thinking. Harvard Business Review Press.

Rivera, R. 2020. *Principles of Managerial Statistics and Data Science*. Wiley.

Robertson, B. 2002. *The Adaptive Enterprise: IT Infrastructure Strategies to Manage Change and Enable Growth*. Addison-Wesley.

Rogers, D. L. 2016. *The Digital Transformation Playbook: Rethink Your Business for the Digital Age*. Columbia University Press

Rogers, D. L. 2023. *The Digital Transformation Map: Rebuild Your Organization for Continuous Change*. Columbia University Press

Rojas, R. V. B., and F. Martínez-Cano. 2025. *Revolutionizing Communication: The Role of Artificial Intelligence*. CRC Press.

Ronteau, S., L. Muzellec, D. Saxena, and D. Trabucchi. 2023. *Digital Business Models: The New Value Creation and Capturing Mechanisms of the 21st Century*. De Gruyter.

Rosenthal, C., and N. Jones. 2020. *Chaos Engineering: System Resiliency in Practice*. O'Reilly.

Roy, R. R. 2025. *Artificial Intelligence-Based 6G Networking*. CRC Press.

Royce, T. 2025. *Symbolic AI: The Power of Rule-Based Intelligence and Knowledge Systems*. Independent Publishing.

Ryan, F. 2011. *The Mystery of Metamorphosis: A Scientific Detective Story*. Chelsea Green.

Sajja, P. S., and R. Akerkar. 2012. *Intelligent Technologies for Web Applications.* CRC Press.

Saldanha, T. 2019. *Why Digital Transformations Fail: The Surprising Disciplines of How to Take Off and Stay Ahead.* Berrett-Koehler Publishers.

Saldanha, T., and F. Passerini. 2023. *Revolutionizing Business Operations: How to Build Dynamic Processes for Enduring Competitive Advantage.* Berrett-Koehler Publishers.

Sandkuhl, K., J. Stirna, A. Persson, and M. Wißotzki. 2014. *Enterprise Modeling: Tackling Business Challenges with the 4EM Method.* Springer.

Schank, M. 2023. *Digital Transformation Success: Achieving Alignment and Delivering Results with the Process Inventory Framework.* Apress.

Scheer, A.-W. 1998. *Business Process Engineering Study Edition: Reference Models for Industrial Enterprises.* Springer.

Scheer, A.-W. 2000. *ARIS-Business Process Modeling.* 3rd ed. Springer.

Schniederjans, M. J., D. G. Schniederjans, and C. M. Starkey. 2014. *Business Analytics Principles, Concepts, and Applications: What, Why and How.* Pearson.

Scott, D. A., S. P. Viguerie, E. I. Schwartz, and J. van Landeghem. 2018. "Corporate Longevity Forecast: Creative destruction is Accelerating."

Schank, M. 2023. Digital Transformation Success-Achieving Alignment and Delivering Results with the Process Inventory Framework. Apress.

Sehgal, Anurag. *Demystifying Digital Transformation: Non-Technical Toolsets for Business Professionals Thriving in the Digital Age.* Apress, 2024.

Sheehan, N. T., and N.J. Foss. 2009. "Exploring the roots of Porter's activity-based view." *Journal of Strategy and Management* 2 (3): 240–260.

Shehory, O., and A. Sturm. 2014. *Agent-Oriented Software Engineering: Reflections on Architectures, Methodologies, Languages, and Frameworks.* Springer-Verlag.

Shin, D. 2023. *The Web3 Era: NFTs, the Metaverse, Blockchain, and the Future of the Decentralized Internet.* Wiley.

Shivakumar, S. K. 2024. *Elements of Digital Transformation.* CRC Press.

Sinclair, B. 2021. *The Private Equity Digital Operating Partner using Digital Transformation for Value Creation.* Eve Allan.

Sinha, Sudhi R., and Youngjun Park. *Building an Effective IoT Ecosystem for Your Business.* Cham: Springer, 2017.

Sisney, L. 2012. *Organizational Physics: The Science of Growing a Business.* Organizational Physics.

Sisney, L. 2021. *Designed to Scale: How to Structure Your Business for Exponential Growth.* Organizational Physics.

Sjafrie, H. 2020. *Introduction to Self-Driving Vehicle Technology.* CRC Press.

Slack, N., and M. Lewis. 2017. *Operations Strategy.* 5th ed. Pearson.

Smallwood, R. F. 2020. *Information Governance: Concepts, Strategies and Best Practices.* 2nd ed. Wiley.

Solanki, V. K., V. G. Díaz, and J. Paulo Davim. 2019. *Handbook of IoT and Big Data*. CRC Press.

Soldatos, J. 2021. *A 360-Degree View of IoT Technologies*. Artech House.

Solis, B., R. Lieb, and J. Szymanski. 2014. *The 2014 State of Digital Transformation*. Altimeter Group.

Smart, T. 2023. *Serverless Beyond the Buzzword: A Strategic Approach to Modern Cloud Management*. 2nd ed. Springer.

Snow, C. P. 1959. *The Two Cultures*. Cambridge University Press.

Srinivasan, R. 2011. *Business Process Reengineering*. Tata McGraw-Hill.

Srinivasan, R. 2023. *Platform Business Models for Executives*. 2nd ed. Springer.

Srinivasan, V. 2017. *The Intelligent Enterprise in the Era of Big Data*. Wiley.

Stata, R. 1989. "Organizational Learning—The Key to Management Innovation." *MIT Sloan Management Review* 63 (1): 63–75.

Stoyanov, S., T. Glushkova, A. Stoyanova-Doycheva, J. Todorov, and A. Toskova. 2020. "A Generic Architecture for Cyber-Physical-Social Space Applications." In *Intelligent Systems: Theory, Research and Innovation in Applications*, edited by R. Jardim-Goncalves, V. Sgurev, V. Jotsov, and J. Kacprzyk. Springer.

Sulis, E., and K. Taveter. 2022. *Agent-Based Business Process Simulation: A Primer with Applications and Examples*. Springer.

Sunyaev, A. 2024. *Internet Computing: Principles of Distributed Systems and Emerging Internet-Based Technologies*. Springer

Susanto, H., F. Leu, and C. K. Chen. 2019. *Business Process Reengineering: An ICT Approach*. Apple Academic Press.

Suteanu, C. 2022. *Scale: Understanding the Environment*. Springer.

Swaminathan, A., and J. Meffert. 2017. *Digital @ Scale: How You Can Lead Your Business to the Future with Digital@Scale*. Wiley.

Szatvanyi, G. 2022. *The Great Digital Transformation: Reimagining the Future of Customer Interactions*. Forbes Books.

Taleb, N. N. 2012. *Antifragile: Things That Gain from Disorder*. Random House.

Tardieu, H., D. Daly, J. Esteban-Lauzán, J. Hall, and G. Miller. 2020. *Deliberately Digital: Rewriting Enterprise DNA for Enduring Success*. Springer.

Taulli, T. 2020. *The Robotic Process Automation Handbook: A Guide to Implementing RPA Systems*. Apress.

Teixeira, T. S. 2019. *Unlocking the Customer Value Chain: How Decoupling Drives Disruption*. Currency.

Tella, V., S. Brinker, and M. Pezzini. 2024. *The New Automation Mindset: The Leadership Blueprint for the Era of AI-For-All*. Wiley.

Tesch, J. F., ed. *Business Model Innovation in the Era of the Internet of Things: Studies on the Aspects of Evaluation, Decision Making, and Tooling*. Cham: Springer, 2017.

Thakur, K., H. G. Barker, and A. K. Pathan. 2024. *Artificial Intelligence and Large Language Models: An Introduction to the Technological Future*. CRC Press.

Tseng, M. M., and F. T. Piller. 2003. *The Customer Centric Enterprise: Advances in Mass Customization and Personalization*. Springer-Verlag.

Tsigkas, A. C. 2013. *The Lean Enterprise: From the Mass Economy to the Economy of One*. Springer-Verlag.

Van Mieghem, J. A., and G. Allon. 2015. *Operations Strategy: Principles and Practice*. 2nd ed, Dynamic Ideas.

Vasudevan, S. K., S. R. Pulari, and S. Vasudevan. 2022. *Deep Learning: A Comprehensive Guide*. Springer.

Venkatraman, V. 2017. *The Digital Matrix: New Rules for Business Transformation Through Technology*. Lifetree.

Verma, D. 2024. *Systems Engineering for the Digital Age: Practitioner Perspectives*. Wiley.

Verma, P., and F. Zhang. 2020. *The Economics of Telecommunication Services: An Engineering Perspective*. Springer.

Voigt, K., O. Buliga, and K. Michl. 2017. *Business Model Pioneers: How Innovators Successfully Implement New Business Models*. Springer.

Vongbunyong S., and W. H. Chen. 2015. *Disassembly Automation: Automated Systems with Cognitive Abilities*. Springer.

Wagner, A. 2014. *Arrival of the Fittest: Solving Evolution's Greatest Puzzle*. Penguin.

Wang, D. W. 2024. *Reaching Your New Digital Heights-32 Pivotal Mindset Leaps of Digital Transformation*. CRC Press.

West, G. 2017. *Scale: The Universal Laws of Growth, Innovation, Sustainability, and the Pace of Life in Organisms, Cities, Economies, and Companies*. Penguin.

Wieringa, R. J. 2014. *Design Science Methodology: For Information Systems and Software Engineering*. Springer.

Wirtz, B. W. 2019. *Digital Business Models: Concepts, Models, and the Alphabet Case Study*. Springer.

Wirtz, B. W. 2020. *Business Model Management: Design—Process—Instruments*. 2nd ed. Springer.

Wirtz, B. W. 2024. *Digital Business and Electronic Commerce: Strategy, Business Models and Technology*. 2nd ed. Springer.

Xu, J. 2014. *Managing Digital Enterprise: Ten Essential Topics*. Atlantis Press

Zielesny, A. 2016. *From Curve Fitting to Machine Learning: An Illustrative Guide to Scientific Data Analysis and Computational Intelligence*. 2nd ed. Springer.

Ziemann, J. 2022. *Fundamentals of Enterprise Architecture Management: Foundations for Steering the Enterprise-Wide Digital System*. Springer.

Zwingmann, T. 2022. *AI-Powered Business Intelligence: Improving Forecasts and Decision Making with Machine Learning*. O'Reilly.

About the Author

Vivek Kale has more than two decades of professional IT experience during which he has worked with consulting organizations like TCS, Tata Unisys (now merged with TCS), i-flex solutions (now merged with Oracle Corp.), Syntel U.S., and a couple of startup businesses. He has handled and consulted on various aspects of enterprise-wide information modeling, enterprise architectures, business process redesign, and e-business architectures.

He also has industrial experience, having worked as Group CIO of Essar Group (now ArcelorMittal Nippon Steel India [AM/NS India]), the steel/oil and gas major of India, as well as Raymond Ltd., the textile and apparel major of India. He is a seasoned practitioner in enhancing business agility through digital transformation of business models, enterprise architecture, and business processes, enabling the process-oriented enterprise, and enhancing IT-enabled enterprise intelligence (EQ).

He is the author of books on cloud and big data computing. He is the author of *Inverting the Paradox of Excellence: How Companies Use Variations for Business Excellence and How Enterprise Variations Are Enabled by SAP* (CRC Press, 2015) and *Agile Network Businesses* (CRC Press, 2017). He is also the author of *Digital Transformation of Enterprise Architecture* (CRC Press, 2019).

Books by Vivek Kale (*additional details on each of the books are available on Amazon.com*)

Unleashing the Startup Unicorn: Breaking Through Constraints to the Entrepreneurial Spirit (Business Expert Press, 2024)
Parallel Computing Architectures and APIs: IoT Big Data Stream Processing (CRC Press, 2020)

Digital Transformation of Enterprise Architecture (CRC Press, 2019)

Enterprise Process Management Systems: Engineering Process-centric Enterprise Systems using BPMN 2.0 (CRC Press, 2018)

Creating Smart Enterprises: Leveraging Cloud, Big Data, Web, Social Media, Mobile and IoT Technologies (CRC Press, 2018)

Enterprise Performance Intelligence and Decision Patterns (CRC Press, 2018)

Agile Network Businesses: Collaboration, Coordination, and Competitive Advantage (CRC Press, 2017)

Big Data Computing: A Guide for Business and Technology Managers (CRC Press, 2017)

Enhancing Enterprise Intelligence: Leveraging ERP, CRM, SCM, PLM, BPM, and BI (CRC Press, 2016)

Guide to Cloud Computing for Business and Technology Managers: From Distributed Computing to Cloudware Applications (CRC Press, 2015)

Inverting the Paradox of Excellence: How Companies Use Variations for Business Excellence and How Enterprise Variations Are Enabled by SAP (CRC Press, 2015)

Implementing SAP® CRM: The Guide for Business and Technology Managers (CRC Press, 2015)

Implementing Oracle Siebal CRM (Tata McGraw-Hill, 2010)

Implementing SAP R/3: A Guide for Business and Technology Managers (Sams, 2000)

Index

www.ingramcontent.com/pod-product-compliance
Lightning Source LLC
Chambersburg PA
CBHW061145220326

41599CB00025B/4355